Engaging
the
Disengaged

This book is dedicated to All Who Dare, especially staff members and students who have been part of Eagle Rock School and Professional Development Center:

Aashli, Adam, Adriana, Alfredo, Amanda, Ana, Andy, Ashley, Bern, Beth, Brianna, Brizeida, Calen, Christian, Christine, Clara, Coral Ann, Cybil, Cynthia, Dan, Danny, Darren, David, Dustin, Edwin, Elliott, Hae-John, Haleigh, Hannah, Heidi, Isabel, James, Jane, Jason, Jen, Jenna, Jeremy, Jesse, Jill, Jimmy, Jon, Jonathan, Josh, Karolee, Katie, Kelley, Kelly, Khalid, Kirk, Lan, Lauren, Linda, Luis, Mahkaea, Manny, Meghan, Melvina, Michael, Miguel, Mohammed, Molly, Nate, Oscar, Philbert, Richard, Rob, Robert, Ryan, Sarah, Scott, Sevi, Sia, Stevan, Steve, Tahnée, Tanya, Tim, Vanessa, Veronica, and Zachary.

LOIS BROWN EASTON

Engaging the Disengaged

HOW SCHOOLS CAN HELP STRUGGLING STUDENTS SUCCEED

CORWIN PRESS
A SAGE Publications Company
Thousand Oaks, CA 91320

For information:

Corwin Press
A Sage Publications Company
2455 Teller Road
Thousand Oaks, California 91320
www.corwinpress.com

Sage Publications India Pvt. Ltd.
B 1/I 1 Mohan Cooperative Industrial Area
Mathura Road, New Delhi 110 044
India

Sage Publications Ltd.
1 Oliver's Yard
55 City Road
London EC1Y 1SP
United Kingdom

Sage Publications Asia-Pacific Pte. Ltd.
33 Pekin Street #02-01
Far East Square
Singapore 048763

Printed in the United States of America

Library of Congress Cataloging-in-Publication Data

Easton, Lois Brown.
Engaging the disengaged : how schools can help struggling students succeed/Lois Brown Easton.
    p. cm.
Includes bibliographical references and index.
ISBN 978-1-4129-4998-9 (cloth)
ISBN 978-1-4129-4999-6 (pbk.)
    1. School improvement programs—United States. 2. Underachievers—Education (Secondary)—United States. 3. Learning strategies—United States. I. Title.
LB2822.82.E27 2008
371.93–dc22   2007020013

This book is printed on acid-free paper.

07   08   09   10   11   10   9   8   7   6   5   4   3   2   1

Acquisitions Editor:	Allyson P. Sharp
Managing Editor:	Dan Alpert
Editorial Assistant:	Tatiana Richards
Production Editor:	Astrid Virding
Copy Editor:	Kristin Bergstad
Typesetter:	C&M Digitals (P) Ltd.
Proofreader:	Ellen Brink
Indexer:	Juniee Oneida
Cover Designer:	Michael Dubowe
Graphic Designer:	Monique Hahn

Contents

Preface

A PORTRAIT OF STRUGGLING STUDENTS

Some sit in the back of the classroom, hidden behind the backpacks on their desks, cradling their heads in their arms or stretched out with their heads hooked on the back of the chair. Some may actually be sleeping; others faking it, perhaps hoping no one will notice or call on them. Some of them act out, perhaps just to keep themselves awake or get attention.

Not all struggling students are like these, of course. Some adapt themselves to the realities of traditional American education and seem to succeed, never letting on that they are struggling. Some can't wait to get out of school, describing their time in school as if they were prison inmates "doing time" or creatures caught in some kind of time warp for thirteen years. Some struggling students adapt only to the extent they must, getting marks that barely pass them from grade to grade, graduating from high school with the minimum number of credits and a "D" average. The latter are the students that Theodore Sizer and others worried about when they studied American high schools in the 1980s—students who did the bare minimum and never pushed themselves to become real learners (Sizer, 1984; Hampel, 1986; Powell, Farrar, & Cohen, 1985).

Even for these students school wasn't always a struggle. They probably liked kindergarten and first grade, maybe even second and third grades. By middle school, however, many of them had decided that the struggle wasn't worth it. They began to ditch a few classes, discovering that their absences didn't make much difference. Some discerned that, whether or not they had warmed the seat during the week, they could still pass Friday quizzes and scheduled tests. Why bother to come to school?

Some noticed that their absences made little difference to their teachers or principals. Apparently, they decided, they were so invisible in class that no one knew when they were gone. No one contacted their parents (who may or may not have cared). In their coterie of friends, ditching was cool and school so very uncool! So, they stopped going to school except to meet friends after seventh period. Eventually, even the Friday quizzes didn't matter to them; they, teenage cynics, decided that education was not worth much if they could pass quizzes and tests after having skipped classes and avoiding homework.

Some struggling students didn't give failure a chance to kick in. They stopped going to classes and didn't show up to fail quizzes or tests. It wasn't that they had failed the tests, quizzes, or classes; they simply weren't there. They took control of their fear of failure by eliminating its possibility.

Eventually, it was okay to flunk a class; flunking their second and third classes just proved the point they had decided to make about themselves. They weren't dumb, just suspicious about the value of an education. The results were ridiculous. Suspensions—talk about a joke!—gave them permission to do what they were doing (not go to school). They may have technically flunked out before they dropped out, or vice versa. Or, they may have been expelled. In any case, the value of completing their formal education and getting a diploma was no longer as important as what was happening in the rest of their lives. The future they had planned for themselves didn't include graduating from high school.

Their alienation from the formal education system is, of course, not the "fault" of the education system alone. Indeed, most struggling students can point to at least one adult in the school system who tried to help them. (Unfortunately, many can also point to at least one adult in the school system who discouraged them from learning or staying in school.) Many came from chaotic homes and, for some, the only way to escape pain was to obliterate it with drugs or alcohol. These solutions sometimes meant joining gangs, running away, or committing petty crime.

Some rebelled against adults they couldn't respect, describing how pointless it seemed to be to learn when their lives were combusting at home, when a parent had left, when the landlord had locked the door against them, when there were fights or drug deals in the hallway. It was hard for them to find meaning in first period when they had been up all night trying to break up a fight between inebriated family members.

These kids have been labeled in a variety of ways. "Dropout" is used to describe them when they get to high school (some never even get that far). Some call them "at risk," labeling them, but I'd rather think of them as "placed at risk," placed there by others. Those cynical about the system these kids have abandoned have called them the "throwaway" kids. At the very least, these are the "go-away" kids. Even if they stay in our classrooms, they have gone away behind their attitudes . . . and their backpacks. I sometimes think of them as the "dis" kids: disengaged, discredited, disenfranchised, disinterested, disenchanted, disaffiliated, disappointed, disassociated, disconcerting, disconnected. . . . They, themselves, speak of being dissed when they feel they are being disrespected.

Frank McCourt in the third book about his life in Ireland and in New York, *Teacher Man* (2005), describes Andrew, a typical "dis" kid:

> In every class there's a pest put on earth to test you. He usually sits in the last row, where he can tilt his chair against the wall. You've already talked to the class about the danger of tilting: Chair could slip, children, and you could be hurt. Then teacher has to write a report in case parents complain or threaten to sue. (p. 149)

Andrew, of course, pushes McCourt, teacher, as far as possible, knowing that as he does so he is getting lots of attention from his peers, especially the girls. McCourt calls Andrew's attention to what he is doing, and Andrew responds, "Wha'?" McCourt says, "That is the teenage sound you won't find in any dictionary. Wha'? Parents hear it constantly. It means, Whaddya want? Why you bothering me?"

McCourt warns Andrew about the chair and asks him to put it down. Andrew's response is typical teenager, "I'm just sittin' minding my own business." McCourt says, "The chair, Andrew, has four legs. Tilting on two legs could cause an accident."

What to do now? McCourt contemplates a variety of responses, turns away, walks to the front, and then turns the incident into a lesson: "Imagine you're a newspaper reporter. You walked into this room a few minutes ago. What did you see? What did you hear? What is the story?" A student challenges Andrew. Andrew rises to the bait, and McCourt almost goes after him. The next day Andrew and McCourt converse in the hallway, and McCourt learns that Andrew's mother—who was in the same class as McCourt at NYU—had died of cancer. "Her name was June" (quoted passages are from McCourt, 2005, pp. 149–151).

Meet another struggling student. Alan Blankstein (2004)[1] tells the story of this child in his award-winning book, *Failure Is Not an Option*:

> I was called to school for an appointment with the teachers of a 10-year old boy, Sidiki, to whom I had become "big brother." When I inquired into the purpose of our meeting, one teacher's analysis of Sidiki's performance was: "Sidiki is not performing at the skill level of his classmates. He has difficulty paying attention and refuses to participate in class. His reading comprehension is well below grade level and his scores on our standardized tests indicate that his math skills are only at third-grade level."
>
> The team leader provided a more succinct analysis: "He just doesn't get it! I think he may be learning disabled."
>
> I shared with Sidiki's teachers that he was an African immigrant who already spoke four languages, the last of which was English. I shared how enthusiastic and excited Sidiki could become once he was engaged in our evening tutoring sessions, remaining

exclusively focused on his homework for hours at a time—often longer than I could! I also explained the tremendous tumult in his family life, and the pressure and abuse he received from his father.

As I spoke, it was clear that neither teacher had been aware of Sidiki's impressive multilingual abilities, his enthusiasm for learning and capacity for intense concentration, his father's status as an international scholar, or the abuse—physical and otherwise— which Sidiki received from him. As I revealed these facts, a look of empathy began to play on one of the teacher's faces. (p. 102)

Now read about another student who could be classified as a struggling student (L. B. Easton, 2002):

James graduated . . . in December 1996, but graduation was not at all what he expected in his life when he entered the school almost three years earlier. His name was different then and his hair was curly and disheveled; he called it a "mop." An administrator in a . . . school district had recognized in James a talent and intelligence no one else had recognized, and she worked hard to get him admitted. . . . Other people saw a druggie who had somehow escaped the fate of two of his friends, who died of an overdose outside on a cold winter night. The anguish James felt about his friends dying while he lived was still deep within him when he came to [school]. So were the memories he had about being separated from his peers and put into special education classes for most of his educational life, where he found he could manipulate his teachers into doing his work for him. He came to [school] convinced he was dumb, ugly, and unworthy.

[In an exhibition of learning at that school] he described the philosophy books he was reading, inviting his panel members and audience to converse with him about Schopenhauer or Nietzsche. . . . James grinned and then said something I will never forget: "I have discovered the secret to learning." He grinned again, moving his eyes to take us all in, especially those of us who were on his panel. "The secret is that we teach ourselves—that's how we learn. I used to think that learning was the teacher's responsibility. Now I know that it's mine." He smoothed back his curly hair. "I used to wait for the teacher to put learning into me, and when it didn't happen, I knew that there was something wrong with me. (pp. 122–133)

The remaining two stories are brief autobiographies from students who attended Eagle Rock School and Professional Development Center. They included these autobiographies in their Presentation of Learning Packets (you'll learn more about these in Chapter 8).

I was a 'fast' baby; I stopped drinking from a bottle early, crawled early, walked early, and talked early. Early in my life, my parents separated and my father lived apart from us in Oklahoma.

I flunked the first grade. At the time, it was not embarrassing for me because I did not know what was going on then. All through my school years I had a hard time in reading. Reading was the biggest challenge for me to cope with in elementary schools. I . . . attended three schools before I was finally tested for a Learning Disability in second grade. From this point on my schooling was unbearable. When I became old enough to understand that I learn differently, I knew that I was going to have a hard time in school. I did not know that I was going to have a hard time at home.

Around the same time that I was tested, my father, who had become very ill, moved back to California. I saw him a few times before he passed. Also, at that time my mom, who was in an abusive relationship, gave birth to my sister. In school, I was put into a pull-out program for special education students. Emotionally, I sometimes felt that my life was "a rolling brown hell."

By the time I entered middle school in sixth grade, I had a lot of anger toward my mom from watching her get beaten. I felt that she was weak and did not love us kids enough to let her boyfriend go. At this point in my life, I felt that I was stupid and ugly. I did not feel good about myself. I felt that no one could relate to me and to what I was going through.

Here is the final story:

I am a seventeen-year-old Mexican American who was born in _____ , _____ , on November 27, 1985. I have lived in _____ my whole life. Right now I live with my mother, stepfather, my three sisters, and my two brothers. After my parents divorced, my father moved to Mexico so I only saw him once in a while. I am the oldest of six children, and it's hard at times because I have the responsibility to set a good example for my siblings. . . .

As I was growing up I did really well in school. I was always on Honor Roll and always had perfect attendance. My mom was really proud of me and she began to have high expectations for me. She put all of her hope into me and wanted me to become very successful. When I started high school, a lot of things began to change. I began to date, to be self-conscious, and to go out more. I hung out with people whose only interests were to have fun and party. I began to follow what they did because I felt they were my friends, and I enjoyed being around them. After a while, I began to drink and I came to a point where all I cared about was being with my friends and getting wasted because it seemed easier than doing everything else I had to do. As a result my grades started to go down and I would try to get caught up, but I would go back to what distracted me from my work. Afterwards, I lost motivation and interest, and I didn't see the point in trying because I was already behind.

As time went on I realized I was very unhappy. I had a drinking problem, I was failing in school, and my mom was really depressed because I was throwing my life away. I didn't recognize myself anymore; I was a different person, a person I didn't want to be. I realized I was going down the wrong way and I decided I needed to do something about it or nothing was going to change.

Perhaps you know students like these students. They are struggling students, ones who make teachers and principals uncomfortable. Though adults try, most can't seem to connect with these kids. Sometimes, honestly, it's a relief when these students stop coming to school.

It is hard to put these vastly different students into one box. It is hard to write a sentence that begins with, "A struggling student is . . . " Here is what participants in workshops I've conducted about struggling students have said after reading these stories:

"Well, they're not the ones we usually label . . . unless we have mislabeled them and they're struggling where they're placed."

"They're the gray children. They're not really good. They're not really bad. They're in the gray area. I worry that they'll wash out when we're not looking."

"We know so little about what goes on in children's lives. The struggling ones manage, but just barely. It scares me—and makes me very angry—when I get a chance to talk with them. No kid should have to go through what some of these kids do. And, one more thing may be enough to tip them over."

A NATION'S PROBLEM

These struggling kids are everywhere, in your school, in mine. They struggle in the school next door or across the city, in suburban, urban, and rural schools. Though dropping out is conventionally seen as a high school problem, it is, in fact, a problem of all educators and community members who want students to learn, stay in school, graduate, and contribute to a world that desperately needs them. Elementary schools have dropouts; more join the ranks in middle schools; and by high school many who start as freshmen do not make it to graduation. According to many educators and researchers, state testing of standards, particularly end-of-grade or graduation tests, may result in even more dropouts.

Elementary Schools

Although most elementary school students don't actually drop out until sixth, seventh, or eighth grade (technically *middle* schools), a far larger number than most people expect leave school (and appear to enter no other school). *The Chicago Reporter* determined that "from 1991 to 1999, an average of 1,400 youth each year left Chicago's public schools in sixth, seventh or eighth grade" (Dumke, 2001). The Consortium on Chicago School Research reported "7,166 students in 6th, 7th, and 8th grades dropped out, disappeared or transferred to nobody knows where" (Duffrin, 2001). Of course, some of these students may have transferred to schools that failed to send for transcripts or otherwise notify former schools. However, according to Patricia Preston, director of alternative education for the City Colleges of Chicago, "'They've been the silent dropouts no one really talks about'" (Dumke, 2001).

The problem in elementary schools is acute enough that at least one state department of education—Kentucky's—has fashioned an elementary dropout prevention resource. The Kentucky Dropout Prevention Resource Guide (Kentucky Department of Education, 2003) describes standards for dropout prevention programs in elementary schools. It also provides descriptions of these indicators of early-leaving potential and a variety of strategies for remedying the problems:

1. Absenteeism

2. Academic Failure and Retention

3. Lack of Connection

4. Low Socioeconomic Background

5. Ethnic Background

6. Lack of Family Involvement

7. Lack of Community Involvement

Whether or not students drop out in elementary school (sixth, seventh, and eighth grades in particular) or begin the process of leaving school as early as elementary school, dropping out is a problem K–12. Kentucky's indicators—and those identified by others—describe the struggles that may cause students to give up on their education, no matter what grade they're in.

One indicator of potential to drop out deserves special attention. What Kentucky listed as "Academic Failure and Retention" is still hotly debated in American education. Should students who have "failed" a grade level, class, or subject be forced to repeat that unsuccessful experience? Should they be promoted regardless of failing a grade level, class, or subject (a process known as *social promotion*)? Should they be required to participate in an alternative learning program or class?

Researchers and practitioners are mostly in agreement that retention resulting in repeating a grade, class, or subject paves the way for more problems. Students who repeat unsuccessful learning experiences seldom make sufficient learning gains to "catch up" with their peers. Indeed, they are likely to be retained again . . . and again . . . and eventually drop out of a system that has left them behind, according to Foster (1993) in her review of the research about retaining children in grade. Indeed, retaining a child more than once in a grade almost guarantees that the student will eventually drop out. According to Debra Viadero (2006) in a special issue of *Education Week*, "Some studies suggest that being retained even once between 1st and 8th grades makes a student four times more likely to drop out than a classmate who was never held back" (p. 20). This is, in fact, "the predictor that 'trumps everything else,'" according to Karl L. Alexander (Viadero, 2006) of Johns Hopkins University. Researchers found that "sixty-four percent of the students who had repeated a grade in elementary school, and 63 percent of those who had been retained in middle school, eventually wound up leaving school without a diploma" (p. 20).

But social promotion doesn't work either, according to Pierson and Connell (1992), who discovered that social promotion may actually increase academic problems.

What does work? A third alternative, participating in an alternative learning program or class, seems to be the best solution. Practices related to this solution include additional time for learning, before- and after-school programs, summer school, and having aides or tutors work with individuals and small groups. In no case should the original learning experience that led to failure be repeated. In fact, the alternative learning program should be tailored as much as possibile to learning styles and preferences; it should be engaging and worthwhile.

A good resource on the policies and practices of retention is the book written by Lorrie Shepard and Mary Lee Smith (1989), *Flunking Grades: Research and Policies on Retention.*

Secondary Schools

Talking about struggling students in middle- and high schools inevitably leads to investigation of who drops out, and when and why. Unfortunately, according to the Education Trust, figuring out who has dropped out and who has stayed in school is a messy business. In a press release on June 23, 2005, the Education Trust declared,

> Some states rely on ludicrous definitions of graduation rates. Others make little effort to accurately account for students who drop out of school. And others still provide no data at all. The final result: Extremely unreliable graduation-rate information that

erodes public confidence in schools and their leadership and threatens to undermine the important work of high school reform.

Even with such wild ways of working graduation rates, state by state the United States "now ranks 17th in the developed world in high school graduation rates," according to the Education Trust (2005).

Jay Greene of the Manhattan Institute reported graduate rates for 1998: 71% graduated nationally, with 78% of white students graduating, 45% of African American students graduating, and 54% of Latino students graduating (Greene, 2002). In another stab at computing graduation rates, the National Center for Educational Statistics (NCES) used something called an *event rate* to estimate the number of dropouts for 2000:

> Event rates describe the proportion of students in a given age range who leave school each year without completing a high school program. In this report, the event rate measures young adults ages 15 through 24 who dropped out during the school year preceding the data collection. (NCES, 2000)

The NCES maintained that, according to the event rate, "5 out of every 100 young adults (4.8 percent) who were enrolled in high school in October 1999 were no longer in school and had not successfully completed a high school program."

Still another measure of this elusive statistic, the Promoting Power Index (PPI), is used by more than 2,000 high schools. Eighteen percent of these PPI schools have an index of less than 60%, meaning that approximately 1 in 3 students starting in ninth grade will not graduate at the end of 12th grade (Hill, 2005). Many PPI schools disproportionately enroll students of color and lower social economic status (SES).

Education Week addressed the issue of dropouts in its June 22, 2006, special issue called "Diplomas Count: An Essential Guide to Graduation Policy and Rates." Here is a summary of the highlights of this impressive publication:

- In the 2005 school year "an estimated 1.2 million teenagers fell by the wayside." (p. 5)

- The effects are economic and social. Economically, high school graduates earn "on average, 34 percent more than those without a high school diploma. College graduates made a whopping 132 percent more." (p. 5)

- Socially, dropouts are more likely to end up in "prison or on welfare and they die, on average, at a younger age." (p. 6)

- "Graduation rates are far worse for members of most minority groups and for boys." (p. 6)

- State goals for graduation rates are sometimes as low as 50 percent, according to Daniel Losen, senior education law and policy associate at the

Civil Rights Project at Harvard University, and propose "timelines that could literally take hundreds of years." (p. 6)

- The General Educational Development certificate (GED) is not equivalent to a high school diploma. "Comedian Chris Rock (himself a GED recipient) . . . claim[ed] it [stood] for 'Good Enough Diploma.'" (p. 8)

No matter how you count them, we can't keep losing young people from learning, not even one young person. One third? No. One out of four? No. Five in one hundred?

The *Education Week* special issue addressed the school's role in ameliorating the drop-out problem. Unfortunately, *Ed Week* writers found in a 2005 survey of teachers in Boston that "more than two-thirds . . . believe that student success or failure is beyond the teacher's control. Almost two-thirds disagreed with the idea that keeping students from dropping out of school is the responsibility of teachers" (p. 10). Teachers reported feeling helpless in the face of problems some students bring to school: being impoverished, a member of a minority group, or male, for example. Also, teachers found it hard to counteract the problems of students who came from single-parent families, had a mother who dropped out, or who were assuming adult responsibilities while still children themselves.

It is no wonder that teachers feel powerless. It takes more than individual teachers to help struggling students succeed. It takes a whole school, supported by community resources and district and state structures and funding. Still, according to *Education Week*, teachers can do something, and so can schools. Among solutions to the drop-out problem proposed by *Education Week* are these:

- Start sooner rather than later.
- Focus on transitions.
- Provide extra help.
- Redesign high schools.
- Create multiple paths to graduation.
- Coordinate services.
- Strengthen accountability systems. (Olson, 2006)

The fourth suggestion above is the focus of this book. Redesigned schools—not just high schools but all schools that serve struggling students—can help keep them in school, learning, graduating, and contributing to a society that needs them. Writers of the *Education Week* special issue suggested that "schools with smaller enrollments, better relationships between students and adults, teachers who are more supportive of students, and a curriculum that is both focused and rigorous tend to have lower drop out rates" (p. 10). *Education Week* also reported that dropouts completing a survey listed as their "major reason for dropping out . . . that classes were not interesting. Nearly seven in 10 said they were not motivated or inspired to work hard in school; two-thirds said they would have worked harder if more had been demanded of them; and 70 percent were confident they could have graduated if they had tried" (p. 10). The results of this survey suggest the power of engagement.

THE FOCUS OF THIS BOOK: ENGAGEMENT

So much about learning comes down to engagement. Engagement is not simply a matter of motivating students extrinsically or intrinsically—although, of course, we know that intrinsic engagement is usually the better of the two. What we want in schools is what Mihaly Csikszentmihalyi (1990) called *flow*. If only our students could be as intent about learning as tennis players are on serving or artists on painting a picture! How wonderful if they could be fierce with concentration, so absorbed they lose self-consciousness, and so focused that space and time disappear.

Bruya and Olwell (2006) describe flow in schools as engaging "learners at their own level and present[ing] them with an appropriate level of challenge" (p. 31). They suggest that Csikszentmihalyi's concept of flow, "the psychological process that describes how people balance skill, interest, and challenge—may hold an important piece of the puzzle of school reform" (p. 31). If the challenge level is too high or too low, learners might disengage from learning, even drop out. If "challenge and skill are well matched," students are more likely to be engaged; if the activity connects "to the rest of their lives and their interests," they are even more likely to be engaged (p. 31). Bruya and Olwell state, "The most powerful learning in schools is often found in activities that harness individual students' interests and creativity . . . also found in activities that connect directly to the world around students" (p. 31).

In this book, flow is evidence of engagement and engagement stands for all the aspects of school that can be changed to help struggling students want to learn and keep learning. *One part of the premise of this book is that engaged students are learning students. Another part of this book's premise is that schools can do something about engagement.* Providing more engaging contexts for learning is not a matter of erecting a three-ring circus tent in the multipurpose room. The everyday nature of schools can be changed to be more engaging: curriculum, instruction, assessment, the school's culture . . .

If interviewed about this notion, most students would say that responsibility for their lack of engagement is not just a school's problem. They would acknowledge that they have some role themselves in becoming engaged and learning. Still, schools cannot reside in the land of "I taught it; they didn't learn it" or "It's their fault; they come from impoverished homes." Given the statistics about students who become lost to learning and the simple moral imperative of education for all, schools must work hard to engage students in their learning, no matter how students come to their opportunities to learn.

No Quick Fixes

Those who have worked with struggling students know that there are no quick fixes, silver bullets, or Band-Aids that will help them. No purchased textbook or program—whether on character development, motivation, or the latest curriculum or instructional strategy—completely succeeds in engaging students in their own learning. What helps is nothing less than changing the school culture for struggling students. This book is about changing the culture of schools so that it is more humane and inhabitable for struggling learners.

For all learners, actually. These strategies are not just for struggling students. All students need a culture that energizes them for learning and affects not only academic but also personal and social growth.

For all ages, too. These strategies for changing culture work with any learner. The strategies may manifest differently at different grade levels, but the strategies themselves are effective for kindergartners through adult learners.

Hard work? Yes, it is hard to change from within: We are seeking to change that which we know and are living. It is hard to change anything that is ongoing: We can't just stop, think, and do it over again. It is hard to change anything by ourselves, except what we do individually. Nevertheless, systems change every time someone in the system begins to do business a little bit differently.

Imperative? Yes, I believe change is imperative, for struggling students and all those who care about them.

EXPERIENCE WITH STRUGGLING STUDENTS

My colleagues and I have been working with struggling students since 1993, a whole school of them. Although this book is not about Eagle Rock School and Professional Development Center, its contents—"lessons learned" and examples—draw deeply from the work done there with struggling students.

I spent nearly 12 years at Eagle Rock School and Professional Development Center, coming to the school as Director of Professional Development in 1994 as the school was beginning its second year. I designed and facilitated the outreach work of the Professional Development Center, but I also worked within the school, with the students and the rest of the staff. I learned firsthand what works with Eagle Rock's population and how to help visiting educators understand and apply these ideas in their own, different settings.

Eagle Rock was established to work with struggling students; it intentionally enrolls such students from across the United States, at no cost to them, their families, schools, or districts. The school serves as a laboratory school, through which educators do everything they can to reengage these students in learning, keep them in school, and graduate them to productive citizenship. The complementary professional development center helps other educators study how to accomplish these same goals in their own schools.

Thus, this book is about struggling students and what they need, with reference to experiences at Eagle Rock. The lessons learned take form as chapter headings, and most of the examples come from Eagle Rock—from conversations with individual students and teachers; from my own experiences teaching there and observing others teach; from my participation in school community events and meetings; as well as from specially held interviews and focus group sessions.

You can read more about Eagle Rock in the Resources at the back of this book.

VOICES IN THIS BOOK

You will hear several voices in this book. One voice is mine; I wrote this book as if you were visiting Eagle Rock and we were talking on the Esplanade, looking out on the granite dome known as Notaiah. You will also read what real students say about issues related to their struggles in school; these students are from Eagle Rock, some of them graduates, some whose education is still in progress. Finally, you'll read the voices of other educators who work with struggling students. Interspersed throughout this book are vignettes from these educators. In these vignettes, the guest authors describe their schools and what they are doing to engage students in learning; they also provide ways you can contact them.

Finally, in the chapter titles, you'll hear the voices of educators who have visited Eagle Rock. Though you may hear skepticism or challenge in their voices, please take their queries as genuine interest. They asked questions during visits to Eagle Rock because they really wanted to know how to improve their own schools. Their voices deserve respect; they work in schools that struggle immensely to work with disengaged students.

THE READER'S RESPONSIBILITY

Although this book draws many of its examples (and voices) from Eagle Rock, Eagle Rock was not meant to be replicated. The environment at Eagle Rock is unique: The school was designed to try out anything and everything that might help reenroll young people in learning. I realize that no other school operates under Eagle Rock's conditions. Some readers may be tempted to say, "Well, we're not Eagle Rock!" and dismiss ideas that would work very well—with a tweak or two—in their own settings. Other schools described in this book have accomplished amazing changes on behalf of struggling students.

I believe that the ideas in this book from Eagle Rock and other schools can be useful to individual teachers, teachers who are part of a Professional Learning Community (PLC), whole faculties, district administrators, and others involved in improving schools for all students (DuFour, DuFour, Eaker, & Karhanek, 2004). They can be helpful to teacher candidates enrolled in teacher preparation programs as well as to practicing educators who are engaged in their own professional learning.

Some suggestions in this book are appropriate for individual teachers to implement in their own classrooms. Teachers can create a culture for learning in their own classes; they can customize curriculum, instruction, and assessment to meet the needs of their own students. Even so, individual teachers may want to unite with others who are trying to find ways to work with struggling students. A network of concerned teachers will help each member make changes that help struggling students. Some suggestions are more appropriate for a whole school to consider—perhaps a building leadership team (including the principal) or a PLC that communicates with the rest of the faculty and staff—perhaps the whole staff. Some suggestions may seem impossible because they involve systemwide decisions. Systemic change may seem impossible, but as my mentor Suzanne Bailey says, "Systems change one lunch at a time" as individuals do things differently and then share in new ways with others what they are doing (personal communication, June 4, 2004).

Never underestimate what a single teacher can do in a classroom in terms of engaging students in their own learning. Teachers can make incredibly effective cultural changes as well as concrete changes in curriculum, instruction, and assessment. Never underestimate what the faculty and staff of a school can do together. They can improve the learning environment for all students and still meet state and district requirements. Never underestimate what districts can do to support schools working toward substantive improvement for all students.

Please read this book with this question in mind: "How can what I am reading about make a difference in my environment, not only for struggling students but for all students?" As an inquiring reader, you'll see many more possibilities than problems.

THE ORGANIZATION OF THIS BOOK

Educators who visit Eagle Rock's Professional Development Center (sometimes for as short as half a day or as long as nine days) are invited through an immersion experience to discover the WHAT of Eagle Rock: "What do Eagle Rock's staff and students do to commit to learning? What aspects of Eagle Rock help/hinder learning?" If they are intent on making change to benefit students in their own schools, visiting educators go beyond WHAT, addressing two more questions: "SO WHAT?" and "NOW

WHAT?" These questions lead them to consider application in their own settings of what they've experienced at Eagle Rock. Eagle Rock staff help them ask and answer questions like these: "So, what does this mean to us? Do we have students like the Eagle Rock students?" Or, "Our school is an elementary school. How does what we investigated here apply to us?" Always, "How is our environment different and similar? So, what can WE do?" Then, they enter a planning phase through the NOW WHAT question: "What do we do first? Second? Third? Now what do we do?"

As a reader of this book—unless you schedule a trip to Eagle Rock (you're invited!)—you don't have a staff member to guide you through the WHAT—SO WHAT—NOW WHAT questions. Therefore, please read the first part of each chapter as the WHAT part. The last two sections of each chapter in this book will help you think about what you've read and how your learning might effect changes in your own environment. The SO WHAT part of each chapter will engage you in a professional learning activity you can do alone and/or with colleagues. The NOW WHAT portion of each chapter will suggest a few steps you can take to improve engagement in your own environment.

This book is organized in four sections:

Introduction: The Importance of Culture

Part I: Improving the Culture for Struggling Students

Part II: Improving Curriculum, Instruction, and Assessment for Struggling Students

Conclusion: The Importance of Looking at the Student as a Whole Person

If you are more interested in school and classroom cultures, focus on Section I. If you are interested in more concrete ideas, focus on Section II because it addresses what can be done in classrooms. In either case, read the Introduction and the Conclusion with an eye toward fashioning an integrated system of support for struggling students.

AN OVERVIEW OF THE CHAPTERS

Introduction: The Importance of Culture

In this chapter you'll consider how important an intentional culture is to struggling students and how an intentional culture can lead to coherence in structure, governance, curriculum, instruction, and assessment and other aspects of school. You'll also explore ways to analyze culture through beliefs, metaphors, artifacts, and practice and how to achieve coherence. Finally, you'll read about engaging students in the culture of the school and how to make sure the school's statement of culture is a living document, not a dusty plaque.

Part I: Improving the Culture for Struggling Students

Chapter 1. "What About Test Scores?"
From a Testing to a Learning Culture

The first question from visitors to Eagle Rock can be a killer. If I answer it one way, the visitor dismisses all that Eagle Rock has done to help struggling students. If I answer it the other way, the visitor eagerly continues the conversation.

Thank goodness I can answer the question positively. Scores on the TAP, the high school version of the Iowa Test of Basic Skills go up—precipitously—from the pretest version (when students first arrive) to the posttest version (when students graduate).

It may seem obvious that learning improves test scores, but I don't mean learning in the test preparation sense. The curriculum at Eagle Rock is unrelated—except accidentally—to the tested curriculum. The methods of instruction in no way match the testing formats (recall, choice among options), yet struggling students do amazingly well on these tests. This chapter explores how real learning improves test scores.

Chapter 2. "What Do You Mean, Build Relationships? My Job Is to Teach History"
Relationships Are as Important as Content

The teacher who asked that question and followed it with a statement of his job responsibilities was completely sincere. His training had prepared him to teach history.

Students, however, repeatedly declare that what helps them learn—more than anything else, individually or in combination!—is the relationships they have with their instructors. This chapter explores what it is about relationships that advances learning as well as how to build relationships with students.

Chapter 3. "What's Community Got to Do With Learning?"
Intentional Learning Communities Foster Learning

This chapter builds on the necessity of relationships. Students as well as staff benefit from an organization that considers itself a community of learners. The recent movement toward building Professional Learning Communities (PLCs) doesn't go quite far enough. The entire community—students as well as all staff—should be a school learning community, an SLC. Having a professional development center helps students and staff, as well as visiting educators, value learning. Seeing adults learning—and, sometimes, struggling with that learning—helps struggling students feel they are part of a learning system instead of outcasts. This chapter considers students as teachers and teachers as students in a Whole-School Learning Community (WSLC).

Chapter 4. "So, What About Discipline?"
How Principles Govern a School Better Than Rules

This is another frequently asked question. Underlying this question is a caveat: "given these kids," meaning students who are disruptive and disengaged. Upon hearing the term "principle-centered," one administrator was disappointed that I wasn't talking about "principal-centered." Stephen Covey writes about being principle-centered and what that means for leaders as individuals and in corporations. This chapter uses as an example the principles that guide Eagle Rock ("8 + 5 = 10") and how they are much more than a plaque on a wall. Principles—not rules—result in a culture that is meaningful and important to struggling students, a culture they'll defend!

Chapter 5. "What's Democratic About Schools?"
A Democratic School Helps Students Learn

The educator who posed this question was right on target. Most schools are autocratic and top-down. Why *should* a school be democratic? One reason is the curriculum our nation's founders envisioned, which prepared students for their civic responsibilities. Students study democratic values from kindergarten on, but in most schools they don't live them. This chapter explores the reasons for schools to behave democratically as well as how they can do so. Struggling students understand the value and responsibility of power and authority.

Part II: Improving Curriculum, Instruction, and Assessment for Struggling Students

Chapter 6. "What About Standards?"
Developing Curriculum According to the Right Standards

Standards are standard. They are part of the lexicon of schooling. Everyone, from national and state policy leaders to students in school, talks standards. However, in the most important transitions schools offer, from grade to grade and graduation, few schools take a standards-based approach. This chapter contrasts the conventional way of giving credit to students (seat time and grades) with a truly standards-based approach. This chapter introduces curriculum that is based on documentation. This chapter also introduces the magic of high expectations. Struggling students become engaged in their own learning when they are in charge of their own learning; this chapter shows how students can be standards-based.

Chapter 7. "How Do You Get Them to Learn?"
Innovative Instructional Strategies Help Students Learn

Several instructional strategies help students engage in learning. This chapter highlights certain conventional strategies of instruction that work especially well with struggling students. It also describes a variety of outlier strategies—power, voice, choice, accountability, transparency of the curriculum, students as teachers, self-directed learning, and service—that are surprisingly effective in helping students engage in their own learning.

Chapter 8. "How Do You Know They've Learned?"
Learning From Assessing Learning

Grant Wiggins and others have distinguished between assessment *of* and assessment *for* learning. Learning happens for students and staff when assessment is *for* learning. This chapter focuses on two mechanisms Eagle Rock uses to assess for learning: documentations of learning and Presentations of Learning (POLs). You'll meet Sevi when you read his first Presentation of Learning packet and read about POLs themselves. You will also learn the logistics of both types of assessment, how they work in a real school setting. You'll get some ideas about what to do if students are not learning.

Conclusion: The Importance of Looking at the Student as a Whole Person

The conclusion returns to the focus of the book: the student. You'll read the near-to-graduation autobiography of Sevi, the student whose first Presentation of Learning packet you read in Chapter 8. You'll probably notice a few differences! You'll look at what educating the whole student means, with a special focus on personal growth without labeling students. You'll also examine a number of strategies—beliefs and culture, structures, program, and curriculum, instruction and assessment—that help a school embed personal growth into the whole of the school.

NOTE

1. From *Failure Is Not an Option* by Blankstein, Alan. Reprinted with permission from Corwin Press.

ACKNOWLEDGMENTS

The author would like to thank the many reviewers of both a very early version of this book and a later version. Their wise and forthright comments helped immensely.

The contributions of the following reviewers are gratefully acknowledged:

Drucilla W. Clark
Superintendent of Schools
Denville Board of Education
Denville Township, NJ

Michelle Collay
Associate Professor of Educational Leadership
Coordinator, Urban Teacher Leadership Master's Degree Program
California State University, East Bay
Hayward, CA

Scot Danforth
Associate Professor
College of Education and Human Ecology
The Ohio State University
Columbus, OH

Jean Cheng Gorman
Licensed Psychologist
Modesto, CA

Steve Hutton
Area Coordinator
Kentucky Center for Instructional Discipline
Villa Hills, KY

James Kelleher
Assistant Superintendent
Scituate Public Schools
Scituate, MA

Margo M. Marvin
Superintendent of Schools
Putnam, CT

Kathryn McCormick
National Board Certified Teacher
Gahanna Middle School East
Gahanna, OH

Greg Oppel
Social Studies Teacher
Edmond Memorial High School
Edmond, OK

Eleanor Renee Rodriguez
Professional Development Consultant
Rodriguez and Associates
Norfolk, VA

William A. Sommers
Associate
Southwest Educational Development Laboratory
Austin, TX

Max Thompson
President
Learning Concepts, Inc.
Greensboro, NC

Introduction

The Importance of Culture

A visitor to Eagle Rock asked me directly, "Why should we concern ourselves about culture? Students have to go to school. We have to teach them. We know what they need to know. They learn what we know. We don't need culture to do that." A colleague of this middle school teacher responded, "School is more than a simple transfer of knowledge and skills." I added, "Learning happens best in an environment conducive to it, and that's what culture is all about." Students and staff joined our discussion group and one student claimed, "Oh, yeah, schools have culture, and you can tell it from the moment you walk in." A staff member commented, "I think we take culture for granted. When we do that, we have what I'd call an 'accidental culture,' one that has not been thought through." One of the visitors added, "I think we need to be very intentional about building culture, especially when we're working with struggling students. We need to build a culture that helps young people learn."

It is true that you can

> walk into any truly excellent school and you can feel it almost immediately—a calm, orderly atmosphere that hums with an exciting, vibrant sense of purposefulness just under the surface. Students carry themselves with poise and confidence. Teachers talk about their work with intensity and professionalism. And despite the sense of serious business at hand, both teachers and students seem happy and confident rather than stressed. Everyone seems to know who they are and why they are there, and children and staff treat each other with the respect due to full partners in an important enterprise. (Jerald, 2007)

You can also walk into a school and sense a prohibitive culture, one that is rigid and repressive, even cold.

There were many reasons for the Columbine tragedy in my home state, but one of them was a culture that the killers perceived as hostile. They described the culture at Columbine High School as one that celebrated jocks and popular students but scorned people who were "different"— nerds, punks, stoners, artsies. They chose their black trench coats and behavior with care to make a place for themselves in Columbine.

At the very least, schools should examine their own culture, just to see what kind of culture they have. One way educators can do this is by shadowing students and teachers in other schools as well as their own school (Easton, 2004c). Another way educators can examine culture is through learning walks, what Carolyn Downey and others call Walkthroughs (Downey, Steffy, English, Frase, & Poston, 2004). Their observations can yield a good starting point for discussion about culture: Is this what we want? What do we want? How can we create the culture we want?

Once a school community has addressed these three questions and knows what it wants, it is ready to take intentional action to create its optimum culture. Mechanisms for creating culture include these:

- Some statement of aspects of the culture and creation of ways the school community can "live" those statements rather than leaving them inert (as on a plaque in the hallway)
- Rethinking structure (use of time and place) so that it enables the desired culture
- Rethinking governance so that it enables the desired culture
- Rethinking curriculum, instruction, and assessment so that they enhance the culture
- Enacting events (celebrations, activities, programs, ceremonies, etc.). (L. B. Easton, 2002)

Jerald (2007) cites the work of Russell Hobby (2004) and the British Hay Group, which "lists five kinds of 'reinforcing behaviors' that send strong signals about vision and values:

- "Rituals: celebrations and ceremonies, rites of passage, and shared quirks and mannerisms.
- "Hero Making: role models, hierarchies, public rewards, and mentors.
- "Storytelling: shared humor, common anecdotes, foundation myths, and both oral and written history.
- "Symbolic Display: decoration, artwork, trophies, and architecture.
- "Rules: etiquette, formal rules, taboos, and tacit permissions." (Hobby, 2004, as cited in Jerald, 2007)

Thus, an intentional culture is realized through a school's structure, governance, curriculum, instruction, assessment, events, and "reinforcing behaviors." In an effective school, everything works together to benefit the

Vignette 1   A School Vignette: Culture

WRITTEN ON THE WALLS OF MY HEART

Ganado Primary School, Arizona

By Sigmund A. Boloz

"I'm going to cry, you know," I told Mrs. Vent, our reading specialist, as we moved through the commons area toward Dana's multiage classroom. "I'm going to cry the tears of a parent's joy." And I was right. I could not keep the tears of pride from filling my eyes. So, I took four deep breaths in hopes that I might at least flush out some of the redness that had overtaken my eyes.

We always announced the awarding of a T-shirt with such ceremony, but somehow the school's large handheld bell seemed louder than usual as our second-grade student council president, April, swung it up and back, "Clang! Clang! Clang! Clang!" I tried to crack one final joke to push back the tears, but the joke stuck in my throat as our little procession entered the classroom.

"Who gets the T-shirt?" Mrs. Vent asked in a dramatic voice.

"Dana!" Everyone cheered.

"Jump up and down Dana, aren't you happy?" Her teacher, Mrs. Barnes encouraged as Dana stood frozen.

Dana timidly complied and did what looked like more of an awkward jump rope skip, without the rope. While we all watched, Mrs. Vent handed the award to Mrs. Barnes who began pulling the navy blue "I Can Read Guaranteed" T-shirt over Dana's head. I breathed deeply a dozen more times.

"Who do you want to have your picture taken with?" Mrs. Vent questioned as she pulled up the digital camera. "Your teacher, Mrs. Barnes? Your mom?" It was customary for the student who received this award to have a parent or teacher honored along with the reader.

"Oh no!" Mrs. Barnes said seriously. "We already decided. Mr. Boloz."

I would have died if she hadn't picked me, but it was not my place to decide. The blue "I Can Read Guaranteed" T-shirt was the highest honor at our K–2 primary school. It signified that this particular student could read at the third grade level, and now Dana's picture would join the picture wall of 65 other readers already honored this year.

I moved over, kneeled next to her, smiled and raised a single index finger into the air. As I waited for the flash, I was taken back to when I first heard Dana's mother's frustrated voice on the phone. She was almost pleading for an answer, "What's going on? Why is it taking Dana so long to learn to read?"

Now it seemed as only moments ago when I first escorted Dana out of her classroom, had her complete a series of diagnostic assessments, and pronounced

(Continued)

Vignette 1 (Continued)

her to be a diamond in the rough, "All we have to do is polish her," I had smiled hopefully to Mrs. Barnes.

Although I had been the principal of this school for 22 years, I was also a reading intervention specialist who found his greatest satisfaction working directly with children. By choice, I had regularly assigned myself to work with children who were struggling with reading. I also found that teaching reading kept me grounded in the real work of schools and in the actual challenges that teachers faced.

With Dana, a second grader, my hardest task seemed to be getting everyone concerned about her lack of reading fluency to leave our follow-up meetings feeling positive and supportive. As I watched her mother hugging Dana, I recalled that another significant goal in my reading work with Dana was to help her to leave our 30-minute sessions feeling supported and believing in herself. It was hard to believe that one hundred days had passed since we first started our work together. One hundred days of making sure I was there every day sitting side-by-side in our guided reading sessions.

As her mom beamed with pride and Mrs. Barnes wiped away her own tears, I remembered that many of our days together felt as if they were harder on me than they were on Dana. Some days Dana simply resisted.

In those early sessions I realized that reading was a painful experience for Dana. Her reading history had been filled with criticism and blame. Even while Dana worked with me, reading was hard work. Often when reading wasn't easy anymore, Dana and I began feeling sorry for ourselves.

At one point, I was asked to stop working with Dana because her mother felt that Dana was getting "stressed out." After a day or two, it was Dana, herself, who intervened and decided to continue. Watching the celebration continue, I realized that this child's faith in herself and in me was vindicated.

Three point zero! Third grade reading! Even those persons who wanted to move Dana back into kindergarten material earlier in the year, as she began to falter, now cheered her on.

Mrs. Vent eventually took our picture and later that day the photograph of our triumph was posted alongside pictures of the other readers who commemorated their success on the "I Can Read Guaranteed" Wall of Fame. Before we left that day to deliver another dark blue shirt, Dana stopped me, "Mr. Boloz, I made something for you. Here."

She handed me an unframed certificate that she and her teacher had signed. The tears began to flow again. This time I didn't have the strength to hide them; I don't even remember breathing.

"You know," I said as I managed to dislodge the lump that now seemed larger than my throat, "I have received many awards over the years, but this is my greatest." I knelt down and hugged the quiet second grader. "I'm proud of you, too." I choked and I dragged myself away to the next room.

I have seen Dana a few times since that celebration four years ago, the year I retired from our public school. She still reads above grade level. That's the first thing she and her mom always want me to know. But, if you get a chance to come to the College of Education at Northern Arizona University, you can see a framed copy of the picture of Dana and me next to the certificate given to me by Dana, the reader. It is the only award I have chosen to display in my university office because it is also posted on the walls of my heart. It keeps me honest and grounded as I now teach reading and writing methods to future teachers. It reads, "Mr. Boloz. You have made a difference in the life of one child." You can't pay a teacher more than that.

SOURCE: Used by permission from Sigmund A. Boloz.

AUTHOR'S NOTE: Sigmund A. Boloz is the former principal of Ganado Primary School, a public school located within the Navajo Nation which in 1995 was named the Number One School in Arizona. He currently teaches literacy classes at Northern Arizona University.

students and adults who teach, learn, and work there. To the extent that the culture is the optimum for all students and all of the elements of the school foster that culture, students and adults will succeed.

An "accidental" culture or elements of a school that are at odds with that culture or even work against it result in—at best—an incoherent environment for learning; at worst—a toxic environment.

CULTURE AS MISSION AND VISION

One of the best definitions of culture comes from Terrance Deal and Kent Peterson (1999), as cited in Jerald (2007), who define it as an "'underground flow of feelings and folkways [wending] its way within schools' in the form of vision and values, beliefs and assumptions, rituals and ceremonies, history and stories, and physical symbols."

In the effective schools research, culture was defined as safe and orderly, but culture is much more. It is a set of beliefs and values that express what is important and guide all aspects of schooling. In many schools, districts, and organizations, culture is expressed through statements of mission or vision (or both). Organizational developers sometimes argue that these two expressions of culture are vastly different and need to be distinguished. Mission, which is sometimes described as "our niche," comes first and then vision, which is an articulation of what the future looks like. I believe that it doesn't much matter what we call the form we use to describe the culture we want—mission or vision—only that we are as concrete as possible.

Here are some mission and vision statements from schools that have been active in creating hospitable cultures for all students. They are mentor schools participating in the Coalition of Essential Schools.

Boston Arts Academy:

The Boston Arts Academy, a pilot school within the Boston Public Schools, is charged with being a laboratory and a beacon for artistic and academic innovation. The Boston Arts Academy prepares a diverse community of aspiring artist-scholars to be successful in their college or professional careers and to be engaged members of a democratic society. (Boston Arts Academy, 2006)

The vision of the Boston Arts Academy projects its future:

By 2014, BAA will be a recognized leader and advocate for the arts and their integration with academics in the national education reform movement. Viewed as the "Center for the Arts" within the Boston Public Schools, BAA will be known nationally and internationally for successfully educating a diverse array of Boston public school learners in all aspects of the arts.

We envision [a school] that continues to be small, student-centered and reflective of the diversity of Boston's neighborhoods. (Boston Arts Academy, 2006)

Their vision statement is followed by specific descriptions of students who are "holistic thinkers who demonstrate interdisciplinary understanding" and faculty who are strengthened by a "vibrant artists-in-residence program."

Another Boston school, Fenway High School, captures its mission in this statement:

Fenway High School's mission is to create a socially committed and morally responsible community of learners that values its students as individuals.

Its goal is to encourage academic excellence and habits of mind, self-esteem, and leadership development among all the school's students. (Fenway High School, n.d.)

On the other side of the country:

The mission of Leadership Charter High School is to serve San Francisco and its diverse students by providing an excellent education and developing effective community leaders.

We are achieving this mission for our economically and ethnically diverse students by offering significant personal attention and support, a rigorous curriculum, cutting edge technology and the first comprehensive high school leadership program in California. LHS is committed to providing a high quality education and personal attention to different learning styles, hence we will enroll 400 students for the entire school, each grade consisting of approximately 100 students. (Leadership High School, 2006)

A Chicago school, the Young Women's Leadership Charter School (YWLCS) of Chicago, expresses its mission simply but powerfully: The Young Women's Leadership Charter School of Chicago inspires urban girls to engage in rigorous college preparatory learning in a small school focused on math, science, and technology that nurtures their self-confidence and challenges them to achieve.

YWLCS's vision: All young women have the skills, tools and opportunities to develop as ethical leaders shaping their lives and world (Young Women's Leadership Charter School of Chicago, June 1, 2007).

These mission and vision statements give direction to the elements of a school, decisions about structure, governance, and more. In turn, these elements should cast the culture concretely, so it can be seen, heard, felt. Theoretically, it wouldn't make much difference which we understood first—the statement of culture or the elements of schooling—because either could tell us what the school stands for.

CULTURE AS BELIEFS

Expressing culture directly as a set of beliefs or values is one of the best ways to anchor a school's critical elements (structure, governance, etc.). The Young Women's Leadership Charter School (YWLCS) of Chicago has a mission and vision, which you have already read, but I find their Core Values more helpful:

- We value equitable access to resources and opportunities for every student.
- We value the contribution a single-sex education makes to educating the whole woman and promoting her leadership.
- We value inquiry, self-reflection, critical thinking, problem solving and real world experience.
- We value the diversity in our school community.
- We value parents and families as partners.
- We value integrity, honesty, and perseverance.
- We value professionalism in education through reflection, collaboration and shared leadership. (Young Women's Leadership Charter School, 2006)

The school with which I am most familiar, Eagle Rock School and Professional Development Center, expresses its culture through a simple statement and a set of principles, expectations, and commitments. It has a catchy (though incorrect) mnemonic: "8 + 5 = 10" which stands for eight principles, five expectations, and ten commitments. These beliefs and value statements together add up to the culture that directs Eagle Rock. (Please note that Eagle Rock regularly attempts to alter the formula, inviting students, staff, and parents to suggest addition or deletion of elements so that it is mathematically correct. No one has yet been able to do so. At least, "8 + 5 = 10" is memorable, and Eagle Rock does teach mathematics better than this formula would indicate!)

Here are the statement (mission or vision) and eight principles, five expectations, and ten commitments that guide the school community at Eagle Rock:

"An Eagle Rock student will have the desire and be prepared to make a difference in the world."

Table 1   Eight Principles, Five Expectations, and Ten Commitments

Eight Principles	Five Expectations	Ten Commitments
Individual Integrity:	1. Expanding knowledge base	1. Live in respectful harmony with others
1. Intellectual discipline	2. Effective communication	2. Develop mind, body, and spirit
2. Physical fitness	3. Creating and making healthy life choices	3. Learn to communicate
3. Spiritual development	4. Engaging as a global citizen	4. Serve the community
4. Aesthetic expression	5. Practicing leadership for justice	5. Become a steward of the planet
Citizenship:		6. Make healthy personal choices
1. Service to others		7. Find and develop the artist within
2. Cross-cultural understanding		8. Increase leadership
3. Democratic governance		9. Practice citizenship
4. Environmental stewardship		10. Devise a moral and ethical code

You'll get a chance to examine these more closely in Chapter 4.

EXAMINING BELIEFS

One way of examining culture involves examining beliefs. Even if we cannot articulate our beliefs, they are manifested by what we say and do.

What we say and do and what we believe add up to culture. Ted and Nancy Sizer (1999) make the case in *The Students Are Watching: Schools and the Moral Contract,* that students watch what we do and learn from their observations much more than they listen to and learn from what we say, including what we say we believe.

Asking the "so what" question is important in terms of considering the ramifications of beliefs. If we believe that all students can learn, what does that mean? So, what should we be doing to help all students learn? What should we *not* be doing? And, what *are* we doing, exactly, to help all students learn?

One way a school's culture (or a district's culture or a department of education's culture, etc.) can be derived is by amalgamating individual beliefs (weeding out duplications) or looking for common elements among individual beliefs, putting aside those that do not fit. One problem with this method is that a list of individual or common beliefs might not yield the "whole" of the organization. The whole is more than the parts.

Another strategy for identifying beliefs that govern an organization is to have individuals come together to cocreate the organization's core beliefs. One very effective way of bringing individuals together to understand the beliefs that undergird an organization's culture is through visual dialogue. Suzanne Bailey (2000, 2004) developed this strategy for bringing diverse people together in a new way. The strategy "provides 'meta moves,'" such as the following, which help participants

- Shift between and align general ideas with specific details;
- Shift among multiple points of view;
- Shift the scope of . . . work from large to small, as well as to reframe . . . thinking;
- Shift perceptions in time—past, present, and future; and
- Shift the media of . . . communication to include words, numbers, pictures, and movement. (Bailey, 2004, p. 246)

In visual dialogue, diverse community members sit in a horseshoe-shaped group in front of a huge piece of butcher paper. They work together according to a design or template on the butcher paper. In the case of organizational beliefs, the template might look like Figure 1.

Thus, individuals cocreate a statement of beliefs that governs not only the culture of the organization but also the practices that emanate from the culture.

Examining Culture Through Beliefs About Schools and Students

The next section of this Introduction focuses on five ways to examine culture: three through examining beliefs, the fourth through metaphor, and the fifth through artifacts.

Figure 1   A Template for Understanding School Beliefs and Culture

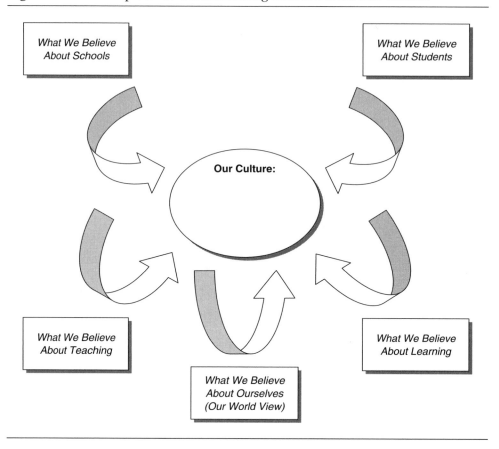

Here are some questions people can ask about what they believe about schools and students:

Do I/we believe that . . .

1. The role of schools is to educate students for leadership? What does that mean for what we do in schools?

2. The role of schools is to prepare students for the future? What does that mean for what we do in schools?

3. The role of schools is to prepare students for further education? What does that mean for what we do in schools?

4. The role of schools is to prepare students for citizenship? What does that mean for what we do in schools?

5. All students want to learn? What does that mean for what we do in schools?

6. Students are, generally, curious? What does that mean for what we do in schools?

7. Students can all learn more than the minimum? What does that mean for what we do in schools?

8. Students can teach each other? What does that mean for what we do in schools?

9. Students bring some amount of experience or knowledge to new learning? What does that mean for what we do in schools?

10. Students learn best through active rather than passive processes? What does that mean for what we do in schools?

No doubt you (and your colleagues) can add to this set of beliefs about schools and students. The most important aspect of identifying beliefs is the second question, "What does that mean for what we do in schools?" Answers to that question should be followed by identification of what you're currently doing. Contrasting what you should do to what you are doing (called *gap analysis)* may lead to steps you'd like to take to change the school culture so that it more closely represents what you believe.

Now take a look at possible beliefs about struggling students. Here is a list of descriptors that might be applied to struggling students. Do you believe that struggling students are

- Lazy?
- Unmotivated?
- Unintelligent?
- Intelligent but not in the ways valued by schools?
- Belligerent or angry?
- Inattentive/distracted?
- Distracting?
- Scary?
- Unhealthy in terms of life choices?
- Poor?
- From families who don't care?
- Social outcasts?
- Immature?
- Members of a minority group?

Again, you can probably add to this list, based on what you've heard in the teachers' lounge or in staffings about struggling students. The politically correct respondent would, of course, claim that none of these descriptors applies to all struggling students, just some, once in a while. A school that surfaces its beliefs about schools, students, and especially struggling students, needs to put these descriptors on the table and encourage honesty about them. "Yes," someone might say, "I worried that these students would be angry and hostile. I was afraid of them." Another might say, "They really don't seem to want to learn." Another might say,

"They only seem that way. That's their way of bluffing. They're really scared they'll fail." Another might say, "I've noticed that most of the students I would describe as 'struggling' are from minority groups. Why is that?" The more honest the conversation about beliefs is, the more headway individuals and groups (faculty, administrators, teachers-to-be, etc.) will make in creating a culture that encourages struggling students.

The most important part of these conversations (which might be called "courageous conversations," based on the work of Glen Singleton & Curtis Linton, 2006), is understanding what the beliefs lead to in terms of culture, structure, curriculum, instruction, and assessment. A school faculty that truly believes that struggling students are "intelligent but not in the ways valued by schools" is going to have different curricular expectations of those students and instruct and assess them differently.

Examining Culture Through Beliefs About Teaching and Learning

What we believe about teaching and learning is as important as what we believe about schools and students. Eagle Rock students and staff came up with the following list of beliefs about teaching and learning:

Learning occurs when people are . . .

- Doing
- Experiencing new input or stimulus
- Practicing, reinforcing, repeating or extending what they know
- Working according to their passions and interests
- Teaching others
- Applying what they are learning
- Problem-solving or struggling with ideas
- Relating what they are learning to themselves; learning about what they value
- Discovering and understanding their place in the world
- Feeling empowered to act
- Working in a safe environment
- Motivated (feeling some compulsion about learning!)
- Reflecting
- Feeling as if they are having fun
- Being part of a continuous connected process of learning
- Learning according to their own style or preferences

Teaching occurs when people are helping each other do what is listed above.
Your own list or a list you and colleagues create may be different from this one. The important step—as it was in the section on schools and students—is identifying what exactly a school should do according to professed beliefs. Contrast what it should do with what it is doing, and you'll have the beginnings of a plan of action.

Table 2   Beliefs About Teaching and Learning

What We Believe	What We Do	What We Should Do	Our First Step
People learn by doing and experiencing.	Our students still sit in classes listening to teachers talking or reading their own books or textbooks silently.	Convert some of our teaching units into experiential units.	Identify teaching units that are most appropriate for conversion into experiential units.
People learn by teaching others.	The adult in the room is the primary teacher. Students address questions to this person and are asked questions by this person, not each other.	Students in the classroom should talk among themselves about what they are learning; they should volunteer to work with each other to ensure that everybody learns.	Have students collect data about who talks in their classrooms and how the interaction works (teacher to student, student to teacher, student to student).
People learn through reflection.	We are in such a hurry to "cover the content" that we don't reflect—as either adults or students—on our learning.	Reflection time should be built into each instructional unit, not just at the end but during the unit as well.	Examine the number of units planned for each year. Consider how to make reflection a part of each unit even if it means shortening the unit or doing fewer units overall.

For example, look at Table 2 to see how these beliefs about teaching and learning might manifest themselves in a school.

Examining Culture Through Personal Beliefs

Ultimately, we teach who we are, according to Parker Palmer. In the introduction to his book *The Courage to Teach: Exploring the Inner Landscape of a Teacher's Life,* Palmer (1998) wrote,

I am a teacher at heart, and there are moments in the classroom when I can hardly hold the joy. . . . But at other moments, the classroom is so lifeless or painful or confused—and I am so powerless to do anything about it—that my claim to be a teacher seems a transparent sham (p. 1).

He warns that his book is not for the reader "who never has bad days, or has them but does not care" (p. 1).

Palmer (1998) directs teachers (and I would expand the definition of "teachers" to anyone—administrator, policy maker, parent, or student— who teaches) to look at the "tangles" of teaching through three lenses:

1. The subjects they teach, which are "as large and complex as life, so our knowledge of them is always flawed and partial"

2. The students they teach, who are "larger than life and even more complex"

3. Themselves, "their inwardness, for better or worse" (p. 2)

"In fact," says Palmer (1998), "knowing my students and my subject depends heavily on self-knowledge" (p. 2).

"Know thyself," inscribed on the lintel of the entrance to the Temple of Apollo at Delphi, has been attributed to a variety of ancient philosophers but most often presented as a quote from Socrates. Palmer further states, "Whatever self-knowledge we attain as teachers will serve our students and our scholarship well. Good teaching requires self-knowledge: it is a secret hidden in plain sight" (p. 3).

Several conditions keep us from knowing ourselves, according to Palmer. One is "objectivism, the academy's most prized way of knowing . . . marked by its insistence that only at a distance can we know things truly and well. (Palmer, 1991, p. 1). If we distance ourselves from the act of teaching—teaching the prescribed curriculum exactly as it is written, reading the words the textbook publishers tell us to say aloud, or pretending to have no opinion about a character's actions in a novel, for example—we run the risk of teaching things, but not life. Palmer (1998) maintains that it is often fear that causes us to back away from putting ourselves into our teaching; we are fearful of being wrong or manipulating students' perceptions. What we fear may be exactly what students fear: "failing . . . not understanding . . . being drawn into issues they would rather avoid . . . having their ignorance exposed or their prejudices challenged . . . looking foolish in front of their peers" (p. 37).

Another condition that hampers self-knowledge is seeing the world in terms of polarities, either-or, black and white, pro and con. Palmer (1998) suggests that we "must escape the grip of either-or thinking . . . to 'think the world together,' not to abandon discriminatory logic where it serves us well but to develop a more capacious habit of mind that supports the capacity for connectedness on which good teaching depends" (p. 62). Palmer describes four ways we indulge in polarities:

1. "We separate head from heart.

2. "We separate facts from feelings.

3. "We separate theory from practice.

4. "We separate teaching from learning." (1998, p. 66)

One other fundamental belief governs who we are as teachers (and learners). How we see people—as essentially good or bad—positions us as teacher. If we tend to see people as fundamentally good, likely to do good things unless obstructed, we will behave differently with others. We will be more likely to see our role as supportive of their natural inclinations. If we tend to see people as fundamentally bad, we will put into place measures to control their natural inclinations.

Though not a belief, our view of how the world works impacts what we do as educators as much as any belief. If we see it as made up of parts, we will be likely to value the teaching of those parts. If we see it as a whole, we will be likely to value the teaching of the whole. If we see it as a whole made up of parts, we will be likely to value the teaching of the whole along with teaching the parts. Although I consider this as strong as a belief, I acknowledge that it also indicates how our minds work as well as how we prefer to learn and teach.

EXAMINING CULTURE USING METAPHORS

Another way to help people identify their beliefs is through the use of metaphors. Suzanne Bailey (2000, 2004) comments, "Metaphors engage both the right and left brain to uncover meaning." The first step in using a metaphor is choosing the appropriate metaphor. The second step involves pushing the meaning of the metaphor as deeply as possible, until beliefs surface.

I have tried two types of metaphors to help people recognize their beliefs. The first is through categories. I ask educators to choose from the following categories the one that most speaks to them about who they are and what they do: animal, tool, container, song, smell, game, growing plant, food. Please note that almost any other category will work as long as it is broad and general. The challenge is to answer the question, "Why?" Why? And why again? Here's an example from a workshop:

> I think of myself as a container because I hold a lot of people—their wishes and dreams, their goals. As a teacher, I hold my students' wishes and dreams and goals. And, I believe my job is to carry my students to places where they can fulfill their wishes, dreams and goals. I am the conveyance. My container is probably porous not solid because I believe that input and output are desirable. Students should read and write and listen and speak, take in new information and create new things.

Table 3   Some Occupational Metaphors

Accountant	Actor	Aerospace Engineer	Air Traffic Controller	Banker
Botanist	Builder	Chemist	Clockmaker	Conductor
Detective	Doctor	Farmer	Fire Marshal	Gardner
Game Show Host	Gemologist	Interpreter	Magician	Manager
Meteorologist	Minister	Navigator	Park Ranger	Personal Trainer
Photographer	Piano Tuner	Pilot	Private Detective	Realtor
Repairperson	Reporter	Scientist	Shepherd	Software Designer
Taxi Driver	Test Pilot	Urban Planner	Weaver	Webmaster

The second type of metaphor is related to other occupations. See Table 3 for a few occupational metaphors that have worked well.

Here's an example of how the occupational metaphor surfaces beliefs:

As a principal, I am most like a scientist because I am continually investigating. I want to find solutions to problems and improvements in terms of what we do in my school. I hear or read about what someone has done—even outside education—and I use the scientific process to see if it will work in my school, you know, hypothesis and testing and all that. I believe my job is to make school the best place it can be for everyone in it.

EXAMINING CULTURE THROUGH ARTIFACTS

Rather than use beliefs or metaphors as avenues for understanding culture, an educational organization can collect artifacts to investigate culture. One way of doing this "backwards mapping" process is by "reading the walls." Downey, Steffy, English, Frase, and Poston (2004) call this activity "walking the walls" in their description of classroom walkthroughs. (Note: By "walls" I mean any part of an organization's structure that is used for displaying what that organization does—could be floors, ceilings, windows, doors, documents, etc.) No matter what you call it (reading the walls, walking the walls, or artifact search), this activity is a more deductive way of understanding culture than beginning with belief statements.

Members of an organization begin with what *is* (as evidenced by what's "on the walls") and then ask what their evidence indicates about culture. Finally, they must ask, "Is this what we want? If not, what do we want? And, how will we make the changes so that our next artifact search yields evidence that more closely matches the culture we want?"

A team can collect enough artifacts in 15 minutes by dividing up the "walls" and having members of the team pair up to investigate different "walls." Here are some sources for artifacts:

- What's displayed in hallways and in display cases
- What's inside classrooms (on the walls, the tables, student and teacher desks, etc.)
- What's in the entryway to the school
- Signs inside and outside the building
- Displayed student work
- Procedures or steps that are posted in some way
- What's in the principal's office (or other offices)
- What visitors are likely to see when they enter the building
- What condition things are in (new, old, in need of repair, etc.)
- What's in the restrooms and common gathering areas
- What's on the school/building grounds
- What the following documents say: yearbooks, policies and procedures, schedules, parent and student handbooks, curriculum guides, and the like

Following their artifact search, participants work together, perhaps in small groups at first and then as a whole group, to identify what their artifacts say about the culture. Here is a discussion that could happen:

Person 1: I saw how many trophies are in the display case. They go back quite a way, but we don't have any current ones. The trophies and the case have not been dusted.

Person 2: That may mean that we used to believe that athletics was important but we don't anymore? Is our culture supportive of athletic prowess?

Person 1: I don't know, but I don't think so. I also looked in the principal's office. All of his pictures are of scholastic events, such as the time the debate club won the regional tournament. He didn't have any pictures of athletics.

Person 2: Well, I looked at the schedule for last year, and it's clear that practices for sports are scheduled, but so are many other student activities.

Person 1:   I suppose we could say that the culture of this school supports sports activities as well as other extracurricular activities. Perhaps we believe in the well-rounded individual. Let's see what others found.

At some point, the whole group will want to identify aspects of culture that are supported by artifacts. This step can be managed with a chart like the one in Table 4.

Table 4   Aspects of Culture Supported by Artifacts

Aspects of Culture	*Support/Evidence/Artifacts*
ABJHS believes that individuals should be well rounded, adept in a variety of skills and behaviors	Trophy case for athletics plus lots of pictures of other student activities; a school schedule showing reserved times for a variety of athletic, scholastic, and artistic activities. A list of end-of-year awards given for a variety of activities. Paragraphs in both the parent and student handbook.

The next step, of course, is to examine the culture derived from real evidence. "Is this the culture we want? If not, what do we want? And what would we do to create that kind of culture?" The last step leads, of course, to new artifacts.

Involving more than those who work in a building in an artifact search can be valuable. For example, students and parents might be invited to participate in a school artifact search. An organization such as a Teacher Center might invite some of its clients. A district might involve Board Members as well as teachers and administrators from schools. Any organization might involve someone from outside that organization to help conduct an artifact search—someone who sees with "fresh eyes."

EXAMINING CULTURE THROUGH PRACTICE

What we do in the classroom as educators—our practice—can be considered artifacts of culture. Examined, classroom practice may prove at odds with the professed culture. Consider what these elements of a *curriculum* say about the culture of two schools (School 1 and School 2):

Example From School 1

The teacher follows a scope and sequence or syllabus that outlines what is to be taught.

Students learn essential skills in reading, writing, and mathematics.

In social studies, students learn names, places, and dates.

In English/language arts, they learn the parts of a sentence.

In science, they memorize the scientific method.

In art, they learn the color wheel.

In music, they learn about famous musicians.

In physical education, they learn group exercises.

Example From School 2

What students are to learn is clearly expressed as standards or outcomes; students know what they are to learn.

These standards or outcomes are the "big concepts" that relate to the various disciplines.

They connect the disciplines on the basis of these concepts.

They use what they learn ("who," "what," and "when") to understand "how" and "why."

They use the past to understand the present and project the future.

They apply what they use through service to others.

Consider what these elements of *instruction* say about the culture of the two schools:

Example From School 1

Students read textbooks to gain most of their knowledge.

The teacher explains key concepts and ideas while students take notes.

Students do the exercises at the end of each chapter or worksheets that the teacher prepares for them.

The teacher leads all-class discussions with students.

The teacher has students take quizzes periodically to understand how well they have learned.

Example From School 2

The teacher establishes some parameters for the learning but otherwise students are free to design their own learning activities.

Students elect to work in groups or individually on their projects.

Students work with original sources (including interviews with experts) as well as Internet resources.

The teacher serves as a coach to each group/individual.

Students/groups share their progress with each other and get feedback, suggestions, and help.

Consider what these elements of *assessment* say about the culture of the two schools:

Example From School 1

The teacher uses a prepared test that correlates with the textbook or prepares a test at the end of the learning.

The teacher grades the test according to an answer key.

The teacher grades according to a scale (90%–100% = A, etc.)

The teacher passes back the papers so students can see their scores.

The teacher awards a grade on the basis of quizzes and test scores.

Example From School 2

Students decide how they will document their learning. They devise a rubric for judging their documentation.

The teacher and the students' peers use the rubric to give students feedback on their documentations.

Students are expected to reach a certain level of mastery; if not, they have options for working toward mastery (more time, different learning conditions, coaching/tutoring, a subsequent attempt at documentation, etc.)

The teacher records whether or not the student has mastered what is expected but does not award a grade. If the student doesn't reach mastery, the teacher records plans to help the student reach mastery.

These artifacts of curriculum, instruction, and assessment reveal a set of beliefs about schools and students, and teaching and learning: the culture of a school. You have probably already decided what the difference is between School 1 and School 2, but here are some ideas for you. (Note: If you haven't already, you'll definitely see a bit of bias here!)

Example From School 1

Some Beliefs:

Students are empty vessels to be filled with knowledge from outside.

The teacher's role is to convey knowledge to students.

Separate, isolated little skills and bits of knowledge are important.

Direct teaching works.

A stimulus-response approach helps students learn and demonstrate their learning.

Learning is an individual activity.

Some Elements of Culture:

Focus on the academic side of the child.

Students as learners.

Power roles: the adult is in charge of the student.

School is like a monarchy.

Example From School 2

Some Beliefs:

Students bring a great deal of knowledge, experience, and skills to the learning process.

The teacher's role is to help students connect what they know with new learning.

Learning consists of making connections, projections, analyses, and applications of learning.

The teacher's role is to be the "guide on the side," ready to impart knowledge if it's need but otherwise stimulating self-directed learning.

Students need feedback in order to achieve quality, but with the proper support they can all achieve mastery of standards.

Learning is a social activity.

Elements of Culture:

Focus on the whole child.

Students as teachers, teachers as learners.

Shared power for learning.

School is as democratic as it can be.

This book is organized into two separate but interrelated sections because culture is closely aligned with curriculum, instruction, and assessment. In a coherent, systemic school, you can use practice (curriculum, instruction, and assessment) to understand culture. You can also use culture to understand practice. Similarly, in this book you can read the first section on culture and understand much about practice, and vice versa. I do, however, encourage, you to read both sections!

STUDENTS AND CULTURE

Students can and should participate in any of the culture-identifying strategies described above. Their insights will prove powerful and may surprise adults engaged in the same exercise. Their honesty will paint a clear picture of a school's culture and its effect on learning.

At the same time, students might think about their own beliefs and how they contribute or do not contribute to the school culture. It is never too early to ask students to begin thinking about what they believe. Even in kindergarten or first or second grade, students can articulate beliefs such as "I believe that it's wrong to hurt another person." At Eagle Rock, students are asked to create a personal moral and ethical code. In fact, they begin it during their first trimester at the school and modify it every subsequent trimester. When they near graduation, they share their personal moral and ethical code with the community and get feedback on it as well as on how well they are living their code. Here are some examples of personal moral and ethical codes from students' Presentation of Learning packets (see Chapter 8):

> *Christine (first trimester):* As a child I was raised to believe in the Christian faith. The beliefs that I live by are simple. I believe that women can do anything men do, but sometimes they shouldn't. Everyone should respect everyone, regardless how much you like or dislike that person, or how disrespectful they are to you. A man should never lay a hand on a woman. People have the right to express their opinion in a respectful way that will not offend anyone around them. Family is too precious to abandon, give up on, abuse, or hate. Life shouldn't be lived one day at a time, but with the future on your mind always. When you jump to conclusions, you are going to be wrong most of the time. You shouldn't put words in peoples' mouths. Help people if they want or need help; if they don't want it, don't help them. We should all live in respectful harmony with the men and women of the world.

Ana (fifth trimester): In everything we do, we must make a choice. Preferably a choice based on one's beliefs, beliefs which are themselves based on a consciousness of choice and developed from honest contemplation. This is my preference, at least, and at most it could go much further. It, like the most appreciated things in life, could become an art, a creativeness and an intelligence of soul open to constant development. I'm working on it.

I believe there is something decent and good in every young person, that youth are powerful when united positively, and that youth will be youth and should have the freedom to succeed and fail. I believe in compassion for others and for myself. I believe in the goodness of ambition, especially for an individual's survival in spirit and ideas. I believe that when ambition becomes arrogant and brutal it is greed and horror. I believe in working within this American society, instead of totally rejecting it, for there is a wide variety within its strict boundaries. I believe in acknowledging a connection to all people through all time. I believe that it is impossible for me to truly know anything, including the truth about right and wrong.

Brizeida (first trimester): Getting respect from others is very important for me since I've always been taught that I should earn other people's respect. I learned to respect others while I was on wilderness [on a three-week wilderness trip during her first trimester} and from being here in the community. I like for people to feel compassion towards me when I am in an intense situation. Because I know that there are always going to be times when I'm going to need it from others, I believe I should earn their compassion as well.

Brizeida (second trimester): When I'm in an unpleasant situation with someone, I have learned that instead of giving attitude or showing rudeness I should ask myself what can I learn from this situation. I believe respect is worth more when a situation is handled that way. I believe that sincerity and honesty are very significant. Sincerity is a way to gain respect and admiration.

Brizeida (third trimester): This trimester I have learned that I should ask for help when I need to. For example, when I have a problem with someone dealing with a class I should ask for help. When I need to give feedback I should not wait until the last minute to say it to someone because it will not be helpful for them or me. If I give feedback from the beginning it definitely can be helpful and will not cause as many problems.

Brizeida (fourth trimester): This trimester I have dealt with more of personal growth and I feel like it has been very important, especially this trimester. For the reason that I have had to learn to deal with issues for myself and to deal with them in a way that I can be understood and not in the way that I was used to doing it all the time. Which was to confront people in a way that they would get angry and that would be because I would take my anger on them. I also have had to learn how to interact with people when I don't have a good relationship with them because I either have to for the reason that I need to work with them.

Brizeida (fifth trimester): In the past, I haven't had such a magnificent trimester like this trimester. I have been able to stay focused and motivated. I have not had trouble with anyone, which says a lot about me being able to control my anger and to think before I act. Of course, there are people that I don't get along with, but that doesn't mean that I am going to do something evil to them. My classes have been great because I have let them be enjoyable. I have learned a lot more academically and that means a lot to me. This trimester I visited a high school with students from all around the world, and when I talked to some of them, I realized the importance of being humble. They taught me to learn from others no matter where they are from.

Over time, it is interesting to watch how students' beliefs change. From a set of platitudes, their statements often become much more personalized (and, sometimes, confusing). They change from being what a school wants them to be to what they really are. They go from being smoothly articulate (and not necessarily real) to being awkward but real.

ENSURING THAT CULTURE IS LIVED

A culture that resides solely on a plaque on a hallway somewhere is not a lived culture. A culture that is lived is evident in structures, governance, events, rituals, and more. What helps make a culture transparent to people—and, therefore, likely to be lived—is to teach it and schedule direct work on it during the school year. Here are some ways to do that:

• Require a School 101 seminar of all new students; during this time have them memorize the statement culture, whether it is as mission, vision, or beliefs. Once they have mastered the words of the culture, have them engage in a variety of activities to personalize it. They can write stories, create artwork, debate its elements, put on skits, compose lyrics, or provide examples and nonexamples. Have veteran students participate in the teaching of the culture to newbies. Ultimately, new students should teach the culture to someone else to ensure that they've learned it.

• Provide the same type of activity for all new staff.

• Schedule regular events that address the culture. For example, schedule student groups to make creative presentations related to the culture during an assembly. Eagle Rock students do this every Tuesday at morning gathering. Have students incorporate aspects of the culture into their work, for example, explaining how a character in a book they've read upholds certain beliefs . . . or doesn't. Have them analyze the effectiveness of a civilization according to the school's culture. They can be encouraged to understand a work of art through aspects of the school's culture.

• Ask students to include in their exhibitions or presentations of themselves as learners (see Chapter 8) how they have incorporated parts of the culture into their own personal lives, both within and outside school.

• Include discussion of the culture in advisories: "What have we done to uphold the culture of our school this week?"

• Ask teachers to incorporate aspects of the culture into their lesson planning. Students studying photosynthesis might be encouraged to think of growth and light in terms of the school's culture.

• Put students in charge of escorting visitors around the school, telling them about the culture.

• Use the language of the culture in student and staff meetings so that it becomes embedded in the language used throughout the school.

• Communicate the culture to parents and ask them to use the language of the vision, mission, core values, or beliefs to talk about school with their children.

• Ask a Question of the Week based on the culture.

• Announce the Theme of the Year based on the culture.

• Ask students and adults alike what they have done today to advance the culture.

• Embed the culture in goal-setting processes for both students and adults. Have them set goals in terms of advancing the culture.

• Include aspects of the culture in assessments—a bonus question on quizzes, for example.

• Report progress that students are making in terms of living the culture.

SO WHAT

In this section of every chapter (including this Introduction) you'll be given a chance to extend what you've read. Use the items in the section titled "Examining Culture Through Beliefs About Schools and Students" as surveys with a 1–4 scale (1 = Not At All; 4 = Absolutely). For the first list of items, respond by choosing a number for each item describing students and write reasons for your responses. Also, please think and write about why many people—secretly at least—see potential dropouts as they do.

Then do the same for the items related to working with struggling students.

Again, think and write about your personal answers and the answers that your colleagues might give. Contemplate the reasons educators might—again, secretly—have these reactions to working with struggling students.

Finally, if you can, invite colleagues to take the surveys and discuss with them the issues that arise as a result.

NOW WHAT

In this section of every chapter (including this Introduction), you'll be given some ideas for what to do next:

1. Make a list of students you know who might be called "struggling students."

2. Focus on one of the students you listed and write as much as you know about that student.

3. Ask your colleagues (perhaps only at your grade level or in your subject, perhaps the whole faculty) to do activities 1 and 2. Compare your lists. How are you seeing students? Do you see them differently? Why? What can you learn from each other about struggling students?

4. Describe some efforts your school or district makes to work with struggling students. Talk with your colleagues about these efforts and their success.

About the Author

 **Lois Brown Easton** works as a consultant, coach, and author. She is particularly interested in learning designs for adults and for students. She recently retired as Director of Professional Development at Eagle Rock School and Professional Development Center, Estes Park, Colorado. A project of the American Honda Education Corporation, Eagle Rock School is a year-round, tuition-free, residential high school for students who have not experienced success in traditional academic settings. The school provides educators who visit the Professional Development Center with experiences in innovative education. As Director, Easton designed and administered the professional development program for preservice and student teachers; practicing teachers and administrators; university and college students, both graduate and undergraduate; and researchers. She designed and administered an internship program for twelve young educators each year and an alternative licensure program accredited by the Colorado Department of Education.

Easton was Director of Re:Learning Systems at the Education Commission of the States (ECS) from 1992 to 1994. Re:Learning was a partnership between the Coalition of Essential Schools (CES) at Brown University in Providence, Rhode Island, and ECS. The Coalition focuses on school-level restructuring based on the research on American high schools that Dr. Ted Sizer and others performed in the 1980s. ECS, an interstate compact that works with state policy makers to improve the quality of education throughout the country, partnered with CES in Re:Learning to orient reform efforts from "schoolhouse to statehouse" and to effect reform systemwide. Easton was director of the systemic side of the reform.

Prior to that, Easton served in the Arizona Department of Education as English/Language Arts Coordinator, establishing the role in the School Improvement Unit and directing the development of the Language Arts Essential Skills, the state's first standards-based curriculum framework.

She became Director of Curriculum and Instruction, and then, as Director of Curriculum and Assessment Planning, designed and implemented the Arizona Student Assessment Program (ASAP), which focused on systemic reform on the basis of curriculum standards aligned with state performance assessments.

A middle school English teacher for 15 years, Easton earned her PhD at the University of Arizona. Her dissertation was a policy analysis of the ASAP. She has held state and national offices, particularly in language arts organizations. She was President of the Arizona English Teachers Association and was elected to the Secondary Steering Committee of the National Council of Teachers of English. She was cochair of the 2001 Conference of the National Staff Development Council in Denver.

Easton has been a frequent presenter at conferences and a contributor to educational journals. Her book *The Other Side of Curriculum: Lessons From Learners* was published in 2001. She is editor of and contributor to *Powerful Designs for Professional Learning*, which was published in 2004.

She lives in Boulder, Colorado, with her daughter and three cats.

List of Vignettes

PART I

---

*Improving
the Culture for
Struggling Students*

1

"What About Test Scores?"

From a Testing to a Learning Culture

One of the first questions educators ask when contemplating school reform or restructuring is, "But, what about test scores?" Their next question is usually, "But, what about college?" They mean, "Will test scores go down if we implement this innovation?" and "Will kids get into college if we do this?" Sometimes they're a little embarrassed to ask these questions because of how unimportant they seem when asked about young people who are failing, or being failed by the system, young people who aren't expected to graduate from high school, never mind go to college.

Let me answer the first question first, with reference to the example I know best: Eagle Rock, with thirteen years of test data. Eagle Rock School (ERS) does not teach toward any test, and yet students do very well on tests. Their scores on a nationally normed, standardized test show differences between pre- and posttest scores that are *significant*. Some score differences are considered *highly significant* or *very highly significant*. These differences almost certainly could not happen just by chance.[1] Students' scores on the SATs and the ACTs match the profile of any American high school—a bell-shaped curve, with most of the scores clustered in the middle. (For specific information about test scores at Eagle Rock, see Resource B at the back of the book.)

Eagle Rock is not the only innovative school that has seen test results improve. Leadership High School (LHS) in San Francisco, California, has its share of struggling students, even though it does not focus on enrolling only "struggling students" (Leadership High School, 2003). According to California's Academic Performance Index (API) for 2002–2003, LHS scored "above average" in comparison to all other schools in the state and "well above average" in comparison to similar schools. Ninety-six percent of its student body took the SAT in 2003, with 42 percent scoring over 1000, an average verbal score of 497 (compared to 494 for all California schools), and an average mathematics score of 493 (compared to 518 for all California schools). New York City's School of the Future reports that more than 90 percent of their students pass the Regent's Exam in English, Living Environment, and Global History, with more than 70 percent in Math, these scores in a city that has an average passing rate of 30 percent (School of the Future, 2006).

Texas's Quest High School posted a mean score on the SAT of 1076 and on the ACT of 21.4 (Quest High School, n.d.). The Met in Providence, Rhode Island, saw math test scores jump from 38 to 68, a 79 percent increase; its reading scores increased over the same three-year period from 64 to 79, an increase of 23 percent (The Met, 2006).

These and other schools demonstrate the principle of "do no harm," a key element of the Hippocratic Oath that doctors take. Even though these schools do not focus on testing, they haven't harmed the students in terms of conventional measures of progress. In fact, it may be *because they are innovative* that their students do well on such measures. In answer to the question, "But, what about test scores?" I respond that, if the innovative school has high expectations as well as a culture of learning, students will equal and, perhaps, surpass scores of students in other schools.

A case in point is Eagle Rock's math computation scores. Eagle Rock focuses on math concepts and problem solving in mathematics and does not drill students on math facts, speed, and automaticity, by choice. Although ERS does not emphasize math facts, students made modest gains in that subtest and significant gains on math concepts. This is an example of the "do no harm" philosophy.

Something happens to students when they are fully engaged in learning within a culture that prizes learning. They seem to do well on tests, too. Students begin to see themselves as learners; they gain confidence in their abilities. Perhaps they are no longer angry at a system that has not served them very well. Perhaps they decide they'll show the test makers what they really can do. Let's look more closely at testing and learning.

(And, to answer the second question, at any given time, more than half of the students who graduate from Eagle Rock, my chief example, are in college. Like many college freshmen, some don't go on to their sophomore year. But about half eventually graduate from all sorts of colleges and universities, and several are pursuing or have completed graduate degrees. Remember, these are students who did not expect to graduate from high school.)

TESTING TODAY

There are, of course, many points of view about testing (see Table 1.1). The Web site for the Public Broadcasting System (PBS) television network describes what advocates and opponents of testing say. Although the Web site is intended as a guide for parents, it is also helpful for educators ("Testing Our Schools," 2002).

I am a critic of what seems to me to be an educational system gone test crazy. According to FairTest, the National Center for Fair & Open Testing, "The U.S. already tests more children more often than any other nation. Despite this, many claim that more testing and accountability based on those tests will improve education, particularly in schools serving predominantly low-income and minority-group children" (FairTest, n.d.). This opinion was written *before* NCLB (No Child Left Behind) legislation was passed.

The main problem with the present plague of testing is the fact that tests have huge consequences, known as "high stakes." Schools, districts, and states make decisions about students, their teachers, their schools, or their districts on the basis of single test scores, rather than multiple indicators. The U.S. Department of Education makes decisions about states based on test scores. Schools live or die according to AYP (Average Yearly Progress) information published in local newspapers. States take over low-performing schools. According to FairTest, "low-income, minority-group, special needs, limited English proficient, and vocational students are most likely to suffer from this unfair use of tests. Such policies should be stopped" (FairTest, n.d.).

In addition, according to FairTest, opportunity to learn is a huge variable among schools in the United States, with many schools lacking funds to help all students learn. "Neither students nor teachers should be held accountable for meeting learning goals, including test results, unless they have been given adequate resources" (FairTest, n.d.).

Time is one of two concrete limits schools face (resources—including expert teachers—being the other). With a finite number of days and hours in a school year for learning—and an expected 12 years to graduate—how students spend time is critical. Spending that time taking tests for other than learning purposes (such as to rank schools in a state or states in a nation) or teaching to the test is a decision that begs reconsideration. Few tests are good enough to teach to. They are limited by costs related to administration and scoring. Teaching to such tests means teaching content that can be scored by machine. According to FairTest (n.d.), "Unfortunately, research continues to show that tests fail to assess many important areas of learning and too often focus on trivia instead of important topics." Tests— and preparation for them—intrude on learning time.

Results of testing usually provide little help to educators. Scores themselves are too general for generating important changes in curriculum and instruction. Item analysis reduces learning to bits of knowledge such as "mass count nouns" (*jury* and *audience,* for example). At one Arizona

Table 1.1   What Supporters and Critics of Testing Say

Issue	What Test Supporters Say	What Test Critics Say
Fairness, civil rights	Advocates say that testing all students is the best way to measure how effective schools are, and that state or local content standards ensure that all students are learning the same curriculum. Supporters also believe that disadvantaged students can be better served by holding their schools accountable when they perform poorly on tests.	Critics contend that tests can contain culturally biased content that may be unfamiliar to minorities and recent immigrants. Moreover, for students with learning disabilities or who process information differently, the nature of the test itself (be it multiple choice or short answer format) may be unfair. Critics also say that tests do not adequately measure student and school performance, and that judging (and in some cases punishing) schools with low test scores results in even fewer resources for the students who need them most.
What the tests test	Advocates say that developing and administering tests that measure students' knowledge against learning standards will ensure that all students have certain proficiencies and are not left behind or falsely promoted from grade to grade.	Critics say that many tests created for national use may not include content emphasized at the state level, resulting in students being tested on material they have not been taught. Moreover, critics warn of a "narrowing" of the curriculum, saying that the heightened attention paid to standardized tests forces teachers to ignore content or even entire subjects that do not appear on the tests.

(Continued)

Table 1.1 (Continued)

Issue	What Test Supporters Say	What Test Critics Say
The use of "high-stakes" tests	Advocates say that tests are an important part of "raising the bar" on student performance. Attaching test results to grade promotion, graduation, and teacher evaluation, they say, will send a strong message to students, teachers, school leaders, and parents that students must meet proficiency levels.	Critics point out that "test anxiety" may affect a student's performance, resulting in scores that do not adequately reflect his or her knowledge. Critics also contend that standardized tests are only one measure of student performance, and must be considered alongside other assessment tools, including classroom work, student portfolios, and teacher evaluations.
The validity of test scores	Advocates say that standardized tests are the most objective and accurate assessments of students' knowledge and skills. By creating norm groups or specific criteria to which students are compared, they say, test makers can measure each student's abilities with precision.	Critics say that test-making is far from a perfect science. Tests may contain errors, making results inconclusive. Furthermore, they say, a test's standard error of measurement may be large enough to throw into question the use of the results.
Using tests to determine school funding	Advocates say that schools should be rewarded financially for performing well on standardized tests, and that providing such incentives will motivate school leaders and teachers to teach effectively and raise student performance.	Critics say that financial rewards for schools in which students perform well is an inappropriate use of funds. They argue that it is unfair to expect students at schools in impoverished areas to perform as well as those in wealthy areas, and withholding additional funding for schools in need will stagnate performance levels.

SOURCE: From Frontline/WGBH Educational Foundation Copyright © 2005 WGBH/Boston. Used by permission.

school, English teachers spent an inordinate amount of time before state testing making sure that students understood when to use the singular and when to use the plural verb form with mass count nouns, all because item analysis showed that most students missed the *one* item on the test that addressed mass count nouns!

Tests are a proxy for the real thing: demonstration of real knowledge and skills. Educators cannot be sure what they are witnessing in students' selected answers. Does a selected answer really represent what students know and can do or simply what they chose to mark on the answer sheet? Moreover, tests seldom point toward what students need to know or do— what errors they might be making when they select the wrong item. As Mina Shaughnessy so wisely pointed out in 1977, understanding errors in thinking—and delving into students' "worldviews" to understand why they made and clung to their errors—is one of the best ways educators can help students learn.

No educator, at any level, would say, "You know, I really don't believe I should be accountable. It doesn't matter to me if students succeed or fail in my class (or school or district or state)." Educators *want* to be accountable for learning, but they want the accountability actions they take to be helpful to them, their students, and the school and district communities of which they are a part.

My ideal system would have the following components:

• *A true standards-based system* (see Chapter 6) created at the school level through adapting district-level standards, which were themselves adapted from state standards. Changes in *conditions for learning*, particularly time, so that all students can achieve standards.

• *State use of a nationally normed, standardized test every other year, in the fall, sampling content, grade levels, and populations* within each year's grade levels. This test would allow national comparisons, but it would be in the fall (when published test scores are less likely to be viewed as a reflection of a year's worth of work with a particular teacher, in a particular school or district, that might force teachers to teach to the test from January on). Sampling content areas, grades, and populations would result in a series of statewide snapshots that could be compared to snapshots from other states as well as snapshots over time.

• *Regular school-level assessments of learning, using classroom work* (student products or outcomes) rather than tests that take time away from classroom work. This type of assessment is often known as a "common assessment" since all teachers collect student work that they will, themselves, score collaboratively using rubrics and, perhaps, anchors for each scoring point (Martin, 2006, p. 53). Douglas B. Reeves (2006), maintaining that schools are "overtested and underassessed," recommends the use of common assessments that "are formative, provided during the year, designed to improve teaching and learning, and accompanied by immediate feedback" (p. 86).

- I would also recommend *public performances (exhibitions) of learning,* not just once a year but several times throughout the year, with the public invited to witness learning. You'll read more about Presentations of Learning in Chapter 8.

- *Multiple sources of information* about achievement (results of examining student work, for example) accompanied by data on perceptions (collected through surveys and interviews), demographics, and processes (what the school does to help students learn, from afterschool programs to literacy hour). See Vicky Bernhardt (2004b) for more information on data collection and analysis.

Big Picture Schools, such as The Met in Providence, Rhode Island, do a particularly good job of using multiple measures to report progress. The Met reports graduation rate; attendance rate; district and Gates Foundation survey data related to parent involvement, school climate, quality of instruction, and teacher availability for students' academic and personal needs; and drug availability . . . as well as test scores (The Met, 2006).

- *Regular, school-level examination of data* from the common assessments, presentations of learning, anecdotal evidence, and other types of data (see "Multiple sources of information," above) resulting in school goals and revisions of those goals to move the school toward success in learning for all students.

Vignette 1.1   A School Vignette: Common Assessments

EVERYONE ON THE SAME BUS

Coal Ridge Middle School, Colorado

By Paul Talafuse

Coal Ridge is the newest middle school in the St. Vrain School District in Longmont, Colorado. Coal Ridge Middle School used to be Frederick Middle School, Grades 5 and 6, in a building once used as a junior–senior high school. Coal Ridge sits high enough on the prairie to provide a good view of the snowy Front Range across the highway. Its profile against the prairie is pristine.

When Frederick Middle School closed in the middle of the 2004–2005 school year, staff and students moved from its "hodge-podge ramshackle building" to this beautiful facility. With the addition of Grades 7 and 8, the school's population jumped from 400 to nearly 800 students.

Frederick Middle School—soon to be Coal Ridge Middle School—was put on academic watch by the district, a very public event, headlined in local newspapers.

We already had a great group of teachers, dedicated to improving our school; the watch was an incentive to get everybody on the bus. It's the teachers and their dedication to working together for kids that make the difference at Coal Ridge.

The teachers formed a Building Leadership Team, at first with just a few of them working with me to improve Coal Ridge. One of the first things staff did was to visit "successful" schools. Then, during the first year, they envisioned power standards—how the entire staff would work on vocabulary, reading, mathematics, and writing. The staff knew they would need to create something concrete to bring the concept of Power Standards down to earth. They began creating common assessments and an accountability system. What's exciting about common assessments is that we give the teacher-made assessments for the same subject as a regular part of classroom work. Teachers involved in giving the assessments score them together (sometimes using a rubric, sometimes using anchors), examine the data, and then set goals for improvement.

At the next Building Leadership Team meeting, the team giving the common assessment presents a PowerPoint on the common assessment, its results, and the goals they set so that everyone in the school keeps focused on improving learning.

The number of people on the Leadership Team expanded from the initial four members to twelve, sixteen, and more "as people began to see the Team as the source of rich ideas." Many participated in order to get and give ideas, but all were there to learn and network with each other.

A staff member commented, "We didn't even have a bus back then. We were going in all sorts of directions instructionally. Now we not only have a bus, but everybody is on the bus. We're sharing strategies and implementing the same sorts of thing across grades and departments."

Another said, "We still have some work to do. The structures are all there, but it's a matter of educating the staff. We designed a process; we have structures that cover everything. It's more like a shared accountability; now, even students are sharing in accountability."

We have a "shared agenda," another leadership team member said. "But, it evolved to this. We certainly didn't have one when we started."

SOURCE: Used by permission from Paul Talafuse.

AUTHOR'S NOTE: Paul Talafuse is principal of Coal Ridge Middle School. He can be reached through e-mail at talafuse_paul@StVrain.k12.co.us

"Above all, do no harm." I believe that schools with innovative programs should do no harm to students in terms of the conventional measures of learning. At the same time, however, testing should, at the very least, do no harm to students. And it won't—if the culture is focused on learning rather than testing.

AN EXAMPLE OF DOING NO HARM

Eagle Rock, with its population of students predicted to fail, serves as my chief example of how a school can teach for learning, not testing, and still

Table 1.2   Pretest and Posttest Scores at Eagle Rock School

Sub-Tests	Average Pretest Scores	Average Posttest Scores	Average Changes in Scores
Vocabulary	55.7	67.4	+11.7
Reading	54.7	67.9	+13.2
Writing	49.1	56.8	+7.7
Math Concepts	43.4	54.6	+11.2
Social Studies	43.5	61.0	+17.5
Science	48.9	60.0	+11.1
Information Processing	47.0	56.4	+9.4
Math Computation	30.1	34.5	+4.4

do well on tests. Eagle Rock students take a pretest when they first enroll at Eagle Rock (in the early years the Test of Achievement and Proficiency, now the Iowa Tests of Educational Development, Complete Battery). These are considered their *pretests*. They take the same test when they graduate; these are considered their *posttests*. The pretest norms are those for sophomores; the posttest norms are those for seniors. This chart shows the differences between pre- and posttest scores.

Remember that Eagle Rock teachers do not teach to any test or use instructional practices that help students choose correct answers on multiple-choice tests. Still, students do amazingly well on these tests. They have been harmed not at all—or very little—by being expected to learn, not just test, well.

Distribution scores tell more of the story. For example, on the *reading* pretest 46 percent of students were below the 50th percentile and 54% above. On the posttest in reading, 25 percent were below the 50th percentile, and 75 percent were above. Averaging all the pre- and posttest scores results in the following distributions:

	Average Scores for All Sub-Tests	
	Below 50th Percentile	Above 50th Percentile
Pretest	55%	45%
Posttest	40%	60%

You can see other data about test scores in Resource B.

In case these score comparisons don't seem significant to you, remember that the students being tested were those who:

- Were deemed most likely to fail, some even when they were kindergarteners
- Sat in the back of the classroom and seemed disengaged in learning
- Dropped out, were suspended, or expelled
- Had given up on formal education
- Were described as lost causes by the education systems in which they struggled

REASONS STUDENTS MIGHT DO POORLY ON TESTS

Students are very clear about why they used to do poorly on norm-referenced, standardized tests. Here are their reasons and a few comments from them to illustrate those reasons.

Lack of Confidence

David said, "I used to hate tests. Everybody thought something was wrong with me, so they kept giving me these tests. I used to freak out, and I'd get all the answers wrong. I knew something was wrong with me." Sevi confessed, "I was afraid the tests would prove that I'm not very good at things, so I messed up on purpose."

Lack of Interest

"I didn't see why we needed to take these tests. They didn't relate to what interested me," claimed Elliott. Calen said, "Mostly I was absent on test days. I hadn't been in school most of the year, so why would I go on the test days?"

Interest in Revenge on a System They Didn't Think Was Fair

Amanda confessed, "It [doing poorly on tests] was one way I could get back at school. I just made random patterns on the answer sheet and I finished first and could do anything I wanted. Well, and [get back at] the teachers and my parents and everybody that took tests so seriously."

Fear and Low Self-Esteem

"I would look around me and all the other kids were finished and I had barely started. I would get more and more nervous and then I would just give up. I knew I wouldn't do well," Manny commented.

Differences in How Students Learn and Think; Apparent Disconnect Between Learning and Test-Taking

Khalid said, "I just don't think that way. I think all the answers are right in some way." David added, "The hurry-up part of tests makes me nervous. I like to think about things."

Group Identification

Well," said Mahkaea, "we certainly weren't the ones getting good grades and looking so preppy on test-taking days. We didn't see the point in having sharpened pencils. Nobody I knew did good on those tests." Luis added, "I definitely didn't want to be one of those kids who do good —well—on tests."

Doubt About the Relevance or Purpose of the Tests

"I never planned to go to college, so I didn't see the point of these tests," stated Adam (who, indeed, went to college and is still working toward graduation). Scott agreed, "It seemed more important to the teachers and the principal. They had a big rally, which was really stupid. And ice cream at lunch."

An administrator summarized a number of these points: "I think learning makes the difference. Our students consider themselves learners. In their previous settings, they considered other people learners, not themselves. Everyone but them, sometimes. As learners, they understand that test-taking is a part of learning—a small part, but a part, nevertheless, of what learners do. They understand that we need an outside reference point for performance. Tests are no big deal."

A science teacher added, "Tests aren't about learning or thinking. They're about little things that don't particularly matter—to me or to students."

REASONS STUDENTS MIGHT DO WELL ON TESTS

Students had their own ideas about why they were able to do well on the posttests even though their school focused on learning.

Self-Confidence as a Learner

Lauren stated, "I just feel more confident. I feel like I can do tests now." Miguel stated, "It's kind of a challenge now. I want to see if I can do them."

Seeing Testing as Part, Albeit a Small Part, of Learning

Aashli suggested, "We just learn so much at [school]. It's like college and, so, I think I can do OK on the tests. They don't bother me."

Seeing Testing as "No Big Deal"

Veronica claimed: "They don't seem as hard to me now for some reason. They're kinda fun even."

Wanting to Perform Well on Tests

Tanya declared, "It's worth it to do well on tests at [my school.] I want [my school] to look good."

Seeing the Challenge in a Test

Nate said, "I just look at tests as one big problem to be solved now. And, I guess, the parts of tests are all little problems to be solved. And I know how to solve problems." Adam added, "It's really funny about what I can do now. I always thought I was too dumb to do tests but now I like to prove that I can do them."

Knowing That Tests Are Neither True Indicators nor the Only Indicators of Their Worth

Vanessa stated, "I know I'm good at some things now. I didn't need a test to tell me that."

The School's Lack of Emphasis on Testing; the School's Focus on Learning

An administrator commented, "We don't fixate on those tests. We know a great deal about our students and how they learn, as well as how *well* they learn. The tests are just an outside measure we consult to be sure that we haven't slipped somehow." The director of students added, "Our students are more than their minds. They are whole people, and testing practices don't recognize that. There's so much happening to kids these days. It's no wonder that a test that wants a kid to choose the best answer on a subject like, say, the area of a triangle, isn't interesting to a kid wondering if his family will be evicted by the time he gets home from school."

TESTING AND LEARNING

Using the "artifact method" of determining culture (see the Introduction), a group of students and adults in a workshop described artifacts from schools that emphasized *testing* and artifacts from other schools that emphasized *learning* (see Table 1.3).

Recall the list of beliefs about teaching and learning in the Introduction? Students and staff determined that "Learning occurs when

Table 1.3   Artifacts of Testing Compared With Artifacts of Learning

Artifacts of a Culture Focused on Testing	Artifacts of a Culture Focused on Learning
Front hallway: Test score results are prominently displayed.	*Front hallway:* Student work is prominently displayed.
Schedule: The official schedule sets aside test-preparation days as well as test-taking days.	*Schedule:* The official schedule notes test days but also a variety of other special days set aside for students' sharing of their learning.
Schedule for Testing Week: Students participate in a pep assembly to get them ready for testing. A special breakfast is held the first day of testing.	*Schedule for Testing Week:* On Monday and Tuesday, students give exhibitions on the expedition they completed; they take tests on Wednesday, Thursday, and Friday.
First Faculty Meeting Agenda: The principal provides last year's test scores during the first faculty meeting in order to aid planning.	*First Faculty Meeting Agenda:* The principal engages teachers in examining multiple sources of data (including results of exhibitions) in order to set goals for the year.
Newsletter: The parent newsletter contains articles about test scores and the need to raise them.	*Newsletter:* The parent newsletter contains examples of student work.
Student Handbook: Some teachers grade "on the curve."	*Student Handbook:* Students are expected to help each other so that the focus is on all students' learning.
Walls: "Brag" walls outside many classrooms highlight the success of certain kids. Charts indicate (sometimes by name) that not all students have succeeded.	*Walls:* Lots of student work—all students? There are no charts indicating which students have succeeded and which have not.
Report Cards: A, B, C, D, and F grades according to percentages (i.e., 90% and above = A). Teachers check comments that apply. The parent signs and returns.	*Report Cards:* The grading system is Proficient, Satisfactory, and In Process. Report cards include narratives from teachers and students themselves. Parents are invited to come in for a student-led conference to look at student work.
Superintendent's Letter: In five out of eight months of newsletters, the lead story is about tests and testing.	*Superintendent's Letter:* Features actual student work as well as photographs of outstanding products. Mentions testing twice.

people are doing and experiencing," for example. Their beliefs about learning describe what happens when a school's culture focuses on learning, not testing. None of these descriptions meshes with the characteristics of traditional tests, the ones that are standardized (such as the ITBS). Few fit the sorts of tests that are given by states and districts in order to comply with NCLB (No Child Left Behind) and indicate AYP (Average Yearly Progress). Some fit the few performance assessments that some states have adopted, especially in the area of writing.

Rick Stiggins acknowledges that assessments need to be tailored to achievement targets. In some cases, multiple-choice tests (the usual form of standardized tests and state or district assessments) are appropriate. For many areas, he advocates strategies such as "running records in which they [teachers] keep track of students' fluency and comprehension" or real (process) writing, problem solving, retelling, and so forth. "The trick is to know which method to use when and how to use it well" (Sparks, 1999, p. 55). He argues for better preparation of educators in the area of assessment.

Wiggins (1998) has written extensively about assessments *for* learning rather than *of* learning. He coined the term *educative assessment* to describe the types of assessment that are oriented toward learning. These assessments not only further the learning of the students "taking" them but also contribute to the learning of educators involved in the process. Most of these assessments are performance based.

Here are some types of educative assessments used at Eagle Rock and elsewhere (such as in schools that are part of the Coalition of Essential Schools, 2002a, 2002b; the Expeditionary Learning/Outward Bound network, n.d.; and other networks). At Eagle Rock these are called documentations of learning because they are the tools students use to make a case that they've mastered the standards.

Various types of portfolios

Oral forms of presentation

Written forms of presentation

Combined oral and written forms

Other forms, such as finished art pieces, sketchbooks, and more

You'll find out much more about these forms of educative assessment and how they relate to standards when you read Chapter 8. You'll also discover what makes these forms of documentation work: the rubric. Finally, you'll have a chance to examine a very important part of using documentations and rubrics (rather than, or in addition to, tests)—how to calibrate scoring through a variety of protocols, such as the tuning protocol.

In addition to documentations of learning at Eagle Rock, the only way students can gain credit toward graduation, students do Presentations of

Learning (POLs) three times a year (L. Easton, 2002). POLs are different from documentations of learning in that they are not related to getting credit in classes; they encourage reflection, synthesis, evaluation, and analysis. Through them, students make a case that they have learned to a panel from outside the school as well as to the learning community of staff, other students, and family members. You'll learn much more about POLs in Chapter 8.

CONCLUSION

Tests have their purpose at Eagle Rock and other innovative schools. They are one way to benchmark quality. They provide some—though limited—feedback. They prove that, at least, a school is doing no harm to its students by focusing on learning rather than test results. They show that students can succeed on tests within a culture of learning.

SO WHAT

Scan a week in your personal and professional life. In a five-minute period, list as many of the things you did as you can. Then, next to each item on your list, describe how you knew you were successful in accomplishing each of these activities.

Randomly select three items on your list. If you were to be given a written, multiple-choice test to determine how successful you were on those activities, what would the test look like? What would the questions be? What would the answer choices be? How well would this test measure what you know and are able to do?

NOW WHAT

Changing the emphasis from testing to learning needs to be done nationally, in all states, and in all schools. We are talking about a huge culture change here. It may seem impossible to any reader of this book, but cataclysmic systems change happens "one lunch at a time," as my mentor and good friend, systems change facilitator Suzanne Bailey says. It happens when one person starts doing something differently and shares that change with one more person, and so on.

You can play a role in changing the culture in your environment. Here are suggestions to get you started:

1. Decide how you can focus on learning throughout your school (or district) environment: How can you make *learning for everybody* (including the adults) the primary target of education? Ask about every decision:

"How does this focus us on learning?" or "What does this have to do with learning?" Ask students and adults daily, "What have you learned today?" (P.S. Persist until the answer you get is more about what they *learned* than what they *did*.) Check out your e-mails, bulletin boards, newsletters, and parent communications. How many are about learning?

2. Decide how to *de-emphasize testing* in your environment. Signs, slogans, cheers, and pep assemblies before testing are nice but rather superficial. Can you eliminate these from the schedule? Prepare students for taking tests (i.e., give them test-taking skills), but be sure they know they're preparing for tests, not for learning. Make sure they eat a good breakfast before testing, but make sure they eat a good breakfast every day. Describe tests as point-in-time feedback, not absolutes in terms of ability, intelligence, or skills. Use the word *snapshot* to describe tests, and point out to students and teachers that they're not the full-length feature film about a student, her teachers, a school, or the district.

3. *Emphasize other forms of assessment* that are public, enhance learning for both students and staff, and are worthwhile. Publicize these new assessments: regular exhibitions of learning to which the public is invited, a class's presentations to which the rest of the school is invited, learning challenges during which students studying the same things challenge each other on what they've learned, learning exchanges during which students teach each other the different things they learned. Investigate ways of making all assessments of learning challenging, personalized, important, and, dare I say it, fun for the whole learning community.

4. *Ask parents and community members* to identify how they know they have done well (and they probably won't say, "Because I selected the right answers on a test"). Start a conversation about what all stakeholders need to know about student success and what would make the results of learning credible to them.

5. Determine how you can help students become more *confident of themselves as learners,* including seeing themselves as problem-solvers (even when the goal is figuring out how to answer items on a standardized test). Post a daily puzzle or conundrum, word challenge, visual puzzle, five-syllable vocabulary word, or brain teaser. Celebrate the learner(s) of the day who attempt the answers as well as those who figure out the answers. Have the principal stop all classes at the same time occasionally and ask everyone (including the adults) to write down what they are learning. Collect their statements and randomly draw one out to read aloud or share via e-mail or a newsletter.

6. Help learners *think about their learning;* help them "go metacognitive." Add more questions to your repertoire and hope others follow suit: "How do you know you know?" or "How did you think about that problem?" or "What led you to that answer?"

7. Be sure students and staff know their *learning styles.* At the beginning of a new grade cluster (such as the first grade in a middle school), or more often, have teachers and students take one of a variety of surveys on learning style and consider what the survey tells them. Make it a norm for students and staff to identify their learning styles to each other. Make it OK for a student to say, "Mr. Teacher, this is how I learn. Can you help me?" Or for Ms. Teacher to say, "I'm going to present the whole idea first, because that's the way I learn. If you learn through the details, hold on, because I'll get to them."

8. Reinforce the fact that *all people can learn* every chance you get, and acknowledge that everyone learns differently but that every type of learner is needed. Make it a point to say, "We really need someone who is a creative learner for this activity" or "Is someone here really good at learning how something works?" or "Who sees the big picture? We need that kind of person for this activity."

9. Plan a way to *recognize many indicators of learning* and articulate those to everyone in the school as well as to the surrounding community. Ask, "How do we know we're learning at this school (class, district)?" and incorporate the answers into a list called Indicators of Learning, which is shared with students, staff, parents, and visitors to the building. Consider a treasure hunt for more or better indicators of learning.

10. Provide *powerful professional learning* for teachers and others who are used to testing as a way of evaluating learning (Easton, 2004b). Have them look at actual student work using a tuning protocol or a descriptive review. Have them examine lessons from the point of view of lesson study. Have them do data analysis on the basis of test scores and myriad other indicators. Have them form study groups to learn about learning. Have everyone—not just the principal—do learning walks (also known as classroom walk-throughs). Have them map the curriculum, not by activities or content but by learning. Have them develop assessments and rubrics themselves as part of their learning.

11. *Join groups* that want to de-emphasize testing in favor of learning. Contact the many regional centers that are part of the Coalition of Essential Schools (www.essentialschools.org), for example.

NOTE

1. The differences were tested using a standard t-test and a nonparametric signed rank test. Both tests indicated that the differences are significantly different from 0 with a significance level of 0.0001 or better.

2

"What Do You Mean, Build Relationships? My Job Is to Teach History"

Relationships Are as Important as Content

The educator who made the statement that serves as the title of this chapter was sincere. He had been trained to be a history teacher. He knew a lot about American, European, and world history. He had worked out interesting lesson plans. He sat in a workshop I was giving on emotional intelligence and fidgeted until he finally felt ready to say something. When he said that it wasn't his job to deal with relationships, most of the group turned to him in shock. It wasn't politically correct to admit that content was more important than students, even in high school. He looked a bit sheepish and then said, "I can barely cover my required content in a year. And, besides, I don't know how to build relationships. They never taught us that."

Let's look at another point of view. "I was just a number, my test scores or something. No one really knew me or about me. They thought I wasn't too smart because of my test scores and that's the way they treated me.

So I got back at them by flunking their classes and dropping out." A student who finally graduated from high school at age 20 (and 11 months) told this story of his past. He had gone to a suburban high school with more than 1,000 students per grade-level. "No one noticed at first when I dropped out. My parents got a call a couple of weeks after I hadn't been at school. One of my friends told me that some of my teachers hadn't even known I was in their classes." His decision to drop out may have been based on faulty logic, but it seemed to him the only way he could get revenge on a system that didn't know him or care about him as an individual.

This chapter is about why relationships are important—especially for struggling students—and how to build relationships within and outside the context of teaching.

WHY RELATIONSHIPS ARE IMPORTANT

Asked by their own teachers, other educators, their own families and others, students consistently—and emphatically—named "relationships" as the key difference between schools that work for them and schools that don't. Why relationships? Here's what staff and students said:

Trust and Learning

Repeatedly, the word *trust* came up for staff and students. Sevi, a student, commented, "It is important for a relationship to exist between students and their teachers for a few reasons. Most important, it builds trust on both sides by allowing something deeper than a relationship limited to the classroom to grow. A sense of community is created which then creates a general feeling of support. When a teacher reaches out to a student on a more individual level, it shows the student that the teacher genuinely cares about supporting the student and is not just trying to pass them through."

Jon, a staff member, commented, "If you don't have relationships with each other, then you don't have anything. Without relationships, you don't have trust. Without trust, you don't have empathy or compassion for the people in your school. I typically find it difficult to communicate with folks with whom I have little or no established relationships, especially on difficult issues such as feedback—either what I'm giving to them, or getting from them."

Josh, a student noted, "The critical thing is making it possible for students to trust staff and realize that staff can understand where they are coming from. A mutual trust and understanding is necessary for students and staff to reach a level that . . . benefits in improved performance in the academic setting (for staff as well as for students)."

Mohammed, a staff member, dwelt on the importance of trust:

Any meaningful and positive learning experience must be built upon a strong relationship. This relationship does not necessitate a friendship, but [it does necessitate] an honest and transparent understanding of intentions and communication. Perhaps the most central theme in any real relationship is trust. Trust allows all agents involved in the learning process to move to the conceptual and theoretical levels of knowledge by letting themselves become more receptive to different forms of analysis and critical thought.

"If a young person does not trust the instructor," he continued,

the attempt by that instructor to teach the student content . . . becomes futile. If the young person cannot trust an adult simply as a human, how can this person trust what the adult is trying to teach? Without trust, a young person won't accept any learning; he or she will only dismiss the information, process, and material as another imposition of values from "above."
    With trust and transparency in a relationship, both parties are receptive to reciprocal advice, feedback, and input. Deep discussions and exchanges can more freely take place. Both young people and adults feel confident that the relationships will not be negatively affected by challenges. Adults can challenge young people on attitudes and emotions and, inversely, young people can challenge adults on treatment and content.

An administrator commented, "Trust is built slowly through repeated honest interactions. A school's culture directly reflects the openness or lack thereof in relationships among its constituents. For people joined in promoting learning, openness and trust are indispensable."

Status and Hierarchy, Power and Authority

Trust is related, in what may seem a strange way, to status and hierarchy, to power and authority. Here is how students and staff frame that relationship.
    Richard, an instructor, addressed the connection:

How can students possibly learn from any person who is not trusted? How can students listen to someone who does not seem caring or understanding about them and who they are? If students do not have trust, rapport and respect for the teacher, and vice versa, the teacher for the students, students will not hear nor integrate anything that the teacher says or does.

Ryan, a student, said, "I personally think that if I have a relationship with someone, I will trust them more and learn from them. I think that is because I believe that a person I know better than a stranger, especially if they have a higher education than me, will know how best to communicate with me. They will know how to teach me in the most effective way."

Sevi, a student, elaborated, "If there is any sense of hierarchy, the student's trust, progress and willingness to listen is not based on genuine respect but on the duties of fulfilling [what] a higher power demands."

Mohammed, an instructor, commented,

Many young adults and adolescents have, for most of their lives, built [up] a distrust and suspicion toward authority. In many cases, authority is manifest in the adults in their lives: parents, teachers, police officers, babysitters, politicians, and principals. In traditional settings, the lack of respect that young people feel from those in authority leads to a repression of emotions and an overall sense of marginalization.

Young people tend to feel that adults do not validate their emotions, thoughts, ideas and experiences. Adults regularly say, "Don't cry!" "Be a big boy (or girl)!" "Don't yell!" "What's wrong with you?" and "I'll give you something to cry about!" Ultimately, this tells the young person that he or she must move away from the current experience because it is unacceptable. All subsequent events with authority only deepen this sense of marginalization.

Mohammed continued, with even more passion,

Marginalization in any context, particularly among the young, creates a suspicion of the dominant group, in this case someone in authority. In other words, young people begin to believe that all authority is equally dismissive of youth perspectives and experiences. The response, among the young, is a dismissal of authority as a whole and, more so, the values that are represented by authority. Young adults have no reason to believe that authority is really there to help them grow and learn.

Richard, a staff member, added, "Many [students] have had adversarial relationships with adults, authority figures, parents, and teachers. They need to feel safe. Maybe they need to be reintegrated into the society from which they feel so alienated."

For Urban Academy in New York City, the word *respect* summarizes how it wants students to feel. A part of Urban Academy's mission states, "Urban Academy is a small laboratory high school which believes that what students think and have to say are important parts of their learning" (Urban Academy, 2006).

Modeling Good Relationships

Students learn what they see (Sizer & Sizer, 1999). Modeling relationships is critical in schools—staff to staff, staff to student, and student to student.

An administrator referenced the Sizers' book as he reflected on relationships: "Human relations are at the center of any school. The way the staff treat each other provides students with a template for interacting with each other. As Ted and Nancy Sizer maintained in their book *The Students Are Watching: Schools and the Moral Contract* (1999) students watch what staff do—not just listen to what they say—and behave accordingly."

Kelly, a student, said,

A strong staff with good relationships is better able to work as a team to create consistency within the curriculum. Students who have relationships with each other are better able to support each other in the classroom, whether that's by tutoring each other or creating positive peer pressure. Staff model teaming for us, working with each other. Students model real caring about how—and how well—other students are doing.

Another administrator captured this idea concisely: "Calm adults make for calm students." Substitute any word you'd like for *calm*.

Richard, an instructor, stated,

Staff-to-staff, student-to-staff, and student-to-student relationships are all important. It is important that staff know other staff members enough to trust each other's judgment in dealing with students. Staff need to know each [other] staff member well enough to know that colleagues have thought through an issue and are making decisions based on experiences as well as their understanding of the school. It's important that students do not believe they can "shop" through staff to find the answer or response that they want.

Students need to know that staff have the best interests of students in mind. Students need positive, healthy role models. Student-staff relationships must develop and deepen before there is a crisis, a problem or an infringement of rules and guidelines. Students can only hear—really hear—feedback, advice, and guidance from an adult they trust and with whom they have rapport. Many students have not had healthy adults in their lives who, they believe, understand and care about them.

The Whole Person

A focus on relationships means that members of the school community are looking at not just the academic side of each other but at each other as whole persons.

Sevi, a student, commented, "If a teacher only knows a student as the student, then it is hard for the teacher to really understand the student's needs, struggles, progress, and interests." Jen, an instructor, added:

It's so crazy. Students don't come in parts. They are whole people, many faceted. So are we. But, in regular schools, we are supposed to pay attention only to how students are doing academically, only to how they learn. How can we pay attention to just their learning, when learning is a function of all of them?

Accountability

Relationships require some form of accountability. Dan, an instructor, addressed this aspect of relationships: "Personal relationships allow for people to hold each other accountable, thus raising the proverbial 'bar.' This concept applies in both academic and personal growth arenas." Ryan, a student, added, "If I have a relationship with someone, I'm not going to let him down. I'm going to work hard for him—and, for me, too."

Vanessa, a student, said wryly: "It's a lot easier not having relationships, I guess. You can just go through life not caring. But when you've built a relationship and you care about others, you really think about them and about who you are and what you do . . . in relation to them."

Summary: The Benefits of Building Relationships

- Relationships construct a safety net of trust so that learning can take place.
- Relationships diminish status and hierarchy, power and authority, so that all can learn.
- Relationships in school provide good models for other types of relationships.
- Relationships recognize that people cannot be parsed into their academic selves and all the rest, but function as a whole.
- Relationships stimulate personal accountability.

It seems crystal clear why struggling students would benefit from an environment that promotes the building of relationships. Trust of adults is frequently quite low for struggling students, who have often had bad experiences with adults; they've been let down, betrayed, or hurt by them. Struggling students are sometimes hypersensitive about status, hierarchy, power, and authority; they often hide behind a carefully crafted "tough guy" persona, using it as a weapon against those who seem to "lord it over them." They may seem arrogant or even belligerent when dealing with an authority figure (even when they are, actually, scared).

Many struggling students have not witnessed healthy relationships at home or in their neighborhoods. Their own relationships may suffer as a result. School people, according to many struggling students, seem to care only about students' academic sides; in fact, for most young people, only a small fraction of what matters to them is the school part of their whole selves. And, finally, impersonal schools (and the people who run them) challenge some struggling students to poke their way through the impersonality, anyway they can. Acting out, being disciplined, suspended, or expelled means that someone has noticed them as a person. In a very strange way, these results demonstrate accountability, but not the sort of accountability that contributes to the well-being of either the school or the individual student. How much better it would be for struggling students to feel some positive connection to their school and those who work and learn there, enough to be accountable for their own actions.

Of course, these aspects of relationships apply to students who don't seem to be struggling, too.

HOW TO FOCUS ON RELATIONSHIPS

Becoming Small

One way to focus on relationships is to become small. According to the Small Schools Project, small schools share the following characteristics.

- **"They are small**. Few effective small schools serve more than 400 students, and many serve no more than 200 students.

- **"They are autonomous**. The school community—whether it shares a building, administrator, or some cocurricular activities with other schools—retains primary authority to make decisions affecting the important aspects of the school.

- **"They are distinctive and focused** rather than comprehensive. They do not try to be all things to all people.

- **"They are personal**. Every student is known by more than one adult, and every student has an advisor/advocate who works closely with her and her family to plan a personalized program. Student-family-advisor relationships are sustained over several years.

- **"They are committed to equity** in educational achievement by eliminating achievement gaps between groups of students while increasing the achievement levels of virtually all students.

- **"They use multiple forms of assessment** to report on student accomplishment and to guide their efforts to improve their own school.

- **"They view** parents as critical allies, and find significant ways to include them in the life of the school community.

- **"They are schools of choice** for both students and teachers, except in some rural areas, and are open, without bias, to any students in a community." (Small Schools Project, 2006)

Eagle Rock and a myriad other schools qualify as small schools. Eagle Rock, for example, enrolls at capacity only 96 students. It enjoys all of the benefits of smallness, noted above, especially the ability to build relationships. Many other schools—elementary, middle, and high schools—have been designed or redesigned to become small. Go online at www.smallschoolsproject.org to learn about other schools that are small.

The head of Eagle Rock School summarizes the difference between large and small schools:

> In a big school, a student can run into another student (or staff member) and escape consequences in a crowded hallway. In a small school, that accidental encounter has to be acknowledged. You know you'll see each other again, many times during the day. An apology is in order. Relationships rule.

Cotton (1996a, 1996b) studied the affective and social benefits of small schools. In a synthesis of 103 studies and reviews, she found that small schools had a positive effect on the following:

- Student attitudes
- Sense of belonging
- Administrator and teacher attitudes
- Extracurricular participation
- Attendance and staying in school
- Social disruption
- Teacher use of innovative practices
- Educational equity

She concluded, "Although the professional literature supports educating children in small schools, the consolidation trend continues to create large schools. This is because factors other than student results—political, economic, social, and demographic factors—typically drive decisions about school size. While such a trend would be difficult to reverse, the research indicates that it would be well worth the effort" (Cotton, 1996a, p. 4).

DIFFERENT KINDS OF SMALLNESS

Smallness is not just a matter of school size. Other kinds of smallness help students build relationships.

Small Class Sizes

Several summaries of research on the effects of smaller class size establish the ideal size of the class at around 17 students (Finn, 1998; Murphy &

Rosenberg, 1998; National Education Association, 2006; O'Connell & Smith, 2000; Pritchard, 1999). Although fewer studies have been done on the benefits of lower class size in secondary schools, most research studies agree that the ideal number of students K–12 is fewer than 20 but more than 13. Eagle Rock has found that between 10 and 15 students is ideal. Fewer, and discussion is less vigorous; more, and the students are less able to make personal connections. Amy Biehl High School, an urban school in Albuquerque, New Mexico, features class sizes of about 15 students, is housed in a 1908 post office building, and uses the downtown as its classroom (Amy Biehl High School, 2007).

One important note from class size research: If teachers conduct smaller classes as if they still had 30 or 35 students, class size reduction will not result in better student achievement. Teachers taking advantage of smaller class sizes can do the following:

Teach, rather than manage and discipline as much.

Provide clear and focused instruction, even individual coaching.

Use a variety of teaching strategies to meet individual learning needs.

Monitor learners, provide follow-up and feedback. Reteach as necessary.

Establish effective processes for whole group work and discussion.

Engage in positive personal interactions and give personal encouragement.

Use cooperative groups and learning centers.

Let students become more self-directed in terms of what they learn and how they learn as well as how they demonstrate learning.

Assign students more written products.

Educators who are transitioning from large to small class sizes may need professional learning opportunities to make the switch. They will benefit from working collaboratively on the process, helping each other through problem solving, coaching, and mentoring.

Class Load

Large class loads are problems for secondary school faculty who teach more than one course per day. One of the Nine Common Principles that resulted from a study of high schools in the 1980s addresses class load, the total number of students a teacher sees in a day:

Personalization. Teaching and learning should be personalized to the maximum feasible extent. Efforts should be directed toward a goal that no teacher have direct responsibility for more than eighty students. To allow for personalization, decisions about the details of the course of study, the use of students' and teachers' time, and the choice of teaching materials and specific pedagogies must be unreservedly placed in the hands of the principal and staff. (Sizer, 1984, p. 226)

At Eagle Rock, teachers commonly teach three courses, with 12 to 15 students in each. Thus, class load may be as many as 45 students each trimester. However, they often team-teach with an intern who is learning from them or with another faculty member.

As with reduced class sizes, secondary school faculty may need to learn what they can do differently because they have fewer students over-all to get to know.

Small School by Design or Redesign

Many large schools are redesigning themselves as small schools. A good example of this process is in my own state, Colorado. Mapleton School District is in an urban area just north of Denver; the area is home to many low-income families. Skyview High School was a large school. Graduation rates were low. Test scores were low. The school had undergone numerous attempts to restructure, including participation in Re:Learning, an effort of the Coalition of Essential Schools and the Education Commission of the States. It took a courageous and imaginative superintendent, Charlotte Ciancio, to make a dramatic decision. She recommended that the large high school be broken up into six small high schools:

Skyview Academy High School

Skyview Big Picture High School

Skyview Early College High School

Skyview Expeditionary Learning School

Skyview Learning Through the Arts School

Skyview New Technology High School (Skyview High School, 2006)

Business Week reported, "A school district outside Denver has galvanized students and parents with a daring experiment in public school choice" (Symonds, 2006). Superintendent Ciancio revealed in this article, headlined "A School Makeover in Mapleton," that "'our schools have been an embarrassment for a long time' . . . just 12% of Mapleton's ninth and tenth graders scored proficient in math on Colorado's standards-based test" (p. 1). Schools opened last fall, some within the old high school building. It's too early to tell if the six small schools will do better than the old, big high school, but in the first year attendance rates climbed from

76 percent to 90 percent. Parent participation was up. Teachers began to seek work in these schools. Students from outside the district applied for admission to one of Mapleton's new schools.

Among other schools reopening as small schools within a school (SSWAS) is Tyee High School in Seatac, Washington, which converted into three small self-directed schools: The Academy of Citizenship and Empowerment; Global Connections; and Odyssey, the Essential School. Leominster High School in Massachusetts became five small schools, numbered Leominster 1, 2, et cetera. In North Carolina, Olympic High School opened in the fall of 2006 as five autonomous schools.

Other schools have opened as small schools. Sometimes these are charter schools regulated by a district. Sometimes these are "special schools" regulated by the state. They may be alternative schools or programs within a high school. They may be independent schools. Several schools that have opened recently as small schools include Connections Public Charter School in Hilo, Hawaii; Memphis City New Small High School in Memphis, Tennessee; Metro High School in Columbus, Ohio; and the Renaissance School at Olympic, Charlotte, North Carolina (CES Small Schools Project, 2002b).

One example of a school that opened as a small school is New Vista High School. It is not a charter, special, alternative, or independent school. It is a public school in Boulder, Colorado. You can read more about it in the vignette in this chapter.

Some schools open small as a result of teachers who became frustrated with the huge size of their former schools and all that meant to them as teachers. The fictional Horace in *Horace's Compromise* (Sizer, 1984) and subsequent *Horace* books exemplified those teachers. Aware of the compromises he had to make about learning and teaching, Horace worked with others to create a new school.

Asked what they would do if they could create a new school for their own communities, esteemed participants in a conference called "Studying the Urban High School," sponsored by the Spencer Foundation on May 17–18, 2001, described their dreams for an urban high school:

- Include "students in the planning and administration of schools"
- Treat "students as though they are all smart"
- Detrack "schools and classrooms"
- Design "small schools with longer than the traditional 45 minute slots so that teachers can have better relationships with students"
- Teach "students about their histories and cultural identities"
- Have "students read out loud and talk to each other, so they can hear their own voices"
- Create "a school where the teachers share a critical pedagogy for social justice"
- "Offer many opportunities to write, so that students can experience the transformative power of writing." (Spencer Foundation, 2001, p. 3)

Vignette 2.1   A School Vignette: Building Relationships

CHOOSING THE RIGHT TEACHERS

New Vista High School, Colorado

By Rona Wilensky

New Vista, a small public high school in Boulder Valley School District (Colorado), serves a broad spectrum of students. Although it's not an alternative school, each year students who could readily be identified as "struggling" enroll in New Vista from middle school (and sometimes as transfers from other high schools) with a history of non-engagement in their learning. Their disengagement can take the form of low grades, poor attendance, disciplinary infractions or all of the above. These students can be divided into two groups, one of which we can help, the other of which we cannot serve at all.

The two groups can be described—bluntly—as follows: Kids for whom school "sucks" and kids for whom life "sucks." The first group can be seen as square pegs in round holes. Who they are does not fit with conventional school practice. This could be due to their non-traditional learning styles; it could be due to their unwillingness to play the "game" of school; it could be due to poor peer relationships; or it could be due to their reluctance to submit to what they perceive as the arbitrary use and abuse of power by adults in schools. These are the kids we can turn around.

The second group of kids, those for whom life "sucks," are the ones who break your heart. Their problems shouldn't happen to anyone and come in myriad forms—physical, emotional or sexual abuse; parents or guardians who are alcoholics, addicts, emotionally disturbed or mentally ill; homelessness; neglect. What it boils down to is that these are the kids who don't have reliable adults in their lives who can really take care of them. And there is little that a public school can do to repair their fractured lives except refer them to overburdened social welfare agencies.

What then can we do for struggling students for whom school "sucks"—the ones we say we can help? It boils down to two strategies embedded in a very intentional school climate. The first strategy is that we make sure that students have enough diverse choices so that they can find some "entry point" into learning. This can take the form of non-academic studies in the arts or applied technology; it can take the form of internships in the community with people earning their living doing something the kid finds fascinating; it can take the form of simply having the ability to make genuine choices about schedules or projects.

The second strategy is that we make sure that they encounter teachers who are prepared to care about them, to guide them to these entry points, and to demand quality work from them. In this vignette, I focus on the second strategy.

We look for four key factors when we hire teachers, the last of which—teaching skills that engage students in active learning—we can coach in those candidates who bring the other three criteria with them.

Philosophical congruence. No one will be hired for a permanent position who hasn't read the materials and visited the school while it is in session. We look for people who agree, at least in principle, with the mission, values and vision of this school. They should at least think that students should be doing most of the work and that it is their responsibility as teachers to create the environment, social and academic, that motivates students to do that work.

Intellectual vitality. Schools are about learning, and the chief learners must be the teachers. We look for people who are smart, well educated in their disciplines, curious, and intellectually flexible. They need to understand the structure of their discipline well enough to be comfortable "teaching" classes on specific topics that might be new to them, but of great interest to their students.

Rapport with students. When it comes right down to it, the essence of teaching at New Vista is forming relationships with students that become the bridge over which the students travel to learn the content. The relationship must be based on genuine respect for students, comfort being *the adult* who keeps the boundaries adolescents need, the capacity not to be put off by students who have developed off-putting styles designed to annoy adults, the capacity to adhere to high expectations and last, the capacity to admit error and to negotiate new arrangements when circumstances truly warrant it.

Most adults have a hard time with this delicate balancing act. In general, they are either authoritarian, adhering to their power and privilege as adults or overly permissive, seeking friendship and a non-confrontational relationship with their students. What we are looking for are adults who expect much of students, behaviorally and educationally, while giving them the personal support, attention, and care that helps them meet those expectations.

Teaching skills. We offer classrooms in which students do the active work of making meaning and genuine learning. We are not looking for people to tell students what they need to know; we want people who can create structures and activities that allow students to genuinely integrate new learning into their cognitive frameworks. This takes different forms in different disciplines but in all cases students are talking about, writing about, and using new ideas in ways that lead to real learning.

As long as they met our other demands, we have hired many teachers who didn't know how to teach. With time and mentoring, someone can learn the pedagogical skills of active learning, but only if they believe in it, know their subject matter, and have the right skills with kids.

The context within which these two strategies are implemented is a very carefully crafted school climate characterized by the following: We eliminate arbitrary rules and the unnecessary exercise of power; we staff the school with individuals who treat adolescents as partners in their own education and as people to be negotiated with; we demand that everyone treat everyone else with genuine respect; and we hold the line firmly when these non-negotiables are violated.

SOURCE: Used by permission from Rona Wilensky, Principal, New Vista High School.

AUTHOR'S NOTE: For more information contact Rona Wilensky, Principal of New Vista High School. She can be reached at Rona.Wilensky@bvsd.org. The school Web site is http://schools.bvsd.org/nvhs. New Vista is a founding member of Goodlad's League of Small Democratic Schools.

Kermit the Frog said, "It's not easy being green." With apologies to the Muppets and creator Jim Henson, I'd like to suggest that it isn't easy getting small. Redesign is plagued with problems, one of which is the Herculean task of trying to change a school from within, while school is still going on. This task has been compared to the impossibility of changing a tire as a jet heads down Runway Three North. Designed small schools have their own challenges, one of which is sponsorship (becoming a charter, for example). Another problem that besets new small schools is start-up funding.

As with all structural reforms, changing the structure is not enough. Many educators remember the thrill of block scheduling. Longer blocks of time for students and teachers to work together—that's all it would take to deepen learning, according to what we heard. For many, block scheduling didn't work . . . because educators did not change much about what happened during those two and a half hours with students: Lecture, practice, and homework, only longer. Educators will become disillusioned with getting small if they do nothing differently, if they do not take advantage of having fewer students to work with during the day. In particular, educators need to actualize one of the main benefits of smallness by building relationships with their students that lead to personal and academic growth.

Many of the ideas in the rest of this book can be implemented in large schools or classes or with large class loads. They are easier to implement, however, if the school is small, the class sizes reduced, and the class load lighter than usual. In addition, the ideas below can apply to schools that are small, as well as those that cannot, for some reason, design or redesign themselves as small schools.

HOW TO BUILD RELATIONSHIPS WHETHER YOU'RE SMALL OR NOT

Building relationships is much easier when there are fewer adults working with fewer students over time. The elementary school practice of looping helps with building relationships, even if the school and class sizes are large. In secondary schools, advisories help adults build relationships with students.

Even if you cannot reduce the size of your school or classes, you can still use some of these ideas for building relationships.

Personalizing Through Learning Styles

Start the year with a focus for all staff and students on learning styles. Schedule time for students and staff to discover and share learning styles (which, for teachers, often become their teaching styles). Have adults in the building share their own learning styles with each other and with students. Have staff and students profile their classrooms and various groups of learners, including the whole staff as a learning group.

Using an instrument such as True Colors© is an engaging way to discuss styles (www.truecolors.org). Also consider Jane Kise's book, *Differentiation Through Personality Types: A Framework for Instruction, Assessment, and Classroom Management,* for a unique and practical way to personalize learning (2006).

Within each class, address questions such as, "What are our preferences? What do we need to work on together to make this a quality learning environment?" Teach students to be advocates for their own learning styles, not in an aggressive way, but as self-directed students. Help them figure out how to recast a task or assignment so that it takes advantage of their learning preferences, asking help if they need it. Help them strengthen their less-preferred learning styles.

Begin the Year With a Focus on Relationships

Spend time at the beginning of each year in each class getting to know each other. This is not wasted time; later, it will have huge payoffs in terms of interdependency, cohesion, engagement in learning, and mutual accountability for learning. See the survey at the end of this chapter for a set of questions that can be used to help students and staff get to know each other.

Rethink Classroom Management

Institute Glasser's (1990) ideas about quality schools by having students hold meetings within the classroom to establish and then monitor how people behave toward each other. Develop and frequently check on norms that will make the classroom hospitable for learning, especially for struggling learners. You'll find some other ideas about classroom management in Chapter 4.

Provide Opportunities for Relationships

Provide as many opportunities as possible for relationships: team teaching, coteaching with students, having students work in groups. Encourage collaboration and interaction to complete meaningful outcomes. Make sure there is class time for students to talk with one another and for staff to talk with students in small groups or individually.

Provide Check-Ins

In elementary schools, consider daily "check-ins" through which students and teachers share a bit of what is going on in their outside-school lives. Have check-ins in secondary classes during homeroom or on one day a week.

Engage in Passionate Teaching

Be willing to share your own passions as a teacher and to work them into teaching if possible. Encourage other teachers to do the same. Become passionate about your own learning. According to Vanessa, a student, teacher enthusiasm "helps students want to learn and, therefore, strong teacher-student relationships are possible." Parker Palmer (1991, 1998) wrote about teaching who we are, especially our passions.

Participate in Advisories

Institute advisories (if you haven't already done so)—regular times when staff members each meet with a small group of students to get to know each other. Focus on the relationships in the group as well as the personal and academic growth of all members (including staff). Consider including in advisories staff who are not certified.

One of the best sources of information on how to create advisories comes from Brown University: *Changing Systems to Personalize Learning: The Power of Advisories,* by Debbie Osofsky, Gregg Sinner, and Denise Wolk (2003).

Give Students Voice

Find ways that students can have a voice in terms of what's happening to them at school or in your classroom. Have forums that allow dialogue among students, staff, and administrators. Provide ways for students to interact in the governance of their school and classrooms. Look at feedback as a two-way process, with students as capable of giving feedback as getting it. You'll discover more about voice in Chapters 5 and 7.

Ensure Open Communication

Sometimes, students *dis*engage because they simply don't know what's going on. They feel left out, and they don't have established relationships to bring them "into the loop" of school. Ask, "Are we overcommunicating yet?" and "Who else needs to be in on this decision?" and "Who else needs to know?" and "How can we take this decision to the level of those who will be affected by it?" An aphorism describes the last of these important questions in a community: "Them's as does the doin' does the decidin'."

Examine the Restrictions

Sometimes—intentionally or not—school structures affect capacity to build relationships. A school administrator candidly reported, "Restrictions are somewhat self-imposed. When I was a public school teacher I was able to create enduring relationships of trust and sharing with my students and the expected norms of behavior." Sometimes "they" say we can't do something. Of course, no one knows exactly who "they" are . . . and perhaps there's no "they" out there at all!

Share Yourselves

Early in my career as an educator, I was told that students should know as little about me as possible. I was also told at that time not to smile until January and to let what students said run off me "like water off a duck's back." I disregarded that advice from the first and have never been sorry. Educators can build relationships if they share themselves, "warts and all." As Mohammed, an instructor said, "Allow young people to humanize adults by relating to them in ways that do not enforce *adultism*." Students need to "realize that adults, like young people, can feel marginalized, sad, angry, and even hyperactive." Students need to understand "the intentions of adults. They need to know that instructors, teachers, and facilitators chose the work they're doing because they like seeing young people grow, learn, and harness their energies into productive endeavors for themselves and for society." Richard, an instructor added, "Self-disclosure may seem frightening to some teachers, but students need to know who their teachers are to trust them. Staff need to share their values, their opinions, their strengths and weaknesses, and their imperfections and flaws with students. They need to share their heroes, their music, their culture, their life experiences."

Cultivate Interactions Outside Class

Find a way to make time for interactions outside the classroom, more informal opportunities for members of the community to get to know each other. Doing service projects together is an excellent example of a relationship-building activity outside the classroom. According to Andy, an instructor, "Building relationships does not take undue time or effort. A few minutes here and there between a staff member and student can foster a meaningful relationship in which each party gets to know the other as a person as opposed to their respective roles."

Begin With Leadership

"Public school leaders can set a tone of openness, caring, empathy, or mutual trust through the way they behave," according to a school administrator. "Open doors, vulnerability, shared hardships. The Buddhist concept of *kun long* is a useful gauge. Are school leaders finding a way to choreograph an environment in which relationships of trust are valued? Slow progress in this direction yields results over time."

Promote a Sense of Equality

Sevi, a student, suggested,

> By removing the sense of hierarchy, you open up doors of trust because no one person is considered better than the other. Also the teacher has to be willing to be taught by the student. If the teacher feels that it is wrong for a student to challenge what they have been presented, he or she has put him- or herself above the student. This removes the bridges of understanding and breaks the foundations of trust. Basically, we are willing to hear our friends out and allow our friends the freedom to disagree with us. If someone is genuinely interested in helping someone learn and grow, those same freedoms should be allowed in the classroom. Those freedoms help us to understand each other on an individual basis.

I acknowledge that this idea can be very threatening. However, it doesn't mean that teachers abrogate all responsibility for teaching, denying the expertise they have cultivated. It means that teachers acknowledge what they don't know, that they're willing to learn from students—who actually might know quite a bit—and that they consciously decide to partner with students in pursuit of learning.

Engage in Unlearning

Help students unlearn much of what they have experienced. Students sometimes think that all they have to do is to sit passively in their classrooms, somehow—magically—absorbing enough to be called "educated." It's no wonder they have this impression of school, but you may want to help them change how school works for them. They need to understand that learning is an interaction, that their opinions count, and that they need to engage in learning, indeed take charge of their learning and demand to learn. Help students become self-directed learners.

Provide Interaction With Authority Figures

Different forms of interaction with authority figures in different roles, according to Mohammed, an instructor, might "include having conversations, participating on a team with students, being mentors, participating in band together or, in some cases, acting as if they are coworkers." Instead of making band, orchestra, and choir for students only, make them available to the whole community, including the adults in the community (might take some schedule wrangling, but it can be done). Create intramurals that feature combined student and staff teams. Have students mentor staff . . . and vice versa. Provide ways that teachers and students can teach together. Don't segregate staff and students during lunch and break times; instead, provide places during these times for the casual conversations that are essential for building relationships.

CONCLUSION

Building relationships. It sounds so simple, but with 35 students in six classes, in a school of 1,500, it's not. Or, if you're responsible for teaching six periods with 35 students in each, it's not. With bells ringing every 52 minutes and bus schedules governing school time together, it's a challenge. With content to teach and tests to give and parents to talk with, it can seem impossible. With nine months in the school year, and a month to review in the fall and a month to prep for the state tests in the spring, there's not enough time. I've been there.

Getting small in some way is one way to enable adults to build relationships with students, but some schools get small and quit there, wondering why smallness alone is insufficient for bringing about the results they want. Effective relationships for learning are usually long term (longer than a single class or semester), mutually beneficial, and cut across the boundaries often set in schools when students are parsed into their academic, personal, and social selves. And, although it helps to be in a small setting, those in large settings can build great relationships. What you'll read in the remaining chapters in this book will help you build the relationships that help students learn and teachers teach . . . and vice versa.

SO WHAT

Begin with yourself. How well do you and your fellow staff members know each other? Invite your colleagues to participate in this interview process with you.

1. Tell your "life stories." How did you get to where you are?

2. What are your best memories of school? Your worst? Your best teachers? Your worst?

3. What do you like doing outside work/school?

4. How do you like to work
   a. In terms of pacing (wait until the last minute, plan from the start, etc.)?
   b. In terms of organization?

    c. In terms of having energy (AM? PM?)?

    d. In terms of space?

5. What drives you absolutely NUTS in the workplace/school?

6. What do you think YOU DO that may drive other people NUTS in the workplace/school?

7. What do you think coworkers or colleagues might say about you and your work?

8. What are some goals you have about being in your workplace/ school this year?

9. What are some challenges or fears you have?

10. What else would you like to say about yourself or ask others?

If you have an opportunity to interact with students, use a version of this interview process with individuals or small groups of students.

NOW WHAT

1.   Investigate ways your school or district can sponsor the building of relationships without getting smaller. Use the suggestions given earlier in the chapter to help you explore possibilities.

2.   Investigate what you can do to become smaller in some way. You probably won't have to look far to find a school that's being designed—or redesigned—as a small school. Find at least one.

    a. Check to see if there are small schools (either by design or by redesign) near you. For example, you'll find some in Chicago (Wasley et al., 2000), New York City (Clinchy, 2000), Oakland (Cushman, 2001), Philadelphia (www.sustainable.org), Los Angeles (The Small Schools Project, n.d.), Seattle (Nova High School and others), Oregon (E3's Oregon Small Schools Initiative), and so many other cities and states.

    b. Contact the Bill and Melinda Gates Foundation (www .gatesfoundation.org) for names of other schools that are working toward being small.

    c. Connect to networks of schools that are designing or redesigning themselves as small schools: The Coalition of Essential Schools, the Small Schools Network, Expeditionary Learning Outward Bound, the Big Picture Company.

    d. Check information provided by the national research laboratories, such as the Northwest Regional Educational Laboratory (www.nwrel.org), WestEd (www.wested.org), Southern Region

Education Board (www.sreb.org/programs), and the North Central Regional Educational Laboratory (www.ncrel.org).

e. Check to see what local colleges and universities are offering in terms of school reform technical assistance, especially small school designs. The Small Schools Workshop, University of Illinois at Chicago, is one example of a university-based initiative. Another is Small Schools Northwest at Lewis and Clark College in Oregon (www.lclark.edu).

f. Check to see what states and large districts are doing. For example, Oregon has a small schools initiative (www .oregonssa.org). Colorado has one (www.cssi.org), and so does Montana (www.mtsmallschools.org).

Note: Many of the sites listed above might lead you to sources of funding!

3. Visit as many small schools as you can. Come to Eagle Rock if you can, or arrange an educational tour of another small school.[1] Shadow students and staff (Easton, 2004b). Ask yourself the What (what do you notice?), So What (so, what does this mean to you?), and Now What (now, what do we do about what we've noticed and what seems important to us?) questions. Experience the school both cognitively and emotionally (in terms of how it feels or how it makes a difference for young people).

4. Read everything you can about small schools and share what you are reading with everyone—including students—who might be involved in changing your own school or opening a small school. The Reference section contains a number of good books and articles.

5. Consider your context and the context of the small schools that you've read about and visited. What are the similarities? What are the differences? How does the idea of becoming smaller fit your context? In what ways might such a decision "go to war" with your context?

6. Work with as many people in your school community as possible to begin to think about your own school as a small school. You will find that designing a small school is not a linear process; it is very organic, and, as you make decisions in one area, you'll find yourself revisiting other decisions. Nevertheless, here in list form are some things you might want to think about:

a. *Rationale:* Why does the school community think the school should be smaller? What data support that move? What data point in other directions? What problems might be solved better if the school were smaller?

b. The overall *structure* of your small school: Many schools decide to become small schools within a school. These SSWASs usually take on some kind of persona. They become houses, neighborhoods, or teams of teachers and students working together.

They may even name themselves. Sometimes small schools are multigrade (mixed classes); sometimes they enroll a cluster of grades but keep classes separated by grade level.

c. The *identity or signature* (Ginsburg, 2004) of your small school. Some small schools have focused on being interdisciplinary. Some have focused on potential vocations (such as law or medicine). Some have focused on interest areas (such as technology or art). Others have simply subscribed to a "less is more" philosophy, determining that they do not have to offer everything a large, comprehensive school might offer students.

d. The *culture* of your small school: You will want to keep (or somewhat modify) some aspects of schooling because they support your new small school culture; you will want to "deep six" other aspects because they were necessary when your school was large but are no longer needed.

e. The *governance* of your small school: How will student and staff voices be heard? How will issues around power, authority, and control be worked out? How will democracy be lived at your school?

f. The *mechanisms* that support possibilities in your small school: Your use of time and space, for example. How—and where and when—will you bring the whole school together? To do what? What rituals will you want to launch your small school, mark its progress (and the progress of students and staff), its endings and beginnings?

g. *Curriculum, instruction, and assessment.* How will you take advantage of being a small school as you decide what and how students and staff will learn and how everyone will know that learning has taken place?

NOTE

1. Schools change. Before visiting, check a school's Web site or ask for current materials. Also call to see if visitors are welcome and to make arrangements for a visit.

3

"What's Community Got to Do With Learning?"

Intentional Learning Communities Foster Learning

Relationships are great. Even better is community. Unfortunately, the concept of "learning community"—once a revolutionary idea—has become a cliché. Every group is a learning community! Everyone in a school is—naturally—part of a learning community!

Calling a school a learning community doesn't necessarily make it so. A real learning community is brought to life intentionally. It is carefully nurtured. It grows and changes. It matures. Without constant care, it soon begins to wither and die.

Jeremy, former gang member, Eagle Rock graduate, college graduate, graduate student, and parent, recalled the importance of community to his learning. "The benefits of the whole school learning community are intentionality (one of my favorite words) and consistency. When all actions of community are in tandem, then goals are achieved easier and with greater success."

THE IMPORTANCE OF COMMUNITY

One way of defining community is through the lens of communitarianism. Although mostly a political and social philosophy, whose best-known spokesperson is Amitai Etzioni (1995), communitarianism has important applications for education (Smith, 2001). Mark K. Smith links the two by describing "ten basic themes [that] run through the communitarian agenda for education:

1. "The family should be the primary moral educator of children.

2. "Character education includes the systematic teaching of virtues in schools.

3. "The ethos of the community has an educative function in school life.

4. "Schools should promote the rights and responsibilities inherent within citizenship.

5. "Community service is an important part of a child's education in school.

6. "A major purpose of the school curriculum is to teach social and political life-skills.

7. "Schools should provide an active understanding of the common good.

8. "Religious schools are able to operate a strong version of the communitarian perspective.

9. "Many existing community-based education practices reflect the features of the communitarian perspective.

10. "Schools should adopt a more democratic structure of operating." (Smith, 2001, pp. 136–141)

Most, though not all, of these principles apply to learning communities as they might operate in public schools. Few would argue that learning communities should have an effect (an "educative function"); otherwise, why would schools as institutions turn themselves into learning communities? They should exemplify esteemed values and virtues, such as trust and the rights and responsibilities of citizenship and democracy. A learning community helps young people learn community service and social and political life-skills.

By far the most important aspect of community, however, is the "active understanding of the common good." Most young people are amazingly egocentric. Some literally do not see someone else's need. Solipsistically, they think the world is exactly as they see it. No one else's perspective is possible. At one point, egocentricity was probably a matter of survival; now, in a crowded, diverse world, solipsism could be civilization's undoing. A learning community helps young people become aware of the greater good.

Piaget noticed egocentrism in young people who were in the pre-operational stage (ages two to seven years). According to Bjorklund (1989), Piaget's description of young children as egocentric "was not used disparagingly. . . . Rather, he used the term to describe young children's intellectual perspective. They interpret the world through preoperative eyes and generally assume that others see the world as they do. Their cognition is centered around themselves, and they have a difficult time putting themselves in someone else's shoes" (pp. 27–28).

Egocentrism does not disappear when young people develop concrete (ages 7 to 11) and formal operations (ages 11 to 16). It just changes. According to his broad definition of egocentrism "as an ability to decenter" (Bjorklund, 1989, p. 34), Piaget believed that adolescents "demonstrate their own form of centration. Piaget maintained that adolescents are often concerned about their future in society" (p. 34). These concerns magnify the need for community because teenagers often want to see how they "can transform society. Therefore, many of their grand social and political ideas may conflict with beliefs or attitudes of others (particularly people in authority)" (p. 34). Most of us have had the opportunity to work with teenagers who know it all. Without community, they may suffer "extreme self-consciousness" and the "mistaken belief that other people are as concerned with their feelings and behavior as they are, which, of course, serves only to increase their self-consciousness" (p. 34).

Addressing the greater good—and helping young people see beyond their egos—is an important aspect of community at Eagle Rock. Rules are few (see Chapter 4), but, as you can imagine in a residential school for teenagers, there is conflict aplenty. One of the commitments that students make when they enroll at Eagle Rock is to "live in respectful harmony." This takes some doing. Students and staff meet regularly in Gatherings or Community Meetings. They have house (dormitory) meetings and gender meetings. They call their own meetings when things get rough. After one particularly bad episode—several students had broken nonnegotiables (no alcohol, tobacco, drugs, violence, or sexual relations) and an underground seemed to be burgeoning—the school shut down for a week academically and devoted itself to repairing and regrowing community. Students (with the help of some staff) organized and ran this event. Both students and staff declared that their week of struggling to understand and reconstruct their own community was the most important learning that had happened that trimester.

The proposal system at Eagle Rock School (ERS) is another mechanism that helps students address the greater good. Students and staff are frequently reminded that Eagle Rock is their community and that it is only as good as they make it. Anyone who has an idea about making the community better in any way is invited to prepare a proposal. This involves doing some research, writing, presenting the proposal both orally and in writing, listening for feedback, perhaps doing more research, revising the proposal, and presenting it again to the community. The proposal system takes the helplessness out of schooling for students by making them feel efficacious, engages them in real-life application of skills, and improves the community.

Community at Eagle Rock, then, has personal and social purposes. It also has learning purposes.

STUDENTS IN COMMUNITY

Ann L. Brown and Joseph C. Campione (1998) describe several essential characteristics of learning communities. For example, learning communities combine "individual responsibility . . . with communal sharing" (p. 158). They also offer "multiple zones of proximal development" (p. 160). Eagle Rock demonstrates these characteristics in a variety of ways. You will learn more in Chapter 6 about how students demonstrate mastery of standards to get credit. They help each other learn and document their learning, often teaching each other in an informal way. Classrooms are set up with round tables (actually, donut-shaped), and students sitting around them can observe each other's confusion or understanding. They ask for and give help, as necessary. Without grades, the system rewards cooperation and assistance rather than competition. It is important to everyone that everyone masters the standards.

Classes are extremely heterogeneous. The word *extremely* is not a mistake (although the word *heterogeneous* may be an absolute). There are no grade levels, so any class may have a range of chronological ages from 14 to 21, as well as the typical range of experiences, background, skills, knowledge, and expertise. Vygotsky's (1978) theories of the zone of proximal development and scaffolding operate in these classrooms. In any classroom, some students are likely to be expert on some things and others expert on other things. With some guidance from the instructor, groups work their way through learning problems, helping each other.

Students sometimes team-teach with the instructors, learning quite a lot through teaching and sharing the expertise they have developed. On a few occasions—for example, after a student returned from a service trip to Vietnam—students have taught classes with a "guide on the side," an instructor to help them think through instructional strategies.

Students frequently serve as discussion leaders. In fact, some classes use a rubric for being a discussion leader as well as a rubric for being a participant in a discussion. In classes that focus on literature or have a literature component, for example, students not only lead discussions but organize reading groups, a strategy adapted from Harvey Daniels (2002) in *Literature Circles*. In addition to selecting their own novels or nonfiction, students set up and conduct meetings themselves, take notes on their discussions, and share with other reading groups what they are discovering.

Documentations of learning (to achieve credit) and Presentations of Learning (POLs; formal, end-of-the trimester exhibitions) are individual and public. Students learn from them as they prepare for them, and they learn from each other when POLs are given (as do the faculty, staff, and administrators).

When the whole school is a learning community, not all learning happens in classes. Tahnée, soon to graduate, commented, "Most of my learning comes from outside the classrooms. Not so much that I learn from the 'whole community,' but I learn from different individuals within the community. I work with Mark constantly in the kitchen, learning how to prepare food and follow my interests in cooking. ERS makes this possible by providing the time and space to make this happen. The schedule is set up so that different people spend time together and it seems that it was the goal for us to be together."

Brown and Campione (1998) note that "ritual and familiar participant structures" are an important part of learning communities (p. 159). Jigsaw is a routine learning activity, with individuals (including the instructor) researching parts of a topic and sharing with others what they have learned. Documentations of learning are regular events in classes since they are the only way students can achieve credit.

Regular POLs have some ritual in them—they are known as "celebrations of learning"—and occur not just at the end of every trimester but for new students when they return from their wilderness trip and for graduates just before they graduate. Graduate POLs bring back students who have already graduated and been "out in the world" to share what they have learned. Students also do Personal Growth POLs before they graduate. Students expect to demonstrate their learning in a variety of ways.

The POL packets, which are sent out to panel members ahead of the POLs themselves, have an element of ritual in them. Students write their moral and ethical code, for example, and ruminate on "I used to be . . . but now I am . . . " in them. Chapter 8 gives examples of these aspects of the packets. Veteran students present their developing moral and ethical codes at Wednesday gatherings and get feedback on them from students and staff alike. Graduates begin to talk about their readiness to graduate a full trimester before they think they'll graduate; other students give them feedback and, themselves, start to think about their own possible graduation.

An intern, Tim, summarized the value of POLs: They

are a great demonstration that ERS is a whole-school learning community. The POLs give students the opportunity to present what they've learned to staff and members of the larger community. The students effectively become the teachers. This also happens through the opportunities students have of designing their own classes and teaching them.

Brown and Campione (1998) note that a learning community is "a community of discourse" (p. 160). One example of the oral nature of the

Eagle Rock community is the morning Gathering. Held for 20 minutes every morning, Gathering brings the community together. The schedule calls for a moment of silence, announcements, a presentation, and music. Gatherings are usually run by students who bring to the community a variety of topics: their personal histories or current needs; community issues; a local, national, or global headline that they want to discuss; a poem they've written or read; or a work of art they've accomplished. Sometimes students structure the Gathering to obtain feedback on themselves. Every Tuesday, veteran students discuss the meaning of the principles (see Chapter 4) by which they live, often engaging the whole community in a discussion of what those principles look like in practice.

Every Monday, the head of school challenges the whole community to consider individually and with each other a provocative idea, such as H. G. Wells's saying, "The past is but the beginning of a beginning." During the week, the head of school stops students on the paths to and from classes to ask them what they think about that quote and how it applies to them.

In fact, Eagle Rock's first curriculum question was, "How can we make this community safe for learning?" At Francis W. Parker School in Massachusetts, coursework revolves around essential questions. When the school opened in 1995–1996, the first essential question was, "What is community?" Subsequent essential questions have also addressed the place of community in schools, for example, "What's the limit?" "What really matters?" "Where's the truth?" "What is unique? What is universal?" (Parker School, n.d.).

"Seeding, migration, and appropriation of ideas" completes Brown and Campione's (1998) list of characteristics of a learning community (pp. 160–161). What a fascinating concept! Members of learning communities *seed*

> the environment with ideas and concepts that they value and . . . harvest those that "take" in the community. Ideas seeded by community members *migrate* to other participants and persist over time. Participants in the classroom are free to *appropriate* vocabulary, ideas, methods, and so forth that appear initially as part of the shared discourse, and by appropriation, transform these ideas through personal interpretation.(pp. 160–161)

Again, Gathering comes to mind. A student shares her interest in the crop walk that is sponsored by a local organization. Suddenly, many students want to go on the walk. Then, the leader of the hosting organization comes out to thank the school for participating and helping to raise money for the project. The chef instructor shares his philosophy about organic farming and takes interested students and staff to visit some local organic farms. Then, next trimester, the science teacher offers a course about the worldwide effects of agriculture. The mathematics teacher and the chef instructor offer a course that leads students to make their own organic juices. Students do a service project to support the local farmers market. They also sell their juice at the market (with profits going to the graduate higher education fund). And so it goes.

HOW WELL LEARNING COMMUNITIES WORK

It sure would be a lot more interesting to be part of a learning community than a student just taking classes. But, do learning communities really have an effect on individual learning? Brown and Campione (1998) are among researchers who think so. They studied a variety of classrooms, but their reported data come from intensive study of a middle school science classroom. They found that students in this classroom—after a unit that incorporated activities that are prized in learning communities, such as the jigsaw and student discussion leaders—scored considerably better on a biology posttest than students who were taught in traditional ways. Students were also able to use "organized knowledge flexibly," including on "novel application tasks" (pp. 163–165). They were able to read better than a "read-only control group" did on a test of reading comprehension, especially on "inferential, gist, and analogy questions" (pp. 165–167). Their reasoning and argumentation skills were improved.

At Eagle Rock, the very public Presentations of Learning, in particular, provide evidence that being part of a learning community is effective. Panel members who come from outside the Eagle Rock community, frequently remark on (1) how articulate students are, (2) how honest they are, and (3) how passionate they are about their own learning. Students present what they've learned, of course, but they also present what their learning means to them. Sometimes students are so assumptive about their academic learning that they need to be prodded to demonstrate their understanding. "Of course I learned this," they seem to say. "Isn't it self-evident?"

As was illustrated in Chapter 1, students also do well on norm-referenced standardized tests. At least, being part of a learning community has done no harm. Jeremy, the Eagle Rock graduate whom you met at the beginning of this chapter, commented, "One benefit of whole-school learning was that we would encourage each other to go beyond the 'normal' limits of education. We created our own learning experiences." He also stated, "Eagle Rock creates itself as a learning community by the way everybody is accountable for themselves."

If you are in a large school—elementary, middle, or high school—you may be wondering how you can learn in a community. Don't give up, even if you think your school will never figure out how to be small. Students report that they have experienced wonderful classes that were like communities. They have been in grade-level communities from kindergarten on. Sometimes their grade-level communities consisted of their own classrooms plus one or two others. Sometimes these grade-level communities consisted of the entire grade, teachers and all. These classroom or grade-level communities

Vignette 3.1   A School Vignette: Communities

COMMUNITIES DON'T GIVE UP ON STUDENTS

Yarmouth High School, ME

By Ted Hall

Although in a suburban setting just outside Portland, Maine, Yarmouth High School has a neighborhood feeling to it. A 9–12 school, it is small, only 500 students. It's a brand-new school in an old, historical shell of a building. Students follow long-trod pathways across neighboring lawns to get to school, and nobody minds. The school has been associated with the Coalition of Essential Schools and the Southern Maine Partnership for quite a while. It has a well-established feeling about it, a history.

At one point, Yarmouth had four levels of academics—four tracks. Now it has two levels in some areas—Honors/AP and College Prep—and one level in other areas, with a goal of getting to one level in most areas by raising the level of College Prep. A Yarmouth English teacher did an interesting study recently. She asked her colleagues to score some writing drafts, without names. The teachers couldn't figure out which tracks the kids were in. My next assignment is to get rid of honors classes entirely; actually, everyone will be taking honors or AP.

So, we're a relatively high-performing district. What distinguishes this district from other high-performing districts is how we take on kids who are struggling. What makes Yarmouth work for struggling students is a focused and determined mind set on the part of its staff. Many of Yarmouth's struggling students come from a population that is economically stressed.

We have barely any drop-outs, single numbers, 1 or 2 a year. That's because we really take dropping out seriously. We'll figure what we need to do for any student. No-out-of district placements for kids. We take seriously the notion that you have to figure out what will work . . . and then what . . . and then what. There's no consideration of letting someone fail. We just keep plugging away. Another plan, a different way. We use Rick DuFour's pyramid of intervention so that we have a year's worth of interventions, but we're quite flexible because we're a small school. We can individualize (DuFour, DuFour, Eaker, & Karhanek, 2004).

Let me give you some examples of our interventions. In response to Monica's needs, classroom teachers had the help of the guidance counselor, special education teachers, and an instructional strategist; they also worked with [her] advisor. In response to Cheyne's needs, they had the guidance counselor, special educators, a speech and language specialist, and instructional strategies, the advisor, and a literacy specialist. In response to Darren's needs, they had the advisor, the SAT (Student Assistance Team) case managers, the guidance counselor, the social worker, a substance abuse counselor, and a literacy specialist. Other people called in to help other students include an occupational therapist, a physical therapist, a nurse coordinator, an alternative education teacher. In all cases, I was involved as were other administrators.

We have the typical structures that help us work with students. For example, Maine schools have to have a Student Assistance Team (SAT); this is a formal structure that brings counselors, social worker, teachers, a nurse, a special education teacher, etc., all together to look at kids who are not doing well; this team stays in touch with parents.

In addition, we have a Student Support Team. This is composed of the school psychologist and others and usually recommends more intervention than the SAT would.

Like lots of schools, we have advisories. Our students have the same advisories for the whole time they're here. It's a small group with built-in, important things to do. For example, the new freshman advisors meet individually with students and parents to choose courses; they get involved with families immediately and involve parents in big decisions, like classes.

Structures are good, but there's this sense with kids. They know they can't flee through the cracks. They'll say, "Even if I try, I can't fall through the cracks." One student who didn't graduate on time and would have dropped out was provided with a math tutor and additional time. He graduated, and we had a little ceremony for him. In many schools, if you hadn't really reached out to him, nagged him, he would have just gone away.

It takes persistence. They'll resist. Sometimes kids can be a real pain in the ass; educators can get burned out by them. There have been a couple of times when we traded off with each other so that another staff member took on a kid who was in danger of dropping out. We got a fresh look at the kid. It's helpful to the kid to have a broadening group of support, too.

We try to avoid labels but provide the services. We have some students who are identified as special education and a whole bunch more who are not but receive services through support teachers working right alongside regular teachers. We provide a study hall in a learning center so that students can work on areas where growth is needed.

We have a literacy person, for example, who works a lot with teachers as well as kids to increase literacy in content classes. She is seen by kids as a great resource; that's how she's seen by teachers, too. She's really good about sharing with teachers the feedback that she gets from students—direct and honest but actionable.

The philosophy behind our instructional support model is simple. We aim to get the right resources to the right students at the right time. Our first layer of protection for kids is comprised of the classroom teachers.

SOURCE: Used by permission from Ted Hall.

AUTHOR'S NOTE: Ted Hall is principal at Yarmouth High School. Formerly, he was principal at Souhegan High School in New Hampshire. Visit Yarmouth's Web site at www.yarmouth.k12.me.us or contact Ted at Ted_Hall@yarmouth.k12.me.us. The school's phone and address are 286 West Elm Street, Yarmouth, ME 04096; ph: (207) 846-5535.

enjoyed many of the aspects of community discussed above, and students felt they belonged and had a purpose outside of themselves because they were part of these communities.

ADULTS IN COMMUNITY

Teachers are used to being developed. Professional development is a given, at least for "back-to-school week." One-shot workshops and seminars, university classes to move up a rung on the salary schedule, and motivational speakers have been the norm, but professional development is changing. Rather than being developed, teachers are encouraged to become learners themselves (Easton, 2004b). In fact, teachers and administrators are being encouraged to form PLCs or Professional Learning Communities.

Professional Learning Communities

Peter Senge, Sharon D. Druse, Karen Seashore Louis, Fred M. Newmann, Gary G. Wehlage, and Shirley Hord were the first to use the term, but Rick DuFour and Robert Eaker have expanded the concept (Blankstein, 2004, p. 55). According to DuFour and Eaker (1998), the characteristics of Professional Learning Communities are these:

1. "Shared mission, vision, and values.

2. "Collective inquiry.

3. "Collaborative teams.

4. "Action orientation and experimentation.

5. "Continuous improvement

6. "Results orientation." (pp. 25–29)

Adults in a learning community are different from those who reside in what has been called "side-by-side caves," a rather apt description of the isolation found in many schools. Adults in learning communities participate in a variety of peer-to-peer learning experiences that contrast dramatically with isolated college classes or motivational speeches. They are not *developed* as much as they develop themselves by doing what Schlecty (2002) advocates, "working on the work."

Characteristics of Professional Learning Experiences

Members of PLCs engage in professional learning activities that share several important characteristics. These characteristics are derived from a book for which I was both the editor and a contributor, *Powerful Designs for Professional Learning* (Easton, 2004b).

Powerful professional learning arises from and returns benefits to the real world of teaching and learning. It begins with what will really help young people learn, engages those involved in helping them learn, and has an effect on the classrooms (and schools, districts, even states) where those students and their teachers learn. Educators who engage in powerful learning first work to understand how a school or district can improve learning for all children.

"Powerful professional development often leads to *collection, analysis and presentation of real data* from student work and teacher practice" (Easton, 2004b, p. 3; emphasis added). Educators identify some powerful professional learning strategies and the people who can lead the learning, people who might very well be in the school or district itself. This kind of professional learning is "content-rich because the content is the school or district itself . . . its staff . . . its learners. This content matters to the people engaged in the experience" (p. 3).

Throughout the professional learning experience (which should be continuous), the focus remains on what is happening with learners (both student and adult) in the classroom, school, and district. Strategies for professional learning *keep the focus on learning (both student and adult)*. During their learning, educators

> return to the learning environment to . . . try out a new technique with learners; set up a research process to obtain data; analyze it and present results to others; design the next steps for professional development; reflect on what was learned; and confer with others. (Easton, 2004b, p. 3)

> *Powerful professional development experiences may not formally end;* they may simply evolve into other powerful forms as participants raise more questions or want to try another strategy. Powerful professional development usually leads to the desire to make continued improvement. It may even change an institution into a learning community. (Easton, 2004b, pp. 3–4; emphasis added)

Powerful professional development is collaborative or has collaborative aspects to it. Educators learn from each other, enriching their own professional lives and the culture of the school or district. They build a shared vision of a school or district, and—contrasting that with realities—they work on what matters and help each other make changes. They set goals, help each other meet these goals, and hold themselves and each other accountable.

Powerful professional learning *establishes a culture of quality*. Powerful professional development encourages discussion about what quality looks like, in terms of the work both educators and their students do.

It *"honors the professionalism, expertise, experiences, and skills of staff"* (Easton, 2004b, p. 4; emphasis added). When educators rely on outsiders, they may communicate the message that those within a school or district lack expertise. Although this can sometimes be the case, with powerful professional learning experiences school and district staff can develop their own expertise and ways of sharing it. A culture becomes a continuous learning community when educators are asked to apply their skills and professionalism to improve student learning . . . and when they recognize the skills and professionalism everyone else brings to the improvement process.

"Using the talent within also *promotes 'buy-in'*" (Easton, 2004b, p. 4; emphasis added). Those who are going to implement change will be more likely to do so if they are involved in the design of the change through powerful professional development. You first encountered this aphorism in Chapter 2: *Them's as does the doin' does the decidin'*. It applies here, as well.

Powerful professional learning *slows the pace of schooling, providing time for the inquiry and reflection that promote learning and application*. We seldom pause in our hectic schedules to make sense of what is going on. We just keep on going. Powerful professional learning is a gift to educators, who seldom have a chance to reflect on their own teaching and learning.

Results of Professional Learning Communities

But do PLCs make a difference? For educators and their schools they did. Shirley Hord's[1] (1997a) research on professional learning communities found the following results for staff:

- Reduction of isolation of teachers
- Increased commitment to the mission and goals of the school and increased vigor in working to strengthen the mission
- Shared responsibility for the total development of students and collective responsibility for students' success
- Powerful learning that defines good teaching and classroom practice and that creates new knowledge and beliefs about teaching and learners
- Increased meaning and understanding of the content that teachers teach and the roles they play in helping all students achieve expectations
- Higher likelihood that teachers will be well informed, professionally renewed, and inspired to inspire students
- More satisfaction, higher morale, and lower rates of absenteeism
- Significant advances in adapting teaching to the students, accomplished more quickly than in traditional schools
- Commitment to making significant and lasting changes
- Higher likelihood of undertaking fundamental, systemic change

Shirley Hord's (1997a) research also validated the benefit of PLCs for students. She found the following effects:

- Decreased dropout rate and fewer classes "cut"
- Lower rates of absenteeism
- Increased learning that is distributed more equitably in the smaller high schools
- Larger academic gains in math, science, history, and reading than in traditional schools
- Smaller achievement gaps between students from different backgrounds

More about her work can be found in *Learning Together, Leading Together* (Hord, 2004).

PLCs—and the professional learning activities that are part of what PLCs do—require some organizational changes.

ORGANIZATIONS THAT SUPPORT PLCs

Schools, districts, intermediary support units (such as BOCES [Boards of Cooperative Educational Services] and teacher centers), and even state departments of education are beginning to change to support professional learning communities. Here are some changes they are making:

Changes in Roles

Teachers become problem-identifiers and solvers; data collectors, analyzers, and reporters; coaches, mentors, and observers; and facilitators of their own and others' professional learning. Teachers know how to learn from each other, how to translate experience into knowledge, and when to find resources from outside.

They use reflection and dialogue as tools for learning, open up their classrooms, and share classroom work so all may learn.

Principals and assistant principals share many of these new teacher roles, including facilitation, coaching, mentoring, reflecting, and dialogue. They also share leadership, especially decisions about professional learning. They are keenly aware of what is happening to learners, both adult and student, in their buildings (walk-throughs or, as I prefer to call them, learning walks) but perhaps in new ways: in the spirit of inquiry, using strategies of inquiry, making no excuses but offering lots of choices, and doing whatever it takes to help everyone learn, including themselves (and sharing their own learning) (Downey, Steffy, English, Frase, & Poston, 2004).

District administrators learn deeply from schools; they spend time in schools, talking with teachers and students and then learn from what they have learned; they also do learning walks. District supervisors or coordinators support what teachers and school-based administrators need to do; they may teach facilitation skills or coaching to school-based staff; those who handle data refocus on how to help others collect, analyze, and report data.

Even the role of consultants changes: They work with schools to help plan and launch new ideas. They might facilitate learning processes on the content the school has identified. Perhaps they'll help with follow-up or problem-solving or observe and provide feedback. Organizations, such as BOCES (Boards of Cooperative Educational Services), intermediary units, and teacher centers, professional organizations, and state departments of education may themselves want to become PLCs. Certainly they'll focus on serving those closest to teaching and learning and their organizations in terms of the new roles suggested above. Policy makers might examine the effects of policy on professional practice; rethink rules and policy that might hinder professional learning; and offer waivers on policies that require accountability but can be customized.

In summary, roles across the spectrum change to support professional learning by focusing on the following:

- Peer-to-peer professional development
- Data collection (various kinds), analysis, sharing
- Reflection
- Application and follow-up
- Working together; sharing learning and need to learn
- Targeting classrooms and schools
- Coaching, mentoring, facilitating

Changes in Use of Time

Use of time may also change. A typical year of professional development looks like this:

Day 1: Beginning of the year motivational speaker

Day 2: Planning and grade preparation

Day 3: Selection from among five whole-day workshops

Day 4: Planning and grade preparation

Day 5: Selection from among five whole-day workshops

Day 6: Planning and grade preparation

Professional learning communities require a different time structure, some whole-day, all-group work, but most partial-day (facilitated by early start or early dismissal) work in small groups. The underlined days below are repeated throughout the year as many times as possible.

Day 1: Focus on school vision, mission, goals, needs, and data (whole school, whole day)

Day 2: Identification of professional learning that needs to take place in the school (whole school, partial day)

Day 3: Powerful professional learning experiences (whole school in small groups)

Day 4: Follow-up and problem-solving (partial days, partial groups)

Day 5: Coaching, mentoring, observing (partial days, partial groups)

Day 6: Data collection and analysis and decisions about further learning (whole school, partial day)

Many schools have rebuilt their schedules to allow professional development time through early or late starts. At Adams City High School, an inner-city high school near Denver, a little tweaking of the schedule made it possible to add professional development time as well as planning time on a daily basis. The school's leadership team has used this time to provide professional learning events related to key goals and then follow-up including coaching, mentoring, and problem-solving.

Changes in Evaluation

Teacher, administrator, school, and district evaluation processes are sometimes the last to change. These processes can sometimes stand in the way of progress, however, and changes in them can leverage other changes. The following two common ways of evaluating professional development do *not* support professional learning:

1. We can evaluate professional development by looking at student test scores.

2. We can evaluate professional development by collecting feedback at the end of the workshop ("I had a great time"; "The room was too cool"; "Thanks for the refreshments").

Both of these ways of evaluating professional development ignore the realization that evaluation of professional learning is complex. We cannot just jump from learning to the effect on student test scores, for example. Between the learning and the test scores, evaluators should note the following:

- How teachers have changed their work as a result of their learning
- How administrators have changed their work as a result of learning
- How the school or district does its business differently

Then—and only then—they should look at student changes in behavior (learning and other aspects of their lives). And, finally, they can look at student growth and achievement using a multitude of indicators.

Even so, evaluators need to acknowledge that cause and effect is a particularly perilous pathway to take in trying to relate professional learning and student outcomes. More helpful is to take a correlative approach: "Our teachers learned this. They began to change their behaviors in school. Administrators did, too. And, our school changed some policies (so did our district). We began to see students doing this. And, interestingly enough, our test scores show improvement in this area."

Evaluators usually target skills or knowledge. Joellen Killion (2002, 2003) of the National Staff Development Council makes the point that many more aspects of human life should be examined in education. An acronym helps us remember the other aspects, KASAB:

"**K**nowledge Conceptual understanding of information, theories, principles and research

"**A**ttitude Beliefs about the value of particular information or strategies

"**S**kills Strategies and processes to apply knowledge

"**A**spiration Desire, or internal motivation, to engage in a particular practice

"**B**ehavior Consistent application of knowledge and skills." (Killion, 2002, p. 212)

An effective professional learning activity would involve a whole school in determining indicators of a desired change in terms of KASAB— for teachers, administrators, the school and district cultures as a whole, as well as students. This activity would answer the question, "How will we know that X has made a difference?"

Changes in Budget

Budget does, of course, change with the move to professional learning and building of Professional Learning Communities, but it may not have to increase significantly. The most expensive change is to support time for educators to work on their own learning; this may be substitute pay or stipends for summer work. Educators will need to be compensated not only for the days they work as a whole school, small group, or independently, but for days they use for follow-up; coaching and mentoring; problem-solving; facilitating their own and each others' learning; and collecting, analyzing, and reporting data. These days must count as professional learning days and be built into the calendar. A hopeful approach here will not work. Administrators, for example, cannot expect teachers to find the time for these follow-up activities unless time is set aside for them.

The good news is that many schools are figuring out how to find the time, from late start to early dismissal days to rethinking the use of meetings, from calling on the larger community to help to school-based use of professional learning days.

Changes in Activities

Activities that enhance professional learning are beginning to replace (or at least supplement) the "sage on the stage" motivational speaker. The most beneficial learning activities are those that are embedded in the work that educators do. A description of such activities—and steps for doing them— can be found in *Powerful Designs for Professional Learning* (Easton, 2004b) and include the following: action research, assessment design, critical friends groups, curriculum design, immersing teachers in practice, lesson study, standards in practice (assignment analysis), study groups. Strategies that can help educators in their learning include accessing student voices, use of case discussions, classroom walk-throughs, data analysis, journaling, mentoring, peer coaching, portfolios, school coaching, shadowing students, training the trainer, tuning protocols, and visual dialogue.

These designs and strategies are powerful ways to address any content area, a variety of ways to improve pedagogy and assessment, and also organizational development—school improvement especially.

Ultimately, Changes in Culture

Finally, the culture of an organization changes when it is focused on professional learning. Everyone in the building, including students, understands the purposes of the school. A teacher cannot say, "My mission is only to teach science." A student cannot say, "Nothing" when asked what he or she learned today. (Unless, heaven forbid, that's true!)

The culture is one of constant questioning and searching for answers. "That's the way it's always been," or "We tried that three years ago and it didn't work," or "Been there, done that" are statements representing the old culture. The new professional culture is one of inquiry.

Being in others' classrooms and school buildings is the norm. Working together is the norm. Individual inquiry is valued, but shared learning is also important. Collaborative teams change as needs require.

Professional learning experiences begin to have an immediacy about them; their genesis doesn't come from far away or a long time ago (or in the future). Five-year professional learning plans don't work (unless they are simply "holding" time for professional learning needs that will be identified yearly or, at most, every two years) . . . nor do "flavors of the year."

Those who work closest with students identify needs for their own learning and the learning of the organization. They courageously step forward to describe what they need and seek resources. There's a results orientation (Schmoker, 2006). Professional learning makes change possible because we must get different and better results.

Attitudes, conversations, and behaviors change. Mental models change. Schools become Philip Schlecty's WOW schools because everybody is working on the work (Schlecty, 2002). Commitment is public and personal. Accessing student voices is part of the process.

THE NEXT STEP: A WHOLE-SCHOOL LEARNING COMMUNITY (WSLC)

Notice the last sentence of the section preceding this section: *Accessing student voices is part of the process.* Recall some of the characteristics of a learning community for students. Compare them to the desired qualities in a learning community for adults. Why not a whole-school learning community (a WSLC)?

Educators may fear that a whole-school learning community—one that includes both adults and students—might *not* work because the whole-school effort might dilute either the community for students or the community for adults. I think, instead, a WSLC strengthens learning for both students and adults.

Eagle Rock is a whole-school learning community. There's a charge in the air when everyone sees everyone else as a learner. As the head of Eagle Rock says, "I am head learner. But you can all be head learner." Staff openly share what they are working on, professionally as well as, occasionally, personally. Students do Presentations of Learning (POLs), and so do staff members. Staff frequently ask students what they need to learn a specific concept; they may ask students to give them feedback about how a particular lesson worked. Students share with staff how they learn and what helps them learn better. As Jeremy noted earlier, there's joint accountability for learning.

Struggle and temporary failure are much more acceptable when both students and adults are learning. Teachers can admit that they don't know something and enlist students to help research the issue. (Students can do so, too.) Teachers can admit that they would have liked to teach a particular concept better and solicit the help of students as well as colleagues. (Students can do so to, in terms of learning better.) Teachers and students can be coconspirators in the quest for learning. At the very least, students feel that teachers are on their side—rather than adversarial—as they are learning.

The professional learning strategies described above are enhanced when students participate. Students can do tuning protocols by themselves on their own work or with the adults in the school; examining work helps everyone. Students can participate in study groups, help to design assessments (especially, create rubrics for quality work), and provide input on curriculum. They can engage in action research by themselves or with teachers, be part of a critical friends group, do lesson study, analyze assignments with their teachers, do walk-throughs, collect and analyze data, coach and mentor each other and their teachers (wouldn't you like to have a student coach you?).

"But what about their real learning?" you might ask. Think how much their real learning can be tied to their work within the community. Which of the strategies above support learning in mathematics, social studies, or science? Which might involve reading and writing, art or music?

Although this may strike some readers as crass, why not get more "bang for the buck" by constituting a school as a WSLC? Schools, of all places, should be learning organizations for all who dwell within. As Isaacson and Bamburg (1992) pointed out, "It is a stinging experience to read about learning organizations and to realize how few schools and districts fit the definition" (pp. 42–44). Thinking and acting as if one were a part of a WSLC is the first step to making it happen.

As an aside, I maintain that we do too much for students. By that, I mean that we try to solve too many school problems without them. When students seem apathetic, the adults take up the problem at staff meetings, trying to solve it. What they should do is ask students about the problem and involve them in thinking up and implementing solutions. Eagle Rock, in fact, did a school tuning (a version of the tuning protocol) on this very subject . . . and all the students participated! When in doubt, ask the students.

If you teach in a primary or an elementary school, you may be thinking, "Oh, I couldn't do any of this with my students. They're too young." In fact, you can, but in a much-modified way. I have heard of first and second graders doing Presentations of Learning. I have heard of processes educators have used to elicit student opinions about learning. I have heard of classroom meetings during which many of the problems of the classroom are resolved . . . by the students.

CONCLUSION

In case you have any doubts about the importance of forming a learning community, perhaps a learning community made up of both the young people and the adults in our educational institutions, read further. Dennis Sparks (2001) states bluntly, "Too many students learn far less than they are capable of achieving. This problem is particularly acute in schools serving high concentrations of low-income students and is a tragic waste of human potential. In addition to the personal loss born [sic] by these students, our democracy and economic well-being suffer when young people are unprepared to fully assume their responsibilities as citizens and wage earners in an increasingly complex world" (p. 1).

Phil Schlecty (1997) also realizes the urgency of change:

> Change in schools is much more urgently needed than most teachers and school administrators seem to realize. Indeed I believe that if schools are not changed in dramatic ways very soon public schools will not be a vital component of America's system of education in the 21st century. (p. xi)

Intentionally changing a school from an institution into a community is a very powerful way to signal that "business as usual" is no longer good enough. Consider how schools might rise to the challenge of the future if students worked in communities, helping each other learn and demonstrate their learning; if adults worked together to learn and to improve themselves professionally; if students and students worked together on the work of learning. Consider the impact if schools thought of themselves as Whole School Learning Communities in which everyone focuses on learning, individually and for all.

SO WHAT

Think about the word *community* and make a list of the various communities to which you have belonged in some way. Choose one or two and make a three-part list with these headings: What I Have Gotten Out of This Community, What I Have Contributed to This Community, What This Community Has Meant to Me. Then consider how some aspect of your environment would be better if it exemplified the values and actions of community.

NOW WHAT

Engage your colleagues in the activities described in the "So What" section. Then, work with them to describe your school in terms of some elements of community. Use these questions as starting points; they'll help you assess the elements that can be used to establish community. Then do a "book" study on this chapter with your colleagues and use the highlights of this chapter to consider how you might go about intentionally creating a learning community, perhaps a whole-school learning community.

Self-Survey on Community

Philosophy and Beliefs

1. Does our school have a set of principles or values that are known by everyone?

2. Are these principles or values known at a deep level (rather than just words on a plaque outside the administrative offices)?

3. Do these values include ideas specifically oriented toward being in a community?

4. To what extent are these applied in classes, extracurricular activities, and the life of the school?

Structures

1. What is the size of the school? How many students? How many staff?

2. To what extent can the whole school get together? In what space(s)?

3. To what extent can the whole staff get together? In what space(s)?

4. What student subgroups are there? What staff subgroups are there? To what extent do the student subgroups mix? The staff subgroups?

5. How well does the schedule accommodate the whole school (including staff) getting together?

6. How do classroom and other spaces accommodate community?

Governance

1. Who makes the final decisions regarding curriculum? discipline? structures in the school (use of time and space)? budget?

2. To what extent—and how—are others (students and staff) involved in this decision making?

3. How do staff meetings work? Who's in charge? Who sets the agenda?

4. What forms of student governance are there? How do they work?

5. Is it possible for students or staff to initiate change? If so, what is the process?

6. In what ways is power centered with the adults? In what ways do students have power and authority?

Events

1. What student events promote community? Are these regularly scheduled or sporadic?

2. What staff events promote community? Are these regularly scheduled or sporadic?

3. What joint student and staff events promote community? Are these regularly scheduled or sporadic?

4. What rituals and ceremonies help promote community? (Adapted from L. B. Easton, 2002)

NOTE

1. From Hord, Shirley M. (1997), *Professional Learning Communities: Communities of Continuous Inquiry and Improvement.* Austin, TX: Southwest Educational Development Laboratory, pp. 33-34. Reprinted with permission from Southwest Educational Development Laboratory.

4

"So, What About Discipline?"

How Principles Govern a
School Better Than Rules

Often unspoken in the question, "So, what about discipline?" is the phrase "given these kids"—students who have dropped out, gotten themselves in trouble, maybe even served jail time. "Surely you must have a muscular set of rules to restrain them?" It is clear to me that the questioner has not yet met Eagle Rock students. After meeting them, visitors usually exclaim, with a sense of relief and disbelief, "They're so nice. They're polite. They were interested in me. They were courteous. Why, one even shook my hand and held the door for me."

Except for the administrator who was disappointed that I wasn't talking about "principal-centered schools," visitors usually want to know just exactly how we've gotten our students to be so, well, disciplined. This chapter contrasts discipline, which is usually based on rules, with guiding principles.

PRINCIPLES

Management guru Stephen Covey (1989, 2004) writes about how organizations can be principle-centered and what that means for everyone within the organization, including the leader. His ideas have helped us understand why Eagle Rock succeeds as a principle-centered community. Our early focus on principles rather than rules led to the formation of a set of principles called "8 + 5 = 10." You first encountered this formula, which is definitely bad math, in the Introduction. Although it is bad math, it is very memorable (which might excuse the math), a five-word mnemonic for eight themes and five expectations, which add up to ten commitments that students make when they enroll. You might want to review the components of "8 + 5 = 10" in the Introduction.

Although the themes, expectations, and commitments were not written to correlate from column to column, you can probably see the connections. There's an internal integrity to these 23 items; they really do work like a formula, with the themes represented in the expectations, which are then restated as commitments. Only the first and last of the commitments are different. The first represents one purpose of 8 + 5 = 10: to help the community live in respectful harmony. The last represents another purpose: to help students develop their personal moral and ethical codes. The first and last commitments unite the rest in common cause.

To work, a set of principles must be much more than a plaque on the wall or a set of rules in a student handbook. Eagle Rock's principles—not rules—result in a culture that promotes concepts about how students treat themselves, each other (even the visitor who is shadowing them), their families, their local and regional communities, and the country, world, and universe of which they are an increasingly important part. These are principles students know by heart, live by while at Eagle Rock, and use to guide their lives after Eagle Rock. These principles are ones students will defend.

Why Principles? Why Not Rules?

Stephen Covey (1989) is very clear about why he wrote about principles rather than rules. He regards principles as

natural law that governs the results you seek. How we apply a principle will vary greatly and will be determined by our unique strengths, talents, and creativity but, ultimately, success in any endeavor is always derived from acting in harmony with principles to which the success is tied. (italics his; p. 7)

He continues, "*Principled* solutions stand in stark contrast to the common practices and thinking of our popular culture" (p. 7).

Rules

Rules, it seems to me, come out of a different culture than principles. Covey (1989) names some aspects of that alternate culture: "'I want it now,' blame and victimization, hopelessness, lack of life balance, 'What's in it for me?,' the hunger to be understood, conflict and differences, personal stagnation" (pp. 8–10). Rules are sometimes the most direct response to cultural conditions of the sort Covey names. For people who want it now, for example, there might be a rule that they can't have whatever "it" is until later. There are several underlying messages in rules:

1. People by themselves (or guided by principles) won't do the right thing. They must be required to do the right things—through rules.

2. People deserve rules, just like they deserve punishment if they break rules.

3. The people in charge are the ones who make the rules; the people who don't have any power follow the rules so that the people in charge can live the way they want to.

4. As Covey says, "Conflicts naturally arise out of . . . differences. Society's competitive approach to resolving the conflict and differences tends to center on 'winning as much as you can'" (1989, p. 10).

Rules are imperfect. First, many are either too specific or too general. I learned about this problem when I worked with policy makers to write a state policy for standards and assessment. I wanted to make the policy more specific than it was, but I was told by a legislative aide that the policy had to be kept general. "Otherwise," she said, "people inevitably find a loophole, something we left out." "But what," I asked, "if they interpret a general policy their own way?" "That's why," she responded, "the United States balances the legislative and executive branches with a court system."

Rules are often a quick fix. "Oh-oh, we need a rule for that," someone says when a miscreant draws attention to a problem. Someone drafts a rule, and it becomes institutionalized, and then people begin to see its long-term, systemic effects . . . and may very well regret that rule. Of course, they can rid themselves of the rule. Remember, that's why we have a court system.

Rules cannot address complexity. A 2000 Harris Poll found "huge differences between values of young adults and older adults" (Taylor, 2000). According to the poll, substantial differences included the following:

1. "Only 27% of people aged 18 to 24, compared to 63% of people over 64 think it is absolutely wrong to take pens or paper from the office for personal use."

2. "Only 42% of 18 to 24 years olds, but 78% of those over 64, think it is absolutely wrong to keep excess change given at a store."

3. "Only 41% of 18 to 24 year olds, but 78% of those over 64, think it is absolutely wrong to smoke marijuana."

4. "Only 17% of 18 to 24 year olds, but 45% of people over 64 think it is absolutely wrong to drive over the speed limit."

5. "51% of adults under 25, compared to a much higher 72% of those over 64, believe it is absolutely wrong to exaggerate one's education or experience in a resume or job application."

6. "55% of people under 25, compared to 75% of people over 64, think it is absolutely wrong not to declare all one's income to the IRS." (Taylor, 2000)

Rules exist for each of these situations, but they lack the punch of principles that incorporate values and beliefs.

Rules seldom attack a root cause. Covey (1989) quotes Thoreau to develop this point: "For every thousand hacking at the leaves of evil, there is one striking at the root." Covey elaborates, "We can only achieve quantum improvement in our lives as we quit hacking at the leaves of attitude and behavior and get to work on the root, the paradigms from which our attitudes and behaviors flow" (1989, p. 31). For Covey, paradigms are sets of principles.

Rules are usually exterior. They emanate from outside us; they come from someone else—a "they," if you will, who has decided how we shall live and has the power to make that image into a law of some sort. If we disagree with the rule imposed on us from the outside, we are free to do something about it—such as go to court—where we can debate the rightness of the law. Principles naturally engage us in determining which behaviors emerge from a principle and which do not. They engage the interior of us. As Heidi, a student, commented, "If we had a list of rules it sure would be easier but not better for us personally, in the long run."

Rules bring out the worst in people, according to a graduate, Brianna. "They get us to 'buy-in' to a concept through fear, reward, or punishment." Ana, soon to be a graduate, commented, "A bunch of rules which we might or might not be inclined to care about, aren't sufficient to govern a structured community."

Of course, we need some rules. None of us would survive Interstate 70 at rush hour without some rules. Airspace would be chaotic and dangerous if there weren't rules with people and machines monitoring them. Schools need to have both rules and principles, with the rules targeted toward the really serious infractions, the ones that might injure the student committing the infraction or others.

Eagle Rock has rules as well as principles. Embedded in the themes, expectations, and commitments regarding health and living in community are five nonnegotiables: No alcohol. No drugs. No tobacco in any form. No sexual relationships. No violence in any form. These are nonnegotiable in the sense that students cannot talk staff into approving or accepting the breaking of just one, even just once. Consequences range from being sent home to doing a solo (a time in the wilderness during which the student is alone—though supervised from a distance) or being restricted from being part of the community. There are always consequences regarding breaking a nonnegotiable.

Yet something called Second Chance ameliorates the most devastating consequence of the nonnegotiables, being sent home. Students who leave Eagle Rock for any reason can apply to return. This they do through a letter to the entire community, for they have, through their actions, deeply affected (perhaps hurt) the community. This letter is read aloud and discussed at a community meeting, and students vote on whether or not to call a panel to interview the petitioner. Students and staff who make up the interview team ask questions the whole community has and, on the basis of the student's answers, make a recommendation for or against reinstatement. There is no third chance.

The principles that constitute 8 + 5 = 10 are negotiable in the sense that individuals and the community as a whole spend considerable time understanding what they mean. This is productive time. It's exactly what young people need to do as they grow up. Hannah, a graduate, writes, "There is a certain amount of wiggle room which allows individuals to mold 8 + 5 = 10 into their own lives in their own specific ways." Some will have more commitment to one principle than another; some people will be able to "integrate 8 + 5 = 10 into their lives more fully than others. But, when I think about 8 + 5 = 10, it all makes sense because they are the essential pieces of being a human being. They are there in my unconscious mind and when I see them I remember that they are what I live by."

Covey (1989) allows that in schools—at least those we currently have—which are

> an artificial social system . . . , you may be able to get by if you learn how to manipulate the man-made rules, to "play the game." In most one-shot or short-lived human interactions, you can . . . get by and . . . make favorable impressions through charm and skill and pretending to be interested. . . . You can pick up quick, easy solutions that may work in short-term situations. But secondary traits alone have no permanent worth in long-term relationships. Eventually, if there isn't deep integrity and fundamental character strength, the challenges of life will cause true motives to surface and human relationship failure will replace short-term success. (p. 22)

However, if you desire more—and people in schools that really want to make a difference with young people probably do—you'll want to incorporate "fundamental principles of human effectiveness" into your culture (Covey, 1989, p. 23). Covey begins his first chapter with this quote: "'There is no real excellence in all this world which can be separated from right living,' according to David Starr Jordan" (p. 16). Let's talk about a code for right living rather than a set of rules to prevent (fingers crossed) people from doing wrong things.

Principles

Covey elaborates on the value of principles:

> Principles are like lighthouses. They are natural laws that cannot be broken . . . that govern human growth and happiness—natural laws that are woven into the fabric of every civilized society through history and comprise the roots of every family and institution that has endured and prospered. (1989, pp. 32–33)

According to Covey, principles "surface time and again, and the degree to which people in a society recognize and live in harmony with them moves them toward either survival and stability or disintegration and destruction" (1989, p. 34). They are "self-evident and can easily be validated by any individual . . . natural laws that are part of the human condition, part of the human consciousness, part of the human conscience . . . seem to exist in all human beings" (1989, p. 34).

Ana, an Eagle Rock student, declared about 8 + 5 = 10, "It just happened that I thoroughly agreed with all of them. I see them as a core list of beliefs that have the potential to make a big difference in me and the world."

To get more concrete, here are some principles that Covey (1989) names: fairness, equity, justice, integrity, honesty, trust, human dignity, service, quality or excellence, potential, growth, patience, nurturance, and encouragement. They are not practices (which are "situationally specific"); nor are they values. "Principles are the territory. Values are maps. When we value correct principles, we have truth—a knowledge of things as they are" (p. 35). You know you have principles when it is absurd to attempt "to live an effective life based on their opposites" (p. 35).

Examples of Principles That Govern Schools

"8 + 5 = 10" is only one example of principles that operate in schools. Principles are known by a variety of names. In the Introduction you read some that were called *mission statements*, others that were called *vision statements*, still others called *core values*. Sometimes principles are called *habits of mind* that focus on both mind and character. Ted Sizer (1992) proposed these habits of mind:

- The habit of perspective
- The habit of analysis
- The habit of imagination

- The habit of empathy
- The habit of communication
- The habit of commitment
- The habit of humility
- The habit of joy (pp. 73–74)

Deborah Meier (1995), founding principal of Central Park East Secondary School in Harlem, turned habits of mind into key questions:

- The question of evidence, or "How do we know what we know?"
- The question of viewpoint in all its multiplicity, or "Who's speaking?"
- The search for connection and patterns, or "What causes what?"
- Supposition, or "How might things have been different?"
- Why any of it matters, or "Who cares?"(p. 41)

As Sizer (1992) points out, habits of mind can be understood as skills, but they "reflect value. They neither denote nor connote mere technical expertise, usable skills. They are loaded with judgments, for teachers and parents as well as for students" (p. 74).

In addition to core values, Fenway High School in Boston has melded habits of mind from both Sizer and Meier: perspective, evidence, relevance, connection, supposition (Fenway High School, n.d.). At Boston Arts Academy, principles are distilled into these four: Refine, Invent, Connect, and Own (Boston Arts Academy, n.d.). At the Met in Providence, Rhode Island, the principles are empirical reasoning, quantitative reasoning, communication, social reasoning, and personal qualities such as respect, empathy, health and well-being, responsibility, perseverance, self-awareness, leadership, cooperation, and enhancing community (The Met, 2006). At Parker School in Massachusetts, the principles are inquiry, expression, critical thinking, collaboration, organization, attentiveness, involvement, and reflection (Parker School, n.d.). Wildwood School in California calls its principles "Habits of Mind and Heart" (Wildwood School, n.d.). The School of the Future in New York focuses on point of view, evidence, connections, alternatives, significance, and communication as its habits of mind (School of the Future, n.d.).

For Urban Academy (UA), also in New York, one word summarizes its principles: respect. UA maintains,

> students and staff are committed to respecting each other. Our school is built around the belief that students have ideas and points of view that can and should contribute to their learning experience. Students are encouraged to ask their own questions, do their own research and come to their own conclusions. (Urban Academy, n.d.)

"Respect is the adhesive that holds the rest together" (Urban Academy, n.d.).

Sometimes schools and districts fear trespassing on family or church territory when they tread on values and principles. The Baltimore County School District solved this problem in the 1980s by asking each school community (including parents) to determine which of the values in the U.S. Constitution and Bill of Rights they wanted to focus on each year. No one could argue with the values espoused in these revered documents.

What is vision? What is mission? What are the values? What are the goals? It's not always clear which is which, and that's probably all right, as long as students and staff know by heart and through hard discussion and experience what a school stands for. As long as what the school stands for is a keystone, locking everything else in.

SYSTEM OF USE

So, how can a school "lock in place" its principles so that they are known and used? The answer is intentionality: Specifically, the intention of building a system of use related to the principles. Alone and lonely on a plaque outside the principal's office, mission, vision, core values, and principles quickly fade from consciousness. They are easily forgotten and consulted only when required for "back-to-school" orientation meetings or parent-teacher nights. Some might call the process I call *system of use* "institutionalization," but I prefer the former, which has a friendlier connotation for me.

We cannot assume that new students—whether they are kindergartners or incoming sixth, eighth, or ninth graders—will somehow soak up the soul of a school. We cannot assume that they'll "get it," as if through osmosis just by being there. We cannot assume they'll notice it. We cannot assume that, having noticed it, they'll practice it. We cannot assume that, having practiced it, they'll weave it into their own knowledge, attitudes, skills, aspirations, and behavior.

It's not a waste of time to help young people learn about the culture of their own school, especially if that culture is one you would like to perpetuate. If you don't, they may remain oblivious to what a school really stands for and accidentally act in opposition to those precepts. They may bring with them beliefs and behaviors that would erode the desired culture. Or, worse, if there's an underground culture operating at the school, they might pick up cues from that culture rather than the healthy culture the school is trying to perpetuate.

So, we must intentionally introduce the principles that serve as the basis for the culture; we must maintain the focus on that culture; and we must use the principles for real-life decision making.

Acculturation

Darren, a graduate finishing up his undergraduate college education in California, recalled "memorizing the 8 themes, 5 expectations, and

10 commitments before attending school at ERS. The head of school asked all the new students to have $8 + 5 = 10$ memorized by day one; he even threatened to send us home if we were unprepared." Darren had to sign a paper promising to uphold the ten commitments when he submitted his enrollment application and, yes, he was expected to have them memorized by the time he arrived at Eagle Rock. New students have a week after their arrival to write $8 + 5 = 10$ until they reach mastery (that's 23 out of 23 right). These are the first steps in the system of use that prevents $8 + 5 = 10$ from moldering away on a wall.

The head of school challenged Darren's cohort and, indeed, each incoming class of students (students are admitted three times a year) to modify $8 + 5 = 10$. So far, no one has succeeded in coming up with modifications, not even to produce an accurate mathematical statement. During their full week of orientation, students not only write the code from memory, they also study it in depth. They define and describe what is meant by each theme, expectation, and commitment. They look for real-life and personal examples of the elements of $8 + 5 = 10$ in use. They debate the value of this code. Finally, they teach it to others—the highest form of learning, according to Dale (1946/1996; though often attributed to William Glasser and other educators).

The work for new students on $8 + 5 = 10$ continues while they are on their three-week wilderness trip. They meet in "strong circles" to settle issues, with reference to the Eagle Rock code. They write in their journals about the meaning of $8 + 5 = 10$. They incorporate the themes, expectations, and commitments into the five-minute group presentations of learning they give to the rest of the community when they return from their wilderness trip.

It is not a waste of students' time to have them take a class on the school itself—a School 101, if you like. In that class, students learn the code at a deep level by memorizing it and analyzing it from a variety of viewpoints. They apply it to a variety of hypothetical and real situations, and they teach it to others (perhaps next year's sixth graders?). Similarly, it is not a waste of time to ask staff members to learn the code. You may not want to test them, but you may want to initiate questions such as these in faculty meetings:

"Which one of our principles have you taught to today?"

"Which principle needs work this week?"

"Which principle do students seem to be living? Which are they ignoring?"

"How can we relate next week's learning experiences to our principles?"

Maintenance

Like almost anything else, once taught, key learnings must be reinforced. For example, while new students are on their wilderness trip, veteran students have contemplated and acted upon $8 + 5 = 10$ regularly in a variety of ways. At every Monday Gathering, the head of school poses a question of the week that is related in some way to the school's code. Tuesday Gatherings are always led by students and are known as TGIF (Tuesday's Gathering Is Fundamental). TGIF's focus is on one or more of the 23 principles that make up $8 + 5 = 10$.

During special evening meetings on Tuesdays, students often deal with the themes, expectations, and commitments that are articulated in $8 + 5 = 10$. These meetings rotate through a trimester from gender meetings (with all adult and student community members of the same gender meeting separately), to house or dormitory meetings, and then to whole-community meetings for considering Second Chance or all-community issues. You can well imagine that these meetings might involve community members in deep discussion of the first commitment . . . or the second expectation . . . or the second theme . . . or any of the other elements of $8 + 5 = 10$.

On Wednesday mornings, at a longer Gathering, veteran students present their evolving moral and ethical codes and get feedback from their peers and staff. The head of school reads aloud letters from members of the community who have moved on; almost universally these attest to the utility of $8 + 5 = 10$ in the real world, sometimes through sentences that express regret: "I wish I had paid more attention to $8 + 5 = 10$ when I was at Eagle Rock. I would have gotten so much more out of my time there. I would have had things much easier now."

Classes that students take have been created with some aspect of $8 + 5 = 10$ in mind. For example, few social studies classes are taught without some examination of the concept of leadership for justice. Most science classes have an element of environmental stewardship to them. Almost all classes have a service component.

When students create their Presentations of Learning (POL) packets, they do so with an eye to $8 + 5 = 10$. In the best packets, the words of $8 + 5 = 10$ are woven into the sentences and paragraphs that students write; so, too, in the actual Presentations of Learning. More specifically, students write their developing moral and ethical codes in their packets, most keeping what they have written each trimester so that they (and their readers) have a running record of how their ideas have changed over time and with experience. You will see examples of POL packets and read a narrative of a POL in Chapter 8.

When imminent graduates create their personal growth portfolios and make a presentation on their personal growth, they inevitably address $8 + 5 = 10$, especially the commitments they have made to themselves.

An Eagle Rock graduate commented, "Without $8 + 5 = 10$ Eagle Rock School would be like the large majority of failing schools. The school has a language, a tool, and a unifying mission because all actions (classes, sports, ideas, meanings) are evaluated for their usefulness to the community living according to $8 + 5 = 10$." It is great to have a common school code (mission, vision, values, and goals) such as $8 + 5 = 10$, but nothing is gained if that code is not regularly activated through a system of use.

You probably do not have evening meetings at your school. But if you don't have morning meetings or gatherings, or even homeroom, you might want to think about such meetings as one way to maintain the focus on the principles that count within a school.

Consequences

Rules have consequences if broken. So do principles. The context for consequences is, however, quite different. Imagine this scenario in the principal's office:

Principal: So, Ben, Mrs. Lake tells me you have broken a few rules.

Ben: Yes, I have, but I have good reasons for breaking them.

Principal: Ben, that doesn't really matter. Once you break a rule, you get a consequence.

Ben: That's not fair!

Principal: This has nothing to do with fairness, Ben. Rules are rules. You can't break them and expect to get away with it.

Ben: But, I . . .

Principal: Enough, Ben! Here are your punishments. First, for breaking the chair, you'll write on the board 100 times, "I will not damage school furniture." Then, for locking the school door, you'll go to the time-out room instead of to class for an hour every morning next week. Then, because you didn't answer Mrs. Lake's question about what you were doing, you'll read two chapters in your health book—the ones about getting along with others and authority—and answer the questions at the end of the chapters.

Ben: But . . .

Principal: You know, Ben, the next time anything like these behaviors occur, you'll be suspended. You'll go right home. What do you think about that?

This description may be a bit extreme. Most principals would be interested in why Ben broke the chair, locked the door, and refused to tell Mrs. Lake what was going on. Perhaps there was a stranger outside the door and Ben wanted to prevent his entry by locking the door and having a weapon ready in case he broke through. Perhaps Mrs. Lake wasn't there (oops!) and, when she returned, no one was outside the door. Perhaps Ben was known for making up stories, and he was afraid his explanation for the door and chair would have been derided as just another of his fantasy adventures.

Had Ben been to the principal's office before? If so, how had he handled previous infractions? Was he known as a troublemaker? Would he be likely to escalate his behavior and cause more trouble?

Finally, were the consequences appropriate to the crimes?

Rules are rules, as the principal said. They carry with them certain consequences. How might this conversation have gone if the school were principle-based rather than rule-driven?

Principal: So, Ben, Mrs. Lake tells me you locked the classroom door, broke a chair, and refused to tell her what happened.

Ben: I did all of those things, but I had a good reason.

Principal: Well, let me hear it.

Ben explains. He was angry at another student and accidentally tipped over and broke his chair when he leapt out of it. He locked the door so Mrs. Lake wouldn't come back before he had set up his chair again and tried to repair it. He figured that everything would be OK when Mrs. Lake returned, so he wouldn't have to confess what he had done, but Mrs. Lake had sensed something wrong when she returned to the classroom.

Principal: Your reasons make good sense, Ben. I understand how what Jasmine said made you angry, but I'm wondering how what you did fits our principle of living in respectful harmony with others?

Ben: Well, I didn't mean to break the chair.

Principal: Go on.

Ben: I guess I didn't need to lock the door. I should have answered Mrs. Lake's question about what I was doing.

Principal: So . . .

Ben: So, I guess I wasn't practicing living in respectful harmony with others.

Principal: What do you think you should do?

Ben: I should apologize to Mrs. Lake . . .

Principal: And . . .

Ben: To the class because I really upset them. And to Jasmine.

Principal: What else should you do?

Ben: Well, I think I should do something to improve the classroom, since I destroyed something in it.

Principal: Those are all good things to do, Ben. I don't very often hear of your acting against what we believe in here at Emory Middle School. Why don't you come to see me next Monday, just for a chat, and let me know what you've done.

Again, this dialogue may be a bit over the top. For one thing, Mrs. Lake should probably have handled the situation herself, rather than send Ben to see the principal. Ben could have decided on appropriate consequences with her. Perhaps the class could have helped Ben decide what was appropriate for interfering with the harmony of the classroom. And, of course, Ben's argument with Jasmine may indicate the need for some mediation, conducted, perhaps, by student peace mediators. Perhaps it goes even deeper, and Ben needs to talk to someone about his problems with Jasmine.

Reference to Principles

In a community where rules reign, discipline is, at least on the surface, quite simple. You break a rule; you suffer consequences. In a community where principles predominate, several steps precede consequences. First, way before a miscreant has committed a crime against the culture, he or she has learned the code that governs the culture. He or she understands at a deep level what the code means, personally and to the community.

One does not break a principle. One acts in a way that is inconsistent with the principle. Some of those inconsistent actions are relatively harmless, worthy of discussion at a classroom meeting (Glasser, 1990) or at a larger student meeting; perhaps worthy of a conversation during advisories. Perhaps an inconsistency is worthy of a one-on-one conversation between peers or between a student and an adult. Students sometimes speak of these conversations as "calling" each other and accept that they need to call someone on something when the deed is inconsistent with the school's principles.

Debbie Meier describes what she did as principal at Central Park East Secondary School:

> As a principal I find [habits] useful when "naughty" kids are sent to my office. I ask them to put their version of the story on one side and that of whoever sent them to me on the other; then we discuss whether what's happened is part of a pattern, how else it might have been dealt with, and, finally, why it matters. ("Habits of Mind," Coalition of Essential Schools, www.essentialschools.org/pub/ces_docs/about/phil/habits.html)

Appropriate Consequences

Appropriate restitution is the best consequence when principles are violated. "What would be an appropriate way to give back to the community?" is a good question to ask. In the second scenario, the principal asked Ben what would be an appropriate way to restore to the class something they lost through his actions. His decided that public apology to the class and to the teacher were appropriate. He also decided that making something to improve the classroom would be appropriate since he had destroyed something in it.

In the first scenario, the consequences were highly inappropriate. Writing teachers shudder when students are made to write as punishment. What good does it do to write the same statement 100 times? The second consequence—reading the chapter and answering the questions at the end of it may seem more fitting because the content of the chapters seemed appropriate, but, once again, it makes reading as well as writing a punishment. Taking Ben out of class to sit in the time-out room and threatening suspension are absurd consequences unless, in the case of suspension, Ben had done something life-threatening (to himself or others). The last thing we should be doing is allowing students to miss out on learning time.

The concept of restitution has surfaced in law enforcement. Often called restorative justice, restitution programs aim "to reduce juvenile delinquency by keeping first-time offenders out of the juvenile justice system and by requiring those offenders to increase personal responsibility by providing restitution for their offense" ("Restitution Program," 2007). Restitution programs can be found in almost every city and state. According to one, "Local police and probation departments make referrals. Maine . . . arranges community service for first-time offenders at local community-based organizations. In addition to community service, participants . . . are required to participate in two family meetings, a pre-employment workshop, and a life skills workshop. Parents of the offenders attend a two-hour session on parenting adolescents." Sometimes restitution is used in place of suspension or expulsion in schools.

Many schools, including Eagle Rock, have a student group to handle minor infractions. This group is not a student council. At Eagle Rock this group is called Peer Council, and its members are elected by the student body. Peer Council operates under the supervision of a staff mentor but, generally, makes appropriate restitution decisions on its own. In fact, it may be harder on students than staff would be. Students involved in Peer Council have gone through peace mediation (sometimes called peer mediation) training. Here is the process that Peer Council follows:

1. Listen to one side. No interruptions. No comments.

2. Listen to the other side(s). Again, no interruptions. No comments.

3. Ask parties to describe appropriate restitution.

Vignette 4.1   A School Vignette: Consequences

ENVISION SUCCESS

City Arts and Technology High School, California

By Anna McCanse

City Arts and Technology High School is a small charter school located in San Francisco; at the time of writing this vignette, it was in its third year. It was started by an organization called Envision Schools, which is based in the Bay Area. Envision Schools aims to create a cluster of small schools to provide an education to students who will be the first in their families to graduate from college. City Arts and Technology has 110 students per grade and each year will add an additional 110 until there are have four grades.

Some students at City Arts and Technology struggle with learning on a daily basis. Sometimes these students have learning disabilities (either diagnosed or undiagnosed) or at some point fell behind when they were in primary school. They have a hard time grasping information while the rest of the class flies through a unit and is ready to move on.

Occasionally City Arts and Technology enrolls students who are very bright, but because of things going on outside of school, usually in the home, they are not engaged and are unable to see learning as important to them at the moment. These students are the most frustrating to watch because solutions to their problems are not as simple as sitting down with them after class to explain a concept. There are bigger things at work that we don't have control over and can't change for them.

As a whole, the school's staff regards each student as an individual. Therefore, there is no set formula for how to address each of these student's needs. When these students are disruptive, they receive consequences that are beneficial to the community and to the student. One consequence might be a long, serious talk with a panel of peers and adults resulting in a decision to apologize to the community. Depending on the "crime," students might do community service around the school to repay the community for the damage they caused. There may be a conference with the advisor, parent, and principal to set up a contract or guidelines for behavior along with consequences that the student creates if those guidelines aren't met. For some students, the appropriate consequence is mandatory tutoring, which doesn't work if not supported by parents.

For the most part, there are lots of conversations to hold the student accountable from every angle (teachers, advisor, parents, peers, principal, outside community networks, etc). Another approach is to get the student involved in something outside of school that they care deeply about. For instance, City Arts and Technology has a student who is very intelligent, very disruptive and disrespectful to the community, and has failed two years of classes so far, but he lives for graffiti. He got involved with an afterschool arts program and started taking classes with them. City Arts and Technology worked with the arts program to have him coteach a class on street art. Luckily, the man he was teaching with became the ideal mentor for this student and was able to hold him accountable for his behavior and act as a friend and tutor. If this student got a bad report from the school, he was not able to teach that day or had some similar consequence. City Arts and Technology has been able to connect with the community so that other outside opportunities are available to students.

The school is run according to a set of parameters that help struggling students—and all students—succeed.

- The number of students per class is kept to a maximum of 23.
- Classes are interdisciplinary and taught from a variety of angles.
- Students put on 4 exhibitions per year of their current work. These require them to be accountable for the work that they do.
- The school is community centered.
- Students build strong relationships with each other and with their teachers.
- Each student has an advisor.
- Students have a voice.
- Students are given opportunities to have leadership roles.
- Peer mediation is beginning to take place.
- Parents are encouraged to be a part of the school.
- Support systems are being employed whenever possible.
- The school is flexible and able to change when necessary to meet student's needs.
- The arts and technology are used as a way to engage students in learning.

Despite all these efforts, of course, City Arts and Technology still has students who aren't ready or able to be a part of the school in a way that is successful for them. Almost 100% of the time it is because they have something going on at home that is causing them to focus their attention on something other than school. They have no real investment in their learning at the moment and can't see the consequences it will have on their future, maybe because they don't think they have a future.

A handful of students dropped out or have been asked to leave because their behavior was not improving and they were a burden on the community at large. It is hard for everyone to see such students leave, and when they do leave we do all we can to help them get into a program or another school that may benefit them more. We keep in touch with almost every student who has left the school so far. As the school grows and continues to build a community of invested learners, we hope to see fewer students leaving the school for those reasons. We anticipate seeing any student who wants to being able to graduate from college.

SOURCE: Used by the permission from Anna McCanse.

AUTHOR'S NOTE: Anna McCanse is a former teacher at City Arts and Technology High School; she was serving in the Peace Corps when she wrote this vignette. For more information about City Arts and Technology High School or about any Envision School you may call them at: (415) 841-2200.

4. Meet without parties involved to discuss.

5. Present resolution(s) to parties and monitor their implementation of the acts of restitution.

6. Convey resolution to appropriate staff and students.

Sometimes the problem is widespread. Students who recognize the problem may be encouraged to solve it themselves, perhaps with the guidance and support of staff members. It may be tempting to the adults in the community to try to solve the problem, but they should not . . . or should do so with students. Here is an example of a schoolwide process students used to address decisions related to breaking nonnegotiables at Eagle Rock.

> At an initial special gathering where [the Director of Students] announced the decision [to let the whole school community address how the consequences of breaking a non-negotiable are decided], a student, Molly, took the lead and asked for guidelines from the community about how to conduct our work together. Some guidelines included "helping each other stick to solutions" or "involve the students who have engaged in the non-negotiable behavior." For two weeks following that day there were numerous informal discussions as well as formal community meetings to address the situation. At one . . . community meeting, we developed guidelines that built upon those we began with on October 6th. One important agreement was that while much of the community needed to be involved we also wanted there to be a "critical mass of agreement" prior to presenting a proposal to [the Director of Students]. Through an exercise, we determined critical mass of agreement to mean about 80% of the community as long as there were 3/4 of the community present for any decision making. This was the beginning of formalizing processes by which the community could arrive at decisions. Proposals were submitted through . . . meetings, advisories, and individual contributions. (Soguero, 2007, p. 6)

Throughout the process, the Director of Students and other adults were determined not to dictate the solution. As Soguero (2007) commented,

> It is far too early to tell whether we have really risen to the occasion to deal with root issues around causes of non-negotiable behavior. However, there are clear signs that the community is beginning to see the situation that has formerly been the sole discretion of the Director of Students in a new light. . . . The outcome of this process may have less to do with the non-negotiables themselves and more to do with how we govern ourselves in healthy and productive ways (p. 10)

You may be thinking, "How can a school take so much time to address such an issue?" It isn't mathematics or science, history or reading. But, it is life, and students and staff alike claim that they see more growth, according to Eagle Rock's principles, through such activities than they see in all the classes at Eagle Rock combined.

WHY PRINCIPLES WORK

Natural Reaction to Rules

An administrator describes teenagers as "born to test the limits." This is true of younger and older children as well. Stevan got it right when he declared,

> I feel that it would be harder if there were a lot of rules. If there were, students would push them and test them to see how much stuff they can get away with. With principles, we live more responsibly because we have think about what we do. We are in charge of ourselves a little bit more.

Steve offered an intriguing point of view about principles and rules: "Rules are meant to be bent, but you can't argue with principles." Clara added, "Rules make people feel restricted, so they try to break them."

"A book of rules," according to Beth, an instructor, "probably caused more trouble in students' lives than anything else in public school. [Our code] makes us think and consider and question what we believe and how we act. It's an active process versus an authoritarian system."

How much time do people at your school spend enforcing the rules? Would that time be better used discussing principles and their application to individual lives?

Hierarchy, Power, and Authority

Teenagers, especially, fight anything that smacks of hierarchy, power, and authority. They may do so in subtle, passive-aggressive ways; they may do so overtly, breaking rules and getting kicked out of school. Rules are part of a "hierarchical system," according to Jen, an instructor. "They're a top-down approach . . . involuntary and forced upon others. Having values gives us all the opportunity to internalize and individualize deeper ideas and concepts and lets us think about why we do what we do and don't do." Principles apply to right living for both adults and young people; they are not simply what adults require young people to do.

Common Language

Few people can memorize rulebooks, but a code of principles can be easily memorized. If everyone in the community uses the language, and school events keep the language at the forefront of people's minds, the code morphs into a common language. Dan, a staff member, commented on the "common language that allows for a common understanding. It's a touchstone that binds us." According to a graduate, Darren, "8 + 5 = 10 is a great way to pack the themes of ERS (Eagle Rock School), the expectations of the students, and the values the students need to practice to be successful, all into one little bundle that can fit on an 8.5" by 11" piece of paper."

Whole Student Emphasis

Rules seem to be written for parts of students. There are rules for classes and rules for out-of-class behavior, rules for the cafeteria, rules for the hallway, sometimes even rules for out-of-school behavior. Principles are written for the whole student, no matter where he or she is. Jesse captured this idea nicely: "8 + 5 = 10 changed the way I talk, the way I look at others and the way I'm not so disrespectful of others wherever I go."

Thinking Deeply

As Jen, an instructor, notes, "A set of principles makes us think deeply and engage in-depth in conversations about values, ideas, etc., and extend [our conversation] from our school community to our larger society." Alfredo, a student, commented, "8 + 5 = 10 makes me struggle. I have to think about it because I don't really understand it. I get others to talk about it with me." Darren, a graduate, recalled, "Upon arriving at ERS, I had discussions about the various elements of 8 + 5 = 10 that broadened my awareness about the importance of responsibility." He added, "Having serious conversations about the elements of 8 + 5 = 10 creates an environment for understanding Eagle Rock's expectations of the students."

8 + 5 = 10 is simultaneously simple and complex. Hannah, an Eagle Rock graduate, commented, "8 + 5 = 10 is both simple enough to remember, some principles being a few words, but complex enough to provide thought-provoking discussions."

Self-Realization

Students naturally want to become more self-directed, as much as or more than we, the adults, want them to become so. They want to take ownership of themselves and their learning. As Oscar said, "Students could not be treated as individuals if there were a book of rules. There would be a mold that students would have to fit in." Coral Ann commented, "The great part of 8 + 5 = 10 is that you can personalize it to your own life.

It doesn't get set as the way life has to be according to rules. It gives you a chance to be an individual. You can decide what each principle means to you. It's a lifestyle, not an outside force." She continues, "8 + 5 = 10 reminds me every morning that the lifestyle that I chose causes many effects. I'm the one who builds my own lifestyle and chooses how I live."

Personal Learning and Growth

Stevan at first didn't see how much 8 + 5 = 10 would mean to him. "It does affect people whether they think so or not." Jonathan wrote to tell me, "It has changed my personality profoundly for the better." Ashley commented, "It stretches my comfort zone and has me thinking about things such as what personally I need to work on and what I am doing with myself constantly." Jenna added, "It's a set of ideas that I think about and act towards." Melvina stated, "ERS would be outrageous [if we had no 8 + 5 = 10]. We would be like any school, and people just wouldn't have to change the way they did things." Hannah addressed learning and growth: "As we begin to internalize and understand these fundamental pieces of Eagle Rock's philosophy, life becomes richer, fuller of energy and compassion." According to Darren, an Eagle Rock graduate, "The benefits that resulted from exploring the 8 themes, striving to meet the 5 expectations, and accepting the 10 commitments have only been paralleled by my efforts to turn my life around."

There's not much room for personal growth in rules. They are just there, fashioned by someone else, meant to be followed, blindly. Principles are a good way to embed character development into education, rather than have it serve as a time-bound activity ("Today, children, we will do character development for twenty minutes.") Thomas Lickona is one of many educators who advocate for character education in schools. Lickona (1991) makes the case that schools naturally—although not always overtly—stand for some values: "There is no such thing as value-free education" (p. 20). He declares that the public "acknowledges the need for values education, based on upward spiraling statistics on violence, vandalism, stealing, cheating, disrespect for authority, peer cruelty, bigotry, bad language, sexual precocity and abuse, increasing self-centeredness and declining civic responsibility, and self-destructive behavior" (p. 20). These, he says, present a "clear and urgent need" and schools are the right place for learning values and principles that lead to healthier living and healthier communities (p. 20).

Future Utility

Oscar commented, "I don't follow them perfectly yet, but I see them as an inspiration of what I would like to live by. It's something I don't think about a lot, but it's always in the back of my mind." Dan, a staff member suggested, "It's something that I aspire to . . . like students." Jason, one of Eagle

Rock's first graduates, wrote to me that $8 + 5 = 10$ "serves as a great guideline for developing young adults who need guidance and fundamentals that will carry them through an array of experiences in life." He continued, "Personally, devising a personal moral and ethical code sticks in my mind as it is something that I have to look at and amend daily." Another staff member, Adriana, reported that $8 + 5 = 10$ has "allowed me to think more critically of my personal life choices and how they impact not only me but those around me as well." Brianna, a graduate, said, "The effect that $8 + 5 = 10$ has had on me personally is huge. I have been able to live life with integrity. Mind, body, spirit—thinking about these has helped me balance my stressful lifestyle."

Darren commented,

> Without $8 + 5 = 10$ I doubt I would be four years into an Environmental Resources Engineering degree. I guess it is possible that I could be where I am today without having $8 + 5 = 10$ in my life, but the path I would have taken to be here would probably be quite different. What I am trying to say is the events that unfolded in my life, that led me to where I am today, were influenced by the conversations I was having with people at ERS in some way. $8 + 5 = 10$ almost worked as a catalyst . . . to boost my involvement in what it takes to be a successful Eagle Rocker.

Jeremy, a former gang member and another graduate, responded to my question about how $8 + 5 = 10$ affects students after they have left Eagle Rock:

> Let me answer by telling you about a conversation I had with a man from Camp Fire USA. It came up that I am an ER graduate, and he stated that he loves ER (from his brief experiences). I showed him $8 + 5 = 10$ (of course, I have it printed out and pinned above my office desk). He stated that $8 + 5 = 10$ is a great tool for any organization to have because it is a standard that all behaviors and actions can be evaluated against. In my 7 years since graduating from ER, I have come to understand the usefulness and complexity of $8 + 5 = 10$ even more than when I was a student. My decision process is more in depth and complex.

Strangely, there's little research on the effect of school on out-of-school experiences. Pugh and Bergin (2005) note, however, "Under the right conditions, school learning can enrich students' out-of-school experience" (p. 15). For example, they note that Dewey stated that education should be a "means for contributing to general growth" (p. 15). The "one way in which education can contribute to the expansion of experience is through the development of general attitudes and abilities, such as an ability to regulate action and an interest in learning" (p. 15). $8 + 5 = 10$ seems to have life after Eagle Rock.

Community

Michael, a staff member, stated,

I think the benefit of a value system is that we are forced into conversation about really important issues regarding community. What does it mean to "make healthy life choices" or "practice leadership for justice"? The very process of referencing values is far more growth-producing than the litigious conversation that occurs around rules. Talking about rules is ludicrous. I remember a student in NYC who claimed, "No, technically I was not late for class because my train was late." We turned that excuse for breaking a rule into a much better conversation about responsibility. "Yes," he finally said, "I was late. I broke the rule. I would have been responsible if I'd taken an earlier train or found another way to get here. I would have been responsible if I'd admitted this from the beginning.

According to Coral Ann, 8 + 5 = 10 makes a community out of people who come together from lots of different backgrounds. "They have to re-evaluate the way they live. They make changes in their lifestyles and stretch their comfort zones because of the principles." Hannah, a graduate, elaborated on this point: "All of us, students and staff, bring our own individual morals to Eagle Rock. However, some of them are not the most effective and healthy of rules to live by. 8 + 5 = 10 helps us look in a positive, healthy, less selfish direction, together."

Democracy

Living according to a set of principles paves the way for living in a democracy, as you will discover in the next chapter. These words from the Declaration of Independence, the Bill of Rights, and the U.S. Constitution are a good beginning for a school's set of principles to live by: Respect. Truths. Equality. Rights. Liberty. Safety. Prudence. Security. Public Good. Peace. Justice. Law. Freedom. Responsibility. Power.

Practicality

Finally, there's the issue of practicality. Rules are short and simple, black and white. They take up little time. They seem fair, since they apply to all. They have consequences, although not always the most appropriate consequences (think of students who are suspended from school because they have been truant!). They're easier to enforce: "If you do this, this happens."

But, as Jenna said, "Rules are not always the best for students. They're limited and they're not easily enforced." You can never have enough rules (someone will always think of something that has no rule written for it . . . yet), but a few carefully chosen principles can lead to discussions of right living in almost all aspects of life. What you think is black and white is a challenge to gray. People are driven to "play the gray," not just in their taxes. Rules may seem to take up little time, at least until someone begins to argue the gray. They are fair and equal—applied to everyone—but not always just. What is just for one person may not be just for another, and students are keenly aware of the difference between the two. With principles, they long for fairness ("The same exact thing should happen to her."); with rules, they long for justice ("Our situations are entirely different, even though we broke the same rule."). Rules are easy to enforce if you have resources for patrolling student behavior. Principles are internalized and don't need enforcement.

One of the best discussions you can have with young people is about the similarities and differences among these concepts: fairness, justice, and equality.

CONCLUSION

The most potent reasons for having a principle-centered community, however, are these:

1. The deep engagement of youthful minds in the messy business of figuring out principles and how they apply to their own lives and their lives with others.

2. The kind of community that both depends on principles to work and generates opportunities for principles to be worked on.

3. The active engagement of young people in how they create a place for learning that is habitable and hospitable for all.

Covey wrote the first edition of *The 7 Habits of Highly Effective People* in 1989. When he revised it in 2004, he declared,

Life is more complex, more stressful, more demanding. We have transitioned from the Industrial Age into the Information/Knowledge Worker Age—with all of its profound consequences. We face challenges and problems in our personal lives, our families, and our organizations unimagined even one and two decades ago. These challenges are not only of a new order of magnitude, they are altogether different in kind. (p. 7)

School is, without a doubt, a knowledge organization, yet it does not always behave as if it were. Behaving according to principles rather than rules is one way schools and districts can contribute solutions to problems that are new and unimaginable, messy and complex, and part of the Information/Knowledge Worker Age.

SO WHAT

Think about rules and principles in your own life. Name one rule you follow rigorously. Describe the number of times that rule is likely to affect your life in a week.

Describe a couple of situations that have required you to follow that rule.

Now name a principle that guides you (such as honesty). Describe the number of times that principle is likely to affect your life in a week. Describe a couple of situations that have required you to think about that guiding principle.

Summarize the differences.

NOW WHAT

Working by yourself or with colleagues, use these three simple (but earth-shaking) questions from Robert Garmston and Bruce Wellman (1999) to think about your school or district:

> **Who are we?** (Related questions are "About what do we care?" and "How much do we dare?")
>
> **Why are we doing this?** (Consider rules, principles, "folk wisdom, tradition, and unexamined habit.")
>
> **Why are we doing this, this way?** (This might be any aspect of school, such as the school's schedule, the division of knowledge into subjects, the afterschool program. Ask, "Who benefits from the current system?"). (pp. 9–12)

Summarize the principles already operating in your environment. Are these principles that make for a right life? Are they principles that help people grow and get better? What principles would you change, delete, or add? Do the same thing with rules.

Then consider whether or not your setting could become principle-centered. What would have to happen? Who would support a principle-centered environment for all learners? Who would not? What consequences would be appropriate when principles are violated?

5

"What's Democratic About Schools?"

A Democratic School Helps Students Learn

Do you think teenagers are more likely to vote for their choice on "*American Idol*" and other contest television shows than vote in political elections? The good news is that for the spring 2006 "*American Idol*" contest "only 21% of poll respondents ages 18 to 24 said they had voted for a contestant, but 53% said they had voted for a candidate for public office (Abcarian & Horn, p. A1).

On the other hand, according to Jared Wadley (2004) in *The University Record Online*,

> Late-night talk shows seem to foster political cynicism among young Americans who rely on these programs for information. . . . "These young Americans tend to undervalue the significance of their votes in the election, and they are also more likely to mistrust politicians," says Nojin Kwak, an assistant professor in the Department of Communication Studies. (p. 1)

Statistics from the U.S. Census Bureau's Current Population Survey show that voter registrations have increased somewhat from 1996 to 2004, as has voting (U.S. Census Bureau, 2007).

Table 5.1   Voter Registration 1996–2004

	Registered	*Voted*
2004	72.1% of eligible population	88.5% of those registered
2000	69.5 % of eligible population	85.5% of those registered
1996	70.9% of eligible population	82.3% of those registered

However, according to the Census Bureau, "The voting rate was higher among the older citizen population than the younger citizen population. . . . A key difference between these age groups was registration" (U.S. Census Bureau, 2007). The Census Bureau speculates that the problem might be transience, a reality in the lives of many young adults.

Democracy is more than registering to vote and voting, however. According to Jim Dator, Professor, and Director of the Hawaii Research Center for Futures Studies at the University of Hawaii, who spoke to the 13th Annual Citizenship Institute at the Richardson School of Law at the University, participation in democracy

> usually involves some form of activity . . . listening to or reading about political debates; discussing political issues with family, friends, neighbors, fellow workers; canvassing; holding signs and waving at people from the side of the road; legal financial contributions; joining interest groups; writing or phoning one's representatives, etc. (Dator, 1992)

Dator (1992) "is absolutely convinced that something much more closely approaching true democratic, participative governance is possible using the concepts of electronic democracy."

Although young people do run for office, they are a rarity according to a *USA Today* news story. According to this news story, "An estimated 800 politicians are younger than 35, from city council to Congress. They represent every party and race. Some are second-generation politicians. Others come from families who stayed out of government affairs" (Weiser, 2004). That's about one in every 20 politicians. For comparison, "of the 56 signers of the Declaration of Independence, 12 were 35 or younger" (Weiser, 2004).

Ben Barnes, former Texas House speaker and lieutenant governor, Washington lobbyist and Democratic fundraiser, has commented that the United States needs to consider a farm club approach to democratic participation. Like baseball's farm club system, a political farm club system would "recruit and groom young people to run for office" (Weiser, 2004). Schools could be that "farm club."

Take a look at almost any set of state standards. You'll find something like this under the broad heading *Civics:* "Students know the fundamental democratic principles inherent in the United States' concept of a constitutional democratic republic." Or, more specifically, "Students understand how citizens exercise the roles, rights and responsibilities of participation in civic life at all levels—local, state and national." (Both standards are from the Colorado Model Content Standards.) The problem is that standards such as this, "Students know how citizens can participate in civic life," are headed by verbs such as *identify, explain, describe, evaluate,* or *know how.*

Thus, many K–12 students may merely *study* democratic values; they may never *live* them in schools. In fact, while they are studying democracy, they may be experiencing contradictions to democracy in their daily school lives. This chapter explores the reasons for schools to behave democratically, as well as how they can do so.

SCHOOLS AND DEMOCRACY

John Goodlad is one of the most outspoken proponents of education in a democracy (Goodlad, Mantle-Bromley, & Goodlad, 2004). Through numerous books and networks, he and his colleagues have laid out a compelling "Agenda for a Democratic Society." The mission of the Agenda has four components:

1. Enculturating the young into a social and political democracy.

2. Introducing the young to the human conversation (providing access to knowledge for all children and youths).

3. Practicing a nurturing pedagogy.

4. Ensuring responsible stewardship of our educational institutions. (Goodlad et al., 2004, pp. 29–32)

As I wrote in an article for the *English Journal,*

Goodlad envisioned the actualization of these components simultaneously in schools and schools of education through partnerships between higher education and K–12 education. To help both K–12 and college and university educators make his vision a reality, he formed the Institute for Educational Inquiry and the Center for Educational Renewal at the University of Washington, the National Network for Educational Renewal that has member partnerships in twenty states, and the League of Small Democratic Schools. The League assists schools that are preparing their students for the complex role of citizenry required of a democratic society. (Easton, 2005, p. 52)

Eagle Rock is one of the founding schools in the League.

Richard (Dick) Clark of the League has developed 25 actions schools can take to enact the "Agenda." Ten of them apply to the concept of "Enculturating the young into a social and political democracy":

1. "The school develops students' commitment to the values of liberty, government by consent of the governed, representational government, and one's responsibility for the welfare of all.

2. "Students learn to act in a manner that reveals an understanding of the interrelationships among complex organizations and agencies in a modern society.

3. "The curriculum includes a strong emphasis on developing students' analytical and reasoning skills.

4. "The curriculum emphasizes students' developing communications skills.

5. "The curriculum includes developing students' ability to function effectively in various sized decision-making groups.

6. "The curriculum develops students' ability to engage in theory-based practice in conflict resolution.

7. "The curriculum includes development of students' understanding of the importance of free and open inquiry.

8. "Educators skillfully practice collaborative decision-making.

9. "The school serves as a model that guides students in practicing democratic ideals in the school.

10. "Students are encouraged to exercise the democratic right to dissent in accordance with personal conscience." (Clark, 2003, pp. 5–8)

The Coalition of Essential Schools, founded by Ted Sizer, added a tenth precept to its Nine Common Principles:

The school should demonstrate non-discriminatory and inclusive policies, practices, and pedagogies. It should model democratic practices that involve all who are directly affected by the school. The school should honor diversity and build on the strengths of its communities, deliberately and explicitly challenging all forms of equity and discrimination. (Cushman, 1998, p. 1)

This principle, addressing democracy and equity, paid attention to "whose voice matters, who gets to decide, who learns what, whose vision of the 'good life' schools foster. From the top to the bottom of the ladder, school people live with the dynamics of power and control" (Cushman, 1998, p. 5).

Debbie Meier, educational reformer, instrumental in creating Central Park East Elementary and Secondary Schools, shared her concerns about authority and power with Sizer and Nancy Faust Sizer. Meier had founded and was codirecting Mission Hill School in Roxbury, Massachusetts, at about the same time that the Sizers founded and were coprincipals of the Francis W. Parker Charter High School in central Massachusetts. Meier and the Sizers exchanged letters about their developing schools that were eventually printed in *Keeping School: Letters to Families From the Principals of Two Small Schools* (Meier, Sizer, & Sizer, 2004). In a chapter called "Authority and Power," Meier addresses democracy in schools:

> Power relationships have always been a difficult subject for school people to discuss, whether among themselves or with kids or families. "Question authority" was the political slogan of the young in the 60s [but] public schools were hardly a place of much questioning— or authority or anything else. (Meier et al., 2004, p. 61)

Even teachers with a union behind them had little ability to change schools. Meier recalls, "Kids, presumably, were fairly powerless, although I soon discovered that they too had, in their own way, a great deal of power over the way we could or couldn't go about our work as teachers— the power to privately resist and sabotage" (Meier et al., 2004, p. 61). She adds, in parentheses, "(Cumbersome as more open and democratic ways are, in schools as in society at large they have enormous efficiency—they give the governed an active stake in seeing that things work out)" (p. 62).

Democracy in schools is the focus of yet another organization. First Amendment Schools "is a national reform initiative designed to transform how schools teach and practice the rights and responsibilities of citizenship that frame civic life in our democracy" ("About the Project," 2007). A project of the Association for Supervision and Curriculum Development, First Amendment Schools has four primary goals:

- Create consensus guidelines and guiding principles for all schools interested in creating and sustaining First Amendment principles in their school.
- Establish schools in every region of the nation where First Amendment principles are understood and applied throughout the school community.
- Encourage and develop curriculum reforms that reinvigorate and deepen teaching about the First Amendment across the curriculum.
- Educate school leaders, teachers, school board members and attorneys, and other key stakeholders about the meaning and significance of First Amendment principles and ideals. ("About the Project," 2007)

One of the most usable tools produced by this network is a chart of Core Civic Habits. These habits serve as a guideline for schools that want to practice the freedoms of the First Amendment. They are Civic Habits of

Heart (such as demonstrating clarity of moral purpose), Civic Habits of Mind (such as valuing inquiry that encourages and appreciates both complexity and ambiguity), Civic Habits of Voice (such as speaking out on matters of conscience), and Civic Habits of Work (such as demonstrating self-discipline) (First Amendment Schools, 2007).

Remember how you learned to ride a bicycle or how you learned to use a computer? You probably did not learn how to do these things by simply reading about them. Of course, you read what was available and you consulted experts, but eventually you had to get on that bicycle or turn on the computer. You fell or faltered, braked too suddenly or hit the wrong key, but you learned and were soon reasonably facile with the bike or the laptop. The premise of this chapter is that we can learn all we want about democracy; we can read about it and seek outside opinions. Eventually, we have to live it. Schools that live it produce young people who expect to live it. Eagle Rock is only one example of a school that strives to "enculturate the young into a social and political democracy" (Goodlad et al., 2004, p. 29). Many aspects of democracy, denied students in many schools, are appealing to struggling students.

DEMOCRATIC SCHOOLS IN ACTION

Eagle Rock graduate Jeremy Martinez, whom you met earlier in this book, gave a speech about democracy at the Coalition of Essential School's Summer Institute in July 2006. His speech illustrates many of the characteristics of democratic living that were described above.

In 1996, I walked into Eagle Rock School and Professional Development Center property as a member of its newest group of students. Before Eagle Rock, I had been suspended and expelled from every school I had attended. These suspensions and expulsions stemmed from gang activity, fighting, drug use, non-attendance and an overall unwillingness to be a student. One morning my mother, in an endless struggle to get me to go to school, asked me: "What do you want to do"? My reply: "Drop out."

So, what changed the mind of a violent, high, young gangster? A young person who, in a span of two years, spent more time in various correctional centers in Jefferson County, Denver County, even Santa Fe, New Mexico, than he did in Jefferson County and Denver public schools. What changed his mind?

Why did that young person, who displayed so many negative behaviors in and out of school, choose to leave his friends, his weed, his sleep, his city to live in the mountains?

Was it the magistrate with a stern and very sincere warning: "Do this or spend the next two years under the state's observation"? No (though that was motivating). Was it his parent's pleas and urging, "Jeremy you have the chance of a lifetime"? No, but those words did help in the decision. Was it the school that said "We want you, the student who has been branded as someone not worth wasting time on. We want you to start off with a clean slate. We want you to graduate from this school.

We want you to participate in every aspect of the school: the cooking, cleaning, learning, building, teaching, inducting, criticism, praise, outreach, organizing, leading, following, designing, and whatever else an involved participant in our community should do." In other words, Eagle Rock asked me to be a part of its democratic process. That is what this young person chose over everything else.

Democracy is more than a vote. Democracy is inclusion in and responsibility for the everyday activities of a community. From the mundane to the enthralling, all persons who are affected by a decision must have some say in that decision. Let me repeat that: all persons who are affected by a decision must have some say in that decision.

Eagle Rock is democratic. During my time there I taught my fellow students and my instructors. Let me rephrase that last sentence: I, as a high school student, taught. I was not only the recipient of information, I was responsible for dissemination as well.

Do you know the power and, thus, the confidence that gives a young person? To be told, you are not only smart, you are so smart we want you to tell other people what you know. We want you to share your ideas and knowledge with the rest of the people in this community. Wait, you are <u>required</u> to share that information! Is this democratic: the sharing of information? Yes.

Democracy includes participating even in those tasks which are boring and/or difficult. Kitchen duty is one democratic activity at Eagle Rock that some loathe. Every student, not just those who <u>want</u> to participate, gets to assist in the kitchen. Not only is cooking involved, but so are washing the dishes, plucking the lettuce, mopping the floors, dumping the compost, and washing the aprons. Why is this part of the democratic process? Because we all ate the food that came from that kitchen. Because we were affected by it; we were responsible for it.

Because Eagle Rock is a democratic school, its classes were democratic. Students with the assistance of teachers designed and taught whole classes. "ISMs" was the class Miranda [an intern] and I taught. Because my Senior Thesis was on the creation and rise of the Ku Klux Klan, Miranda wanted me to help teach a class about the different "isms": racism, sexism, ageism (you get the point). So she and I created lesson plans, checked out books, articles and movies and built a curriculum. I, at the time, was also the video equipment expert on campus, so we built into the class that a video must be made by each person in the class. We interviewed experts and laypersons. I taught about the history of the KKK and did tutoring on how to edit text and lay music to the videos. The class was a success. We all learned new things and had our concepts challenged. This class, for me, was not simply a 10-minute presentation. It included the whole process of teaching. During my time as a college undergraduate, I was not given this opportunity. It is not until now as a Master's degree student that I am trusted to do something of the same importance. I repeat my theme: because I am affected by them (classes), I am responsible for them (teaching and learning).

The most democratic process that I was a part of at Eagle Rock was Peer Council. A few other students and I were elected to a council that made decisions about other people's inappropriate behavior. We not only recommended consequences, but what we decided was the consequence. Do any of your schools have

*this? Do your students, who are chosen by their fellow students, have the author-
ity to hand out consequences for misbehavior? Let me ask a more interesting question. If you do have that student group, would they be allowed to make decisions
about a staff member in addition to students?*

*Did we ever expel or suspend a student from Eagle Rock? No, we knew that
such a heavy consequence would need to involve the whole school. Did we hand
out early curfews, extra kitchen duty, suspensions from intramurals, or require
public apologies? Yes. Were we ever challenged about our consequences? Did
people argue with our decisions? Yes. But, the community stood behind us and
what we required eventually occurred.*

*We were occasionally asked to consider the behavior of some staff members.
We as a group would decide if it was appropriate for us to take on that decision-
making process. In one case, we did take on a problem with a staff member who
had knowingly allowed a student to participate in intramurals when that student
had called in sick for the day.*

*So with the power to hand down a consequence on someone who had, for so
long, given us homework, challenged us, at times punished us, called us out at
times, we asked this staff member to make an apology to the community. We made
this decision on the basis of the information we had. We knew this decision would
solidify our legitimacy for the whole community. And we made a fair decision,
which was fully accepted by the person charged.*

*We, members of the community, were asked by our peers to represent them in
matters that affected the whole community. We were selected by the very people
who might be affected by our consequences.*

*What happens to the least powerful at Eagle Rock happens to the most power-
ful at Eagle Rock because we are all one. We all chose to participate and make efforts
for the well-being of the community. Isn't that what democracy is, the people coming together to find solutions to common problems and then act on those behaviors?*

*I was once told at another school, after my smart-aleck remark "It's a free
country," that the country is free, but this school is not. I did not stay there too long.
I came to understand freedom includes pain and hard work. It also includes results
from my behaviors. Eagle Rock gave me the freedom to put my efforts toward something larger than myself. In return my education and life were greatly improved.*

*The process of democracy at Eagle Rock is not incidental. Democracy is built
into the curriculum and morals of the school. Democracy is continuously being evaluated and searched for. Eagle Rock is effective because it is democratic. I am now
married—to a fellow Eagle Rock graduate, expecting my first child in 4 weeks;
I have a high school diploma; I also have a Bachelor's degree from Maryville College;
I am currently at the University of Colorado at Denver working on my Master's
degree. I have designed and am running a program for at-risk and adjudicated youth
in West Denver. Most of all I am an active participant in my community because
I am still, to this day, an Eagle Rock student.*

*I asked at the beginning of my talk, what caused that young, lost person—
me—to choose school over all the other things he was doing. I've given you some
answers. I hope your school offers enough democracy so that a young person like
me could choose it.*

SOURCE: Used by permission from Jeremy Martinez.

Vignette 5.1   A School Vignette: Democracy

A SIMULTANEOUSLY TIGHT-LOOSE SCHOOL

Westside Village Magnet School, Bend, Oregon

By Wendy Winchel

Westside Magnet is a small, tight-knit group of kids, teachers, parents, and volunteers who work together to create a unique learning environment. It's a K–8 school, completely inclusive, and non-graded.

Some of our students have barely attended school before they enroll at Westside. Academically they have maybe never fit into the mold of conventional schools. We can tell even in kindergarten or first grade. Some come to us in kindergarten with no idea how to have a relationship. But, we always like it when we get those children at an early age and start working with parents and the family.

We think of ourselves as a community of learners—I know that's a cliché, but it's true. Our focus is on learning how to work with each other as part of a democratic society. We are part of John Goodlad's League of Small Democratic Schools.

Our children are not segregated in any way, though they're grouped flexibly throughout the day, sometimes according to skill, sometimes according to interest. We look at each child as an individual and help each one move as far ahead as possible. We start with what's in the child, listen to the child, take what's there, and help each one move ahead.

Some of our students may qualify for special education or a learning disability placement, but we believe in full-inclusion. No pull-out whatsoever. When we have special services, such as physical therapists, we have a group of kids, not just the one who needs the help, who work with the therapist in a group activity. Special staff who come infrequently are not used to this kind of work with their "client" so we ask them to teach our own staff and we do the work, again with a group of kids. We have this one little guy with a huge eating disorder—very young—and some of the older students have been trained to be sure he's being monitored.

Westside is all about everybody knowing what everybody needs and pitching in to help, kids, too. It's all about helping each other. The bottom line is that we're a listening school. We begin with relationships and self-advocacy.

Every year we start off the first or second week in September with goal setting. We have students present their current plan—goals for the emotional, social, and academic aspects of their lives. Then staff members sit down with each of them and ask them what they would like to have as goals. We invite parents to be part of this process. For example, for a struggling student who has anger issues, we might have a couple of goals dealing with anger, a plan for how to meet those goals, and a plan for how everyone around this child will help meet those goals. Kids keep track of how they're doing; they check on themselves. Parents are part of it. There's a lot of mutual responsibility going on.

We want our eighth graders planning their lives when they leave here. They have a little journey ahead of them, and we know they are going to need to get help.

At the beginning of year, we also work on rights and responsibilities for all kids in a community meeting. Then, when someone does something wrong, we hold another community meeting and refer to those rights and responsibilities to decide on consequences. Often it's a case of someone taking away someone else's rights or someone being irresponsible. Issues are brought to the community in a respectful manner.

If there's fighting on the playground, someone gets a student mediator. If the student mediator can't solve the problem, then it's brought to the community. A community meeting is hard, but kids know they're cared about. Struggling kids don't always know how their actions are affecting others. They also may need to be heard by others: "This is what some of you have been doing to me and that's why I'm angry." It's not like tip-toeing around issues or sweeping them under the rug, which is how "discipline" is handled in a lot of schools.

It's really about teaching self-advocacy and how to work in a society where you have choices. You can choose, and you can choose bad or good behavior. Your choice is reinforced throughout community.

We have as many adults at the school as possible, adults who spend time with the kids, giving them choices and teaching them that responsibility allows them to have more choices. Adults also involve the kids in the outdoors, take them mountain bike riding, backpacking, and hiking; they even teach students how to do laundry and make a healthy meal (life skills). If we focus on what makes a person healthy in their "soul," "heart," or "body," then academics come naturally.

Our students do pass state tests, even though our curriculum is not centered around the content or the processes of testing. We designed our curriculum with choices, interests, interconnectedness, according to the real world. We have a lot of hands-on learning, creating and making projects. Struggling students suddenly have a lot of ways to express themselves. We set kids up for success. Last year, we discovered a student who was an incredible sculptor, but no one knew that until he chose to make a sculpture.

We provide many, many opportunities for conversations in Westside Magnet. These conversations provide scaffolding for learning. We have a focus for the conversation, some content, but we take from what the kids are concerned about and interested in and make it into the work. They research, we research, and then we talk more.

I've begun to see schools as loose or tight. You know how you go into schools and everything's tight, tight, no room for movement? "This is the way we're doing it, no change. Halls, rooms, lunch at this time. No movement." You can also walk into a school and it's loose-loose, anything and everything goes, whatever you want to do. Rules are made up as you go; there's no planned curriculum. Some schools are loose-tight; they let things go until the school culture begins to fall apart and then the powers that be tighten up. Suddenly there are rules. I think Westside Magnet is tight-loose. We have scaffolding, structure embedded in what we do, a curriculum with big expectations, but when you become responsible and able to grasp concepts, you can make all sorts of choices. Then, it's loose.

SOURCE: Used by permission from Wendy J. Winchel.

AUTHOR'S NOTE: Wendy Winchel is principal of Westside Magnet School. The school's Web site is http://bend.k12.or.us/wsv. Their address is 1101 NW 12th Street, Bend, OR. Their phone number is (541) 383-6205. Contact Wendy directly at wwinchel@bend.k12.or.us.

Practices That Build Democracy in Schools

Jeremy's speech illustrated a number of practices that help make a school democratic.

Voice

The opportunity for students to have a say in matters that pertain to them is especially important to students who are struggling in school. Many students—especially those who are contemplating leaving school early—do not "get" school. They think it is some form of baseball's "hidden ball trick." How and why they are required to do the things they do seems a secret, almost a mystery to them. "Will that be on the test?" "I have to take a PE class to graduate?" "Why did she get an 'A' and I got a 'C' and we did the same thing?"

To have voice, students must have information. School needs to be transparent to them. They need to know as much as they can (without violating state laws). Thus, Eagle Rock students attend and speak up in staff meetings. They participate in the hiring process (though not on personnel issues). They know how to graduate. They know the curriculum standards or requirements as well as the instructors do. They know the qualities of good work—through rubrics they have helped to design themselves or have been given beforehand. They know how to present their learning publicly. They know the code of the school because it is taught, learned, and reinforced; it is not sequestered in a rule book somewhere on the principal's desk. School is obvious to them.

As informed citizens of the school, they can then use their voices to affect what affects them. One way they can use their voices is formally, through a proposal process. Anyone in the community—adult or student—can write a proposal to change something at Eagle Rock. Proposals are great for learning how to write, requiring deep thinking about different sides of an issue or problem and its possible resolution. Proposals often require some research and then the most genuine of persuasive writing. Writers present their proposals to the most appropriate people (perhaps the whole school), both orally and in writing, and then consider feedback even to the point of rethinking and rewriting. Few proposals are accepted immediately; their writers must have patience before their ideas actually become a part of the culture.

One of the conventional ways of providing students voice is through committees and leadership roles. At Federal Hocking School in Ohio, students participate in the Mentor School Committee (which organizes the school for its mentorship role as part of the Coalition of Essential Schools), the Interview Committee, the Site Based Committee, the Technology Committee, and the Senior Year Committee (focused on Senior Projects and Senior Portfolios) (Federal Hocking High School, 2007).

A most important aphorism speaks (so to speak) about voice: "You have no right to no opinion." Embedded in that statement is the expectation that students will speak up and be accountable for what they say. Also embedded is the notion that students who do not speak up will be responsible for their silence.

Katie, a new student, commented, "Democracy affects me by allowing me to hear my voice (having my voice heard)." I think she, wisely, spoke to both sides of having voice.

Choice

Choice at Eagle Rock. Eagle Rock students have the ultimate in choice: They can choose to attend . . . or not. So, too, can staff. Students can choose—through their behavior—whether or not to stay (and, sometimes, that's a daily choice). Students know what they need to master to graduate. They graduate when they have mastered everything they need to master, so they can choose when to graduate. School is not necessarily a routine of four years, nine months each, of required classes and a few electives. They graduate when they are ready to do so.

Students choose courses much as college students do. When students chose the class "Blood and Guts" one trimester, they were choosing, essentially, a biology class, but because they chose it over other science classes such as "Moo" and "Ecological Ethics," students were invested in learning in that class. (The snazzy title and curious approach helped too.) Instructors create such classes according to their own passions and those of their students, so they and their students are often engaged in learning what intrigues or excites them, not just the regular "ho-hum" curriculum. All classes are, therefore, both elective and "required" in the sense that they offer opportunities to students to learn, master, and demonstrate the graduation requirements.

What helps make curricular choice possible is the school's approach to curriculum. Classes are not units of credit. Students do not get grades for seat-time. Classes are vehicles for learning and demonstrating mastery of graduation requirements, which are based on the Colorado Model Content Standards (2007). Students either achieve mastery or not through a class; if they do not, they take a later class (something that appeals to them more, offers a chance for a different style of learning, or provides a variety of ways to document mastery). There's no failure. The school doesn't have grades, GPA, or class rank. Still, our students get into—and graduate from—the colleges they want.

Students can often choose to follow a passion *within* their chosen courses. Danny, a graduate, pursued a puzzling aspect of light for more than two trimesters. He didn't know, of course, that the phenomenon he was observing was explained by mathematics (and neither did his instructors, at first). All he knew was that light spread as you moved the source of light away from what it was shining on. "We started talking about whether light spread in pixels like on an LCD screen, so the pixels would be further and further apart as we moved away from it, or did it spread like butter, thinner and thinner" (L. B. Easton, 2002, p. 166). Danny tweaked the phenomenon and recorded his findings. He did research online and in the library. He wrote elaborate explanations of what was happening. He tried to explain his findings orally to anyone who would stop by, snagged by the spheres he'd strung up across the room. Science, mathematics, writing, reading, using technology—all these were part of Danny's natural inclinations as he followed his passion. (By the way, Danny rediscovered the inverse square law.)

Another choice that seems to turn around disengaged students relates to learning style and preference. Students can often choose not only how they'll learn, but also how they'll express their learning. Some may want to work with others conducting research and creating a service project related to the content. Others may want to work alone but doing hands-on work, such as building a model, to show what they have learned. Another student may want to apprentice to an expert in the field and prepare a computer presentation to demonstrate learning.

Finally, students can choose how to document their learning. Many will do a paper and an oral presentation. Some will do portfolios. Others will combine artwork and mathematical formulas. Still others will demonstrate how to do something. Some might write a script and enlist others in acting it out. "How are you going to show us that you have learned?" is a key question in classes. "How will we know?" You'll learn more about these and POLs (Presentations of Learning) in Chapter 8.

Choice-making occurs with Presentations of Learning. Students have 15 minutes (which seems interminable when they are newbies, a speck of time when they are veterans) to make the case that they have learned. How they do that is up to them, leading to highly creative or virtuoso presentations, even techno wizardry. Students even construct a rubric for their own POLs so that the choices they have made can be scrutinized by panel members from outside of the community.

Choice in Other Schools. At the Boston Arts Academy, students specialize in one of the five arts subject areas. In their senior year, students work on a "unique capstone experience, writing a grant proposal to fund an independent community outreach arts project" (Boston Arts Academy, n.d.). At Central Park East Secondary School (CPESS) in Harlem, students go through their senior year according to a personal program of study, presenting the work to a graduation committee of choice. The portfolio at CPESS is how the school emphasizes individualized education ("Professional Development," 1994). Similarly, at Parker School in Massachusetts, seniors create their own portfolios and present and defend them in order to graduate (Parker School, n.d.). At Quest High School in Humble, Texas, seniors choose a modern-day social issue and create a social action plan (Quest High School, n.d.). Middle school students at the School of the Future (SOF) in New York City, enter SOF's high school on the basis of a portfolio; as high school students, they expect to graduate on the basis of four exhibitions and a portfolio, all of which they tailor to their interests (School of the Future, n.d.).

The Met in Providence, Rhode Island, and other locations, gives students a choice of internships within 16 career clusters upon which all their other learning is based. Students work at the Audubon Society or the Providence Film Commission, for example, and then, back at school, "work with their advisors to build and reinforce the skills and knowledge needed" (The Met, 2006). Internships are also a prominent feature of Chicago's Young Women's Leadership Charter School (a 7–12 school) that provides an array of choices for students (Young Women's Leadership Charter School, n.d.).

The K–12 Wildwood School (n.d.) in California is project-based, a mechanism through which the school lets students follow their passions. Many schools include service projects as part of their curriculum, offering students a wide range of choices related to their interests.

Choice in Your Own School. "Regular" schools can also offer students lots of choices. Providing some choices may require systemic change. A district would have to change, for example, if it were to be composed entirely of magnet schools, a system in which every student has what Margery Ginsberg calls a "signature," a specialty for which it is famous, a feature that draws students and staff alike to it (Easton, 2004b, p. 14). What if every school were a school of choice and those who participated in each one did so because they wanted to?

An alternative—one that can be found in a number of large schools that have converted to small schools within a school (SSWAS)—is to have a school composed entirely of "houses," each with its own signature to attract students and staff. Some houses might feature the arts or technology, careers, or themes, allowing students choices while assuring a core curriculum. SSWASs don't have to be limited to high schools; they can occur in elementary and middle schools, too.

Even within a school, groups of teachers at a grade level or teaching the same subject can offer choices. For example, grade-level teachers can offer choices to students through a focus for the year; two teachers at a grade level may want to focus on space travel; another teacher may want to focus on medieval times; another one might choose to focus on games. Students can choose their teachers according to their interest in the focus. In high school, the three teachers who teach American history can offer choices according to the approach they take, one looking at history through the eyes of immigrants, another through enacting dramatic court cases, and a third through the experiences of everyday citizens. Biology can be offered as an investigation into extinct species, or through an internship in a zoo, or through dissections.

In their last years in a school (5th grade, 8th grade, and 12th grade, for example), students might be able to choose a specialty or major for the year, a cross-curricular investigation that culminates in an exhibition, project, or portfolio. In some schools, this is called a *capstone* project.

Some choices can be offered by individual teachers in their classrooms. One good example of choices in elementary schools is the practice of using centers. Another might be allowing students to choose units they'd like to work on individually or with a partner or small group in order to learn and document learning of a standard. Or, students can follow their passions within the subject or content of a unit. They can choose how they'd like to learn and present their learning, according to their learning styles and preferences. They can propose their own processes for learning and set their own deadlines, perhaps according to a contract. The teacher is a coach, mentor, advisor, and cheerleader, dispensing information at the start-up, perhaps, and then to individuals and groups as needed. Students are doing the real work in these classrooms in an environment carefully crafted for them by the teacher.

Project-based learning is another mechanism for allowing students to make choices. Individually, with a partner, or in small groups, they can tackle an essential question or problem, presenting what they have learned to the whole class—an excellent way to get both depth and breadth out of the curriculum. In order to meet particular standards—which are usually stated rather broadly—students can draft lists of questions they have and research them alone or with others, presenting what they have learned to others. When internships are part of the curriculum, they can make choice possible, as can service learning opportunities.

As much as possible, individual teachers can offer choices in *what* students focus on within a content or subject area or related to a particular standard as well as *how* they learn (learning style preferences, for example) and present their learning to others.

You may be wondering how schools with large class sizes find ways to allow students to find their own learning pathways through the curriculum? One way, of course, is by getting smaller. Another solution is getting more adults in a class—interns, student teachers, researchers, practicum students, parents. Another is trusting students with more responsibility for learning. In terms of time, the best strategy is "less is more," a concept developed by Ted Sizer and the Coalition of Essential Schools. Classes might be seen as vehicles for learning rather than ways to cover the curriculum, which is a futile enterprise at best. Teachers might recognize that students cannot master everything, but they can learn what they care about in ways that work for them. They can demonstrate what they know and can do so in ways that are appropriate for them. Through choice, they can go deep into learning and naturally find breadth, too.

Choice is one way to engage students in their own learning. Without choice, students—and not just those who struggle—may disengage from learning or learn little.

Accountability

A natural adjunct to choice is accountability. When you choose, you are automatically responsible for your choices. Students want to be accountable; it's part of being respected. They can say, with pride, "I am responsible for my own learning."

In schools that work for struggling students, there's no doubt that students will learn—it's just that they may choose how to learn. There's no doubt that they'll be accountable for their own learning—it's just that they may choose how to demonstrate that they've learned. Similarly, they may choose how to live the principles that govern the school . . . but there's no doubt that they will do so.

Respect and High Expectations

Students of all ages bring something to their learning. They are not, as was once thought, tabula rasa, blank slates to be filled with knowledge. Calling upon their expertise, even to the extent of having them teach what they know to others, is one way to respect them as learners. Students, in turn, respect each other as learners.

When students first look at what they are required to accomplish at Eagle Rock, they despair. No one had shown them what was expected in their other schools. They just marched through a year, taking subjects and courses, five or six at a time. When they are told what they are expected to accomplish, they may blanch, but they also will feel respected. They are worthy of meeting high expectations; they won't be excused from meeting them. They know themselves and can be in charge of meeting the expectations.

And, they're flattered. Many struggling students have been put in Special Education or in pull-out programs. They know the curriculum has been "dumbed down" for them. James, one of Eagle Rock's early graduates, figured out early in his Special Education career that his teachers would do the work for him. Mostly he liked that . . . until he hit a crisis and began to doubt himself.

Of course, students need plenty of support in order to meet high expectations. "You can do that," veterans say to the new students. "You can do that," say staff members. At Eagle Rock, there's no competition for high grades, so everyone helps everyone else master the requirements.

One of the most respectful opportunities that students have at Eagle Rock is when they are asked to teach visitors, and this happens regularly. They almost burst with pride about what they know. Also, students are frequent presenters at local and national conferences. They are trusted to listen to understand, speak knowledgeably and personably, and share their stories with educators who want to figure out how Eagle Rock works.

Flexibility is an adjunct of high expectations and accountability. Students see flexibility as a willingness to trust them to meet high expectations. Iron-clad rules and expectations communicate the opposite: "We don't trust you to live up to our expectations and be accountable, so we're going to tell you exactly when and how to accomplish what we ask." Of course, a little structure—especially if it's offered in a personal way—always helps.

The expectation that everyone in a democratic society will contribute to that society in any way they can, and respect for what everyone contributes, is part of democracy within a school.

A Code

All democracies have a code of some kind. The code for the United States is included in the Constitution, the Bill of Rights (the first ten amendments to the Constitution), and the rest of the amendments. You have already read about the code at Eagle Rock known as $8 + 5 = 10$. As Sevi, a new graduate, commented, "ERS [Eagle Rock School] without $8 + 5 = 10$ would very much resemble the United States without the Constitution. It would lack the ideals that lay the foundations for its brilliance and success." Above all, the code must be known and practiced according to a system of use.

Governance Strategies

Governance is the school feature that most often seems to fly in the face of democracy, at least according to students. Rather than democracies, schools seem more like monarchies (with the principal as king) or oligarchies with the assistant principals in cahoots with the principal. Students don't know exactly where rules come from, except from someone in The Office. They don't know how rules are made; why, for example, there's a rule about this but not a rule about something that seems much more important. They're not sure what to do if they believe a rule is wrong, but unless they're willing to be a nuisance, they won't ask. Sometimes they break a rule just to see if anything happens. Sometimes they'll push the limits just to see how far they can venture into the gray area surrounding most rules.

As a result, schools seem arbitrary to them. They don't make much sense. Some students begin to feel some disrespect toward school. This is particularly true for students who are disengaged from school. They feel powerless in the face of what seems a monarchy. They feel they have no authority or control over their own lives. School is done to them. They don't get to do school.

They look on the typical student governance structures with a bit of disdain, seeing them as relegated to choosing the decorations for the dance and overseen by a staff member who limits what they can do. Student Councils are often pseudo-democratic bodies, their members elected because they are popular, but denied real responsibilities.

Eagle Rock has not solved all of the aspects of governance, and students still chafe when they think school is being done to them. However, they have some mechanisms that give them an important role in the running of the school, such as Peer Council, which was described by Jeremy. Peer Council does not participate in major decisions (such as whether a student who has broken a nonnegotiable should be sent home), but it does handle lesser infractions that would be resolved by assistant principals in most schools. It also addresses issues before the community, such as how to help struggling students get their work in on time. The Council is a small body of trusted veteran students elected by the school; it meets only when there's a need. It gets the respect it deserves.

A group called the Magnificent Seven consists of the seven most veteran students at Eagle Rock. These students have "duty" one night a week with a few staff members (remember, Eagle Rock is a 24–7 enterprise). They have a master key and share equal responsibility with staff during their duty, including monitoring activities on the campus, supervising campus clean-up, performing bed checks, and supporting staff as needed. Certainly there are veteran groups of students at other schools who can be entrusted with some responsibilities relegated to staff.

Frequently, students form ad hoc groups to address issues that have come to their attention. Recently, when students became aware that an underground culture was beginning to flourish, the students themselves held a meeting to remind each other why they were at Eagle Rock and how fragile its culture is. Adults did not attend this meeting; students resolved the issue themselves. Another temporary group designed a shadowing day for Eagle Rock's own staff so that they could experience a day at Eagle Rock as they would have if they were students. Another temporary group redesigned the Presentations of Learning process. The important aspect of these groups is not so much what they do—although their actions make a difference—but the fact that the students know they can form such groups to address issues that seem to get in the way of their learning. There's also an unspoken message to the adults in schools: The adults don't need to solve every problem for students; in fact, the more the adults can trust students to solve their problems through an approved structure, the less "buy-in" staff will need to get for solutions that staff devise.

Like most schools, Eagle Rock has elected representatives and committees involving students. House leaders represent each house (dormitory) by attending staff meetings, during which their ideas are sought as eagerly as ideas from adults. They have real input on the issues. Communication is two way, with house leaders reporting on what happened in staff meetings and taking ideas from students to future staff meetings. Committees also help Eagle Rock function well; they regulate how the kitchen is run, how intramurals are held, and what happens in the houses.

Gatherings and community meetings are an informal governance structure. Usually run by students, these regular events bring the whole community together "to share important ideas and information. Many students take advantage of a Gathering to share important concepts or situations affecting the entire community," according to Donnie, ERS graduate and current social studies instructor. "Student-run Gatherings have focused on recycling, AIDS, fund-raising for worthy causes, anger management, giving and receiving feedback, providing service to others, and many other topics" (Eagle Rock, 2006).

Some Pitfalls of Becoming and Being a Democratic School

One of the biggest challenges to schools desiring to be more democratic is that it's much easier *not* to be democratic. Just have a bunch of rules and monitor their compliance. The many reasons for having democratic schools—described at the beginning of this chapter—make the hard work of democracy worthwhile. Preparing students to be active citizens is one reason; another reason relates to the needs of students to have voice and choice, and to participate in other aspects of a democratic structure, especially students who are struggling to stay in school.

Few current educators have, themselves, had experiences in a democratic school; they are used to the way things were when they went to school and may find it hard to imagine a school that is not authoritarian. One way to help educators understand how democratic schools work is by having them visit such schools, immersing themselves in the experience of democracy. Among the best schools to visit are the First Amendment Schools (2007).

Educators may fear a change that may give students more power than they should have. They may have always associated their work with being in charge—of a school or a classroom, for example. They may see themselves as the authority, not just in terms of what they know (the subject they teach) but also in terms of their experiences as adults. They may fear that the school will be out of control if it's democratic. And, finally, they may have become teachers because they were seduced by images of power—there, in the front of the classroom, knowing everything, and being in charge of 30 young people.

It's not easy to change beliefs, but several strategies may help to do so. I've already mentioned the value of visiting democratic schools. What's most important during such a visit is talking with the students, asking how they feel about their roles in the school, their learning, and the success of the school. Asking students if they ever worry about the school being "out of control" may result in some interesting answers. Involving students and their parents in the conversion of a typical school to a democratic school may also result in changed beliefs, at least relief that the school will not descend into chaos, because those who designed it won't let that happen. Finally, beliefs are sometimes changed when small successes are achieved. Changing one aspect of school, such as instituting a proposal system, might be so successful that doubters are ready for more spectacular changes.

Being democratic seems to take more time, although I suspect that if a rule-driven, monarchical society were closely examined, as much time is taken setting, monitoring, and enforcing rules as would have been needed if the whole community were involved in the issue in the first place. Think about the many hours wasted in faculty meetings talking about rules about chewing gum!

Space may also be a problem. For a democracy to work well in schools, the whole community needs to meet together—or at least a subset of the community—and to have mechanisms for two-way feedback with the rest of the community. One solution to this problem is to have meetings according to grade levels or subject areas. Another is to use advisories as the main structure for advancing democratic principles. If schools become small schools with a school (SSWAS), they can function like states in terms of their own democracies, electing representatives to serve in the more national, whole-school effort.

Like the adults, older students have probably experienced schools that were far from democratic. They may resist a change from what is familiar to them; playing an active role—which they must—in a democratic school may seem a bit scary. They may need to undergo some form of "unlearning school" in order to thrive in a democratic school. One way to do this is through what I called School 101 in Chapter 4, a "class" that students take as newcomers to the school in order to learn the school's code or set of principles, one of which might be democracy.

Donnie, the staff member mentioned above who graduated from Eagle Rock and then from the University of Colorado, Boulder, and is the current social studies instructor, has a keen interest in democratic schools (Eagle Rock School, n.d.). He reports that the "foundation of democratic living is indeed idealistic and . . . its integrity constantly tested." For example, he sometimes observes that staff members "are only paying lip service to the ideas and suggestions" that come from students.

Staff are also the source of many "student leadership ideas, which then percolate down to students. Consequently, many of the leadership roles students fulfill do not originate with them and may not be what they desire. Students are challenged to buy into the idea of a greater good, and to contribute to making the greater good happen" (Eagle Rock School, n.d.). Students don't always realize that they have the opportunity to "design and implement their own structured leadership opportunities instead of taking hand-me-downs" (Eagle Rock School, n.d.).

Students do not always "embrace the leadership opportunities they are afforded with full integrity and commitment. For example, some students contribute to an underground culture that undermines the stated values of 8 + 5 = 10" (Eagle Rock School, n.d.).

Donnie also worries about introverted students, of whom there are many at Eagle Rock. Leadership comes from the more vocal and extroverted students. "Informal leadership possibilities are usually filled by those who have the charisma and feel comfortable being public figures. When more introverted students are forced into leadership positions, they are often hesitant and quiet and that behavior may be considered dysfunctional by the others and seen as complacent" (Eagle Rock, 2006).

CONCLUSION

John Goodlad begins *Education for Everyone: Agenda for Education in a Democracy* with these words:

> For some time—increasingly since World War II—too many of us occupying this richly endowed part of the world have assumed that the work-in-progress we call democracy will take care of us. This is a dangerous assumption. Things thought not to need our caring attention deteriorate. (Goodlad et al., 2004, p. ix)

We owe it to our students and their children not to let democracy deteriorate.

SO WHAT

What are your own Civic Habits? Make a list of your personal Civic Habits of Heart (such as demonstrating clarity of moral purpose), Civic Habits of Mind (such as valuing inquiry that encourages and appreciates both complexity and ambiguity), Civic Habits of Voice (such as speaking out on matters of conscience), and Civic Habits of Work (such as demonstrating self-discipline). Go to the First Amendment Schools' Web site (www.firstamendmentschools.org) to compare your own habits with those listed by the network's schools.

NOW WHAT

Work individually or with your colleagues on the following survey to decide how well your school enculturates the young into a social and political democracy. Share results with other colleagues or present them at a faculty meeting.

Survey on the Characteristics of a Democratic School

Characteristic of a School That Enculturates the Young Into Democracy	1 = Not Well	2 = Adequately	3 = Satisfactorily	4 = Extremely Well
"The school develops students' commitment to the values of liberty, government by consent of the governed, representational government, and one's responsibility for the welfare of all."				
"Students learn to act in a manner that reveals an understanding of the interrelationships among complex organizations and agencies in a modern society."				
"The curriculum includes a strong emphasis on developing students' analytical and reasoning skills."				
The curriculum emphasizes students' developing communications skills."				
"The curriculum includes developing students' ability to function effectively in various sized decision-making groups."				
"The curriculum develops students' ability to engage in theory-based practice in conflict resolution."				
"The curriculum includes development of students' understanding of the importance of free and open inquiry."				

(Continued)

Survey (Continued)

Characteristic of a School That Enculturates the Young Into Democracy	1 = Not Well	2 = Adequately	3 = Satisfactorily	4 = Extremely Well
"Educators skillfully practice collaborative decision making."				
"The school serves as a model that guides students in practicing democratic ideals in the school."				
"Students are encouraged to exercise the democratic right to dissent in accordance with personal conscience"				

SOURCE: From R. Clark (2003). *Goodlad's Agenda for Education in a Democracy: A Framework for School Renewal.* Seattle, WA: Institute for Educational Inquiry. Reprinted with permission from Richard W. Clark.

PART II

Improving Curriculum, Instruction, and Assessment for Struggling Students

6

"*What About Standards?*"

Developing Curriculum According to the Right Standards

"Step right up, folks. Today, yes, today, is the chance to choose your classes. Make room, make room for the students who are just now arriving. First to go . . . drum roll, please . . . Janet!"

"Have you ever wondered [sound of a bird] just what people mean when they say, 'It's just for the birds'? Well, this class will answer [bird sound] all of your questions. If you take this class [multitude of bird sounds apparently coming from a CD player], I guarantee you will find out all about bird breeding—oooooh [students echo this sound] aaaaaah [again]. And not just about breeding, all about their behavior. You'll get to map breeding sites within Rocky Mountain National Park and identify birds based on their characteristics and songs. And, you'll be doing all of this for the Cornell University Lab of Ornithology. Be prepared to get up early, get credit in environmental science, and work on your science credit. Remember, sign up . . . for . . . *For the Birds*."

A scattering of applause. Then, the head of school says, "But, wait, there's more." Students are apparently used to this, most of them joining in dramatically on the last two words: "there's moORRE!" He gestures toward the entryway to the hearth. Jen, fully clad in climbing gear and clanging with carabiners, comes around from the back of the fireplace. "Huff, puff, puff, puff. This is so hard, but it's worth it," she says as she tries to climb the red rocks that jut out from the fireplace. "You . . . know . . . *Colorado Rocks* is . . . really . . . a rigorous academic course. It focuses on science, environmental science, and environmental writing. Yes, we'll do some climbing around here and study some geology. We'll do some top rope climbing and we'll climb a few peaks, but if you want to work on a science portfolio, environmental science credit, write an essay of explanation about some literature—well, come take this class." She lets herself down from one of the rocks that she's been clinging to while delivering this invitation.

The head of school has no chance to introduce the next class. The teacher, Jimmy, jumps right in. "Don't want to climb? Think it's too hard? Do you get winded just climbing the stairs? Well, this class is for you. It's *Social Statistics and Fantasy Baseball*. Yes! You, too, can play fantasy baseball and learn descriptive statistics, then apply those concepts to real-world situations. Politicians and lobbyists use statistics to support their claims and shape our world. We will analyze their studies, debate their claims, as well as generate our own policy suggestions, backed, of course, by the powerful world of statistics!"

"But, wait," the head of school says, and then everyone joins in, "there's more." One by one, the teachers peddle their classes: *Shape O' the World, From the Gravitron to Gravity: Amusement Park Physics, Eco-Challenge, Free Form Funkafide Fiddles, Chick Lit, Peacing Together the Middle East, Waiting for the Barbarian.* At the end of these sales pitches, the head of school wraps up the event with "But wait . . . ." Instead of ending as he usually does, he says, "For only $5.00 more, folks, you can get your genuine imitation steak knives," and the students boo and hiss with genuine pleasure and go off to work with their advisors to sign up for classes.

What kind of school *is* this?

This chapter is about how schools can offer classes that jazz both the instructors and students. (It's not about *Freshman English* or *U.S. History*.) It's about curriculum that's based on a school's set of standards—related to state and national standards. It's about mastery of the curriculum. (It's not about promoting and graduating students according to seat-time and grades.) It's about choice and self-directed learning. (It's not about required classes seasoned with a dash of electives.)

The scenario above occurs three times a year at Eagle Rock, as instructors "pitch" next trimester's classes to students. It's almost like a pep rally for learning. You, too, can invigorate curriculum that is standards-based (never mind the knives).

USING STANDARDS AS THE BASIS OF CURRICULUM

Most schools, districts, and states claim to be standards-based. Most are not. They still promote from grade to grade and graduate students on the basis of seat-time. Seat-time in high school translates into credits or Carnegie units and passing grades. For example, if high school students take enough classes in English—usually four years' worth—and pass them all with a "D" or better, they are candidates for graduation. Ditto mathematics, science, social studies, foreign language (sometimes), and physical education.

Prior to high school, seat-time translates into passing grades in all subjects for a year and leads to promotion to the next grade. Not passing one or more subjects sometimes leads to being retained in a grade. The same is frequently true for students who do not pass high school courses; they are not promoted to the next higher grade, or they are required to repeat a class during the summer or the following year. The main problem, however, is the use of credits to determine eligibility to graduate.

Most states require a minimum number of credits for graduation. Credits stand for time: One credit is equal to one year; a half credit is one-half year. For example, in California, "Section 51225.3 states that commencing with the 1998-99 school year, all pupils receiving a diploma of graduation from high school must complete all of the following while in Grades 9 through 12, inclusive:

- Courses in the subjects specified, each course having a duration of one year, unless otherwise specified.
- Three courses in English.
- Two courses in mathematics, including one year of Algebra I beginning in 2003-04. (California *Education Code* Section 51224.5)
- Two courses in science, including biological and physical sciences.
- Three courses in social studies, including U.S. history and geography; world history, culture, and geography; a one-semester course in American government and civics, and a one-semester course in economics.
- One course in visual or performing arts or foreign language. For the purposes of satisfying the requirement specified in this subparagraph, a course in American Sign Language shall be deemed a course in foreign language.
- Two courses in physical education, unless the pupil has been exempted pursuant to the provisions of *Education Code* Section 51241.
- Other coursework as the governing board of the school district may by rule specify. (California Department of Education, 2006)

Some states have given the nod to alternative ways of graduating students by requiring additional, worthy projects, such as a "High School and Beyond Plan" and a "Culminating Project." California offers these alternatives:

- "Practical demonstration of skills and competencies,
- "Supervised work experience or other outside school experience,
- "Career technical education classes offered in high schools,
- "Courses offered by regional occupational centers or programs,
- "Interdisciplinary study,
- "Independent study, and
- "Credit earned at a postsecondary institution." (California Department of Education, 2006)

Please note that most states that offer alternatives have not abandoned the credit way of graduation; they've just added some elements. Some offer differentiated diplomas based on doing something extra or more than the required number of credits.

According to the Carnegie Foundation, which no longer has a

position on the unit system . . . the Carnegie unit (credit) was developed in 1906 as a measure of the amount of time a student has studied a subject. For example, a total of 120 hours in one subject— meeting 4 or 5 times a week for 40 to 60 minutes, for 36 to 40 weeks each year—earns the student one "unit" of high school credit. Fourteen units were deemed to constitute the minimum amount of preparation that may be interpreted as four years of academic or high school preparation. (Carnegie Foundation, 2006)

The Foundation

became linked with the unit in the early 1900s, after other groups, like the National Education Association, defined and adopted a "standard unit" for high school work. At that time, high schools, a new phenomenon in themselves, lacked any uniformity in the courses they taught, the number of hours students spent in class, and the amount of homework assigned. (Carnegie Foundation, 2006)

The unit system served as "an eligibility requirement for universities interested in participating in its pension program. Entering freshmen were expected to have completed 14 'units' of academic preparation before entering the college or university" (Carnegie Foundation, 2006).

Many educators believe that the Carnegie unit or credit has outlived its original purpose, especially now that states are specific about standards or competencies. In fact, in 1993, Ernest L. Boyer, President of the Carnegie Foundation, stated, "I'm convinced the time has come once and for all to bury the old Carnegie unit. Further, since the foundation I now head created this academic measurement a century ago, I feel authorized this morning to officially declare the Carnegie unit obsolete." (Wisconsin Department of Education, 2006)

Most national organizations, such as the National School Boards Association (NSBA), have agreed that the Carnegie unit should be scrapped. In their important book on high school reform, *Breaking Ranks II: Strategies for Leading High School Reform,* The National Association of Secondary School Administrators (NASSP) describes eight options (see Table 6.1) for "moving from time-based to standards-based education" (Westerberg & Webb, 1997, p. 92).

In most schools, however, the Carnegie unit or credit has *not* been scrapped. It coexists with standards in a policy setting that is sometimes confusing, sometimes downright contradictory. Some states run two systems for graduation:

a. Mastery of competencies or standards (according to each district's measures) and earning a requisite number of credits (seat-time and passing grades) OR

b. Passing state tests on standards as well as earning credits.

What happens when students take all the right courses in the right amounts and get a "D" or better in each one . . . but don't demonstrate mastery of the standards? Or, they don't pass the state graduation exam(s)? Or, they have all the credits they need and have passed the state examination but have not shown mastery of standards?

The dilemma is real. Michael Skube (2006), in a special for the *Washington Post,* wrote, "In California this year, hundreds of high school students, many with good grades, faced the prospect of not graduating because they could not pass a state-mandated exit exam" (p. 15A). In 2006, they were rescued by a judge who "overturned the effort," a solution that has been forced in other states and at the end of other years when the two systems for graduation have skirmished.

There are other, more subtle, problems with the Carnegie unit. Back in the early 1900s, the Industrial Age was in full swing. Henry Ford had established the assembly line. Time and efficiency were paramount as developing countries rushed to provide a spending public with the products they sought. It was only natural that the factory model would migrate to education. Schools were expected to contribute to the culture children who understood the factory model and would perpetuate it as workers. Thus, school was a production process. Students progressed from class to class and year to year as if they were raw material being manufactured

Table 6.1   Options for Moving From Time-Based to Standards-Based Education

---

Standards-based model: Eliminate Carnegie units as the basis for earning a diploma and adopt standards-based graduation requirements centered around identified essential learnings.

Combined model: Retain some or all of your Carnegie unit graduation requirements, but supplement them with a limited number of standards-based requirements.

Endorsement model: Disassociate the standards from graduation, but add "endorsements" to the diploma (or transcript for each standard or requirement met.)

In-class model: Disassociate the standards from graduation requirements, but build them into required courses as major assignments. Attach significant weight to these assignments when determining course grades. Possibly eliminate "D" grades.

Dual diplomas: Offer students/parents a choice of following either the credit track or the standards-based track to a diploma. Attach incentives to the standards-based track.

Dual diplomas and endorsements: Students who elect to and do accomplish all standards are awarded a standard-based diploma (plus incentives). Students who elect to or are advised to pursue a credit-based diploma are given a regular diploma plus endorsements.

Internal compliance: Disassociate the standards from graduation requirements, but develop a building system for monitoring student and teacher accountability.

School within a school: Students and teachers could elect to be in a special standards-based system, possibly combined with dual diplomas, endorsements, and/or incentives.

SOURCE: From Westerberg, T., & Webb, L. D., *Providing focus and direction through essential learnings.* Copyright © 1997, National Association of Secondary School Principals, www.principals.org. Reprinted with permission.

into usefulness. Thinking was that standardization was everything. So, classes were scheduled for about an hour, with seven or eight in a day. A year of schooling existed within an agricultural calendar and was, therefore, about nine months in length to allow for planting and harvesting. Eight years of school were enough for most children; only a few went on to high school and, there, they followed an efficient, easily understood seat-time or Carnegie unit plan for graduation.

Specifically, seat-time meant sitting in a desk (perhaps bolted to the floor, in line with other seats) and being filled with information by a teacher at the head of the room. Instruction was usually lecture, and learning was passive. Tests required the regurgitation of learning. Seat-time was, therefore, very efficient—as were the factories of the day—one teacher handling 35 products every 50 minutes or so. Content came in bits and pieces, just like the nuts and bolts that factory workers used to make products. Enough little things in the right order, and the product is complete (the student educated). Defective products either dropped out of the assembly line through some mechanism or were relegated to the trash heap at the end of the process.

So, Carnegie units became associated with a type of education that was depersonalized, operated according to a cost-benefit model, and efficient, if nothing else. Getting rid of Carnegie units, then, is one way to reform education so that the focus of school is on creating thoughtful human beings rather than well-machined products.

Another problem with Carnegie units or credits is that people still think they regulate college or university admissions (along with class rank and GPA, which are both products of units and grades). Please notice that I used the words *still think,* for these indicators are less a gatekeeper than people believe them to be. Many members of the Coalition of Essential Schools worried that the "less is more" focused curriculum they had established would prevent students from being accepted into college. The May 1994 issue of *Horace,* the newsletter of the Coalition, announced that "most selective colleges say they're used to unusual transcripts, and big universities are looking for new ways to work with schools in change" (Cushman, 1994, p. 1). In fact, "Alternative assessments like exhibitions, projects, and portfolios appeal to colleges and universities seeking thoughtful students" (Cushman, 1994, p. 1). SATs and ACTs still count, but class rank and GPA are less important.

The key to college admissions for a school that has abandoned Carnegie units and grades is to work with the colleges and universities that most students want to attend. At Eagle Rock, a person whose job bears the title Life After Eagle Rock does just that, phoning admissions officers, meeting them at higher education conferences, and preparing materials that explain Eagle Rock's standards-based mastery requirements. In fact, in states where standards are strong, state universities actually look for students who have graduated according to mastery of the state's competencies.

Other colleges and universities want students who demonstrate "habits of mind," such as critical thinking skills, inquiry and questioning, conceptual thinking, analysis, perseverance, research skills, independence, ability to solve problems, tolerance for ambiguity, and more. Check out several Pennsylvania colleges whose academic deans drafted "What We Expect: A Statement on Preparing for College" (Cushman, 1994, p. 5). In the same issue of *Horace*, you can examine expectations from Harvard and the State University of New York. As Eagle Rock has discovered, most colleges and universities have an admissions route for students from nontraditional programs.

In a study of how school reform related to going to college for minority and low-income students, Martinez and Klopott (2005) found four practices that seemed to help such students succeed:

- "Eliminating academic tracking by enrolling all students in an academically rigorous core curriculum;
- "Providing relevant curriculum and pedagogy;
- "Developing small learning environments for students; and
- "Providing a balance of academic and social support for students for the purpose of developing social networks and relationships." (p. 58)

Students—especially those who struggle with school—do not always see the point of taking classes for a certain amount of time: "Why do I need chemistry? A whole year???? When will I ever use chemistry? Forget it!" Most see the point of standards or competencies, however. Sitting in a class they are sure they'll never need is much more onerous than working toward a standard in a context that is relevant, even exciting, to them. Also, standards are visible and understandable: "Oh, I need to show you that I can do this. Okay." They are not as formidable—even in a pack—as a whole year of a course (or even a half year). Students who struggle to come to school every day can face standards, especially if they are asked to learn and demonstrate their learning in ways that are meaningful.

Not Just Any Old Standards

Many schools working with struggling students have found that developing their own standards is more effective than wholesale adoption of state or district standards. Schools that begin with these questions— "Who are our students? What do they need to know and be able to do?"— find that their customized curriculum leads to more personalized teaching and learning.

It is prudent, of course, to make sure that your own school standards relate to state or district standards, especially if you are subject to state or district testing, and more especially if scores on those tests are high stakes (see Chapter 1 for my thoughts on state and district testing). Most states allow a "meets or exceeds" approach that provides for customization.

Eagle Rock began its approach to standards with the questions above, developed 8 + 5 = 10 (see the Introduction and Chapter 4), and then developed curriculum. Here are a few areas where Eagle Rock's standards have been *adapted* from state standards.

- Science: Environmental science appears separately in the Eagle Rock curriculum because environmental stewardship is part of the Eagle Rock code.

- Social studies: Students do not merely learn about the social studies; because of the fifth expectation, they learn to become leaders for justice.

- Social studies: They also focus more on *using* the elements of civics— part of the theme of democratic governance.

- Social studies: In order to activate cross-cultural understanding, many social studies classes focus on non-European history and culture. In fact, the subject once called *Social Studies* is now known at Eagle Rock as *Societies and Culture*.

- Physical education and health: These are given more emphasis than they are in most schools, partially because many Eagle Rockers developed unhealthy lifestyles before enrolling.

- The arts (music, drama, visual art): Students are expected to develop the artist within and to express themselves aesthetically at Eagle Rock, so art is not an elective. For many students, some kind of artistic expression is a healthy way of handling the emotions that have hijacked their ability to learn (see also Goleman, 1995).

When Eagle Rock staff asked the question, "Who are our students?" and considered 8 + 5 = 10, they found they needed to augment the state standards. They added standards in the following areas:

- Career Development
- ERS Orientation, ERS Transition, and Wilderness Experience: These are the processes new students go through to acculturate themselves to Eagle Rock and to begin to make personal changes.
- Food Service: A part of service to others.
- Personal Growth: Many elements of 8 + 5 = 10 and the nature of the population make this requirement especially important at Eagle Rock. It includes spiritual development, which is documented through students' personal growth portfolios and presentations; it is not focused on any religious principles.
- Service Learning: This is actually a graduation requirement.

As they were developing standards for curriculum, Eagle Rock staff had to face the dilemma most educators face, whether they're in the classroom or administering a district: "How can we cover the curriculum?" They were realizing—rightfully so—that "there's too much to cover." Eagle Rock staff, however, refused to ask that question in the first place. If they had, the answer would have been, "We can't." They would have added, "And, we don't want to."

Eagle Rock staff are not alone in this approach to curriculum. Some educators think about it this way: Imagine that what students need to know and be able to do is fine parquet or multifaceted, richly colored mosaic tiled flooring. They should *uncover* rather than *cover* that knowledge (or elegant flooring). Ted Sizer (1984), founder of the Coalition of Essential Schools, described uncovering as having simple, but profound, goals:

> The school's goals should be simple: that each student master a limited number of centrally important skills and areas of knowledge. While these skills and areas will, to varying degrees, reflect the traditional academic disciplines, the program's design should be shaped by the intellectual and imaginative powers and competencies that students need, rather than by "subjects" as conventionally defined. (1984, pp. 225–226)

This concept became the second principle in the set of Nine (later Ten) Common Principles that were adopted by schools across the country that joined the Coalition. Sizer (1984) specified,

> That is, students' school experience should not be molded by the existing complex and often dysfunctional system of isolated departments, "credit hours" delivered in packages called English, social studies, science, and the rest. Less is more. Curricular decisions should be guided by the aim of student mastery and achievement rather than by an effort to 'cover content.'" (p. 226)

Other reformers have echoed this principle in their own strategies, and "less is more" has approached proverb status in the world of educators. The National Association of Second School Principals (NASSP, 2004) made "less is more" its first strategy for "breaking ranks" in high schools: "Establish the essential learnings a student is required to master in order to graduate, and adjust the curriculum and teaching strategies to realize that goal" (p. 7).

What is interesting at Eagle Rock is that over its 15-year history, uncovering a limited number of essential learnings leads students on an individual basis to understand a lot more curriculum. As they go deep to explore a few ideas, they necessarily go broadly, as shown in Figure 6.1.

Here's an example of how depth simultaneously achieves breadth or coverage. Eagle Rock students, interested in the 1960s and the Vietnam War, worked for three months to make sense of it. As they worked, they naturally explored history preceding and following the Vietnam War. They naturally learned about what led up to the Vietnam War and what followed it. Their learning was deep as well as broad.

But make no mistake about it; Eagle Rock staff are content *not* to cover the curriculum. They acknowledge that not all students can know everything. They work to make sure, however, that what students do learn is

Figure 6.1   Breadth and Depth

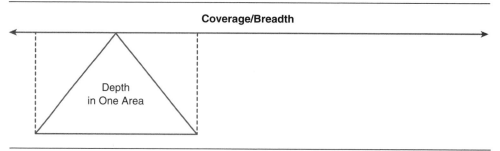

meaningful to them, has some impact on their lives, will be memorable, and will generate further need to know. It's okay if students graduate without knowing why the Franco-Prussian War was fought (which they would have had to learn if their World History teacher were covering the curriculum), but they certainly need to know why wars happen.

Many networks of schools—such as the Expeditionary Learning/ Outward Bound (ELOB) network—help educators translate standards into living curriculum. ELOB schools, for example, organize curriculum around learning expeditions. Check the Paideia Plan (Adler, 1982). Also look at what is available through the International Baccalaureate Middle Years Program. Foxfire (2002) offers an integrative approach to curriculum. For elementary schools, the Developmental Studies Center in Oakland, California, offers curriculum that unites content area standards in reading and mathematics with a personal and social growth curriculum.

Both the National Council of Teachers of English (NCTE) and the National Council of Teachers of Mathematics (NCTM), as well as other subject-area groups, offer examples of curriculum based on standards.

A variety of schools have implemented extraordinary curriculum related to state standards. Check out Boston Arts Academy's (BAA) curriculum, organized so that students can pursue their own specialty in the arts but also engage in the other subject areas under broad headings: Humanities, Mathematics, Science, World Languages, and College and Career. BAA focuses on writing through *slateblue*, its literary magazine, and also organizes senior year according to a capstone project: writing a grant for community art projects (Boston Arts Academy, n.d.).

The High School for Recording Arts in St. Paul, Minnesota, has shaped state standards into a dynamic curriculum related to the music business (High School for Recording Arts, 2007). San Francisco's Leadership High School has schoolwide outcomes that focus on four areas: Communication, Critical Thinking, Personal Responsibility, and Social Responsibility (Leadership High School, 2003). The Met in Providence and other cities, links standards and curriculum to the internships its students serve (The Met, 2006).

The Francis W. Parker School in Massachusetts integrates the traditional disciplines into domains: Arts and Humanities; Math, Science, and

Technology; Spanish; and Wellness. It has performance standards in reading, writing, listening, oral presentation, research, artistic expression, scientific investigation, mathematical problem-solving and communication, systems thinking, technology, wellness, and Spanish (Parker School, n.d.). The Urban Academy in New York City focuses on six academic proficiencies: Creative Arts, Criticism, Literature, Mathematics, Social Studies, and Science (Urban Academy, n.d.).

THE PROCESS OF DEVELOPING STANDARDS-RELATED CURRICULUM

The process of developing standards is as important as the standards themselves. Most schools find it beneficial to work with their larger school community (parents, students, citizens, administrators, teachers) to answer the two key questions: Who are our students? What do they need to know and be able to do? A smaller committee drawn from the whole community group can check the school's list against district and state standards. Checking the standards created by the national subject matter groups such as the National Council of Teachers of Mathematics (NCTM) and the National Council of Teachers of English (NCTE) is also important.

Communities and students change. So, too, should schools and the standards they have written. Curriculum needs to be in "perpetual draft" form, so that it can change as conditions do. The best questions a faculty can ask itself at the beginning of each year is, "Who are our students?" "How have students changed?" "What do we know and need to know about their learning?" "How should our *never-finished* curriculum be revised this year?" Data—both subjective and objective—about how well the curriculum is working can inform its revision.

Expressing Curriculum

A school can express its curriculum in a variety of ways. Most schools express curriculum requirements according to grade level. Movement from grade level to grade level (and, ultimately, graduation) signals completion of the required curriculum. "Passing" indicates that sufficient learning in a variety of subjects or classes has occurred. Of course—as I argued above—it doesn't, really. Seat-time and passing grades cannot prove that a student has learned. Perhaps the student has simply been present for enough time and has done barely enough work to get a "D" in enough classes or subjects. That is hardly testimony to learning.

Deciding What a Credit Is

The unit of credit in such schools is the subject, class, or course. Fifth grade is made up of several subjects; students move from fifth to sixth grade by passing enough subjects (seat-time and grades). Students pass from freshman to sophomore status in high school similarly, spending enough time and earning a passing grade in each course (or most courses) they take, required or elective.

Standards or competencies are usually shelved in subjects, classes, or courses—they may, in fact, be the required curriculum (rather than the table of contents from a textbook or a course outline) in a course—but decisions about promotion or graduation may not be based on having mastered them. Decisions are usually based on passing the subject, class, or course and, ultimately, moving from grade level to grade level. To climb from grade level to grade level, students must complete homework, take tests, complete projects—to earn at least the "barely passing" level of "D"—and be in class enough to meet the time requirement. There's a huge assumption here: that the standard or competency is embedded in the teaching and learning, in the homework, tests, and projects. I think that standards are beginning to wiggle their way down to the work that teachers assign, but I have also heard from classroom teachers too many times, "What standards?" I know this is a fine point, but it's important, especially to those who are casting a curriculum that works with struggling students.

When students fail to pass a subject, class, or course, they may fail a grade. The result: Students retake the subject, class, course, or grade level. The statistics on failing are dismal. According to the National Association of School Psychologists (NASP, 2003):

> It is estimated that as many as 15% of American students are held back each year, and 30%–50% of students in the U.S. are retained at least once before ninth grade. . . . The probability of dropping out increases with multiple retentions. Even for single retentions, the most consistent finding from decades of research is the high correlation between retention and dropping out. A recent systematic review of research exploring dropping out of high school indicates that grade retention is one of the most powerful predictors of high school dropout. (n.p.)

Many struggling students have failed a subject, class, course, or grade level at least once. Some have done so twice. Those who have done so more than twice probably never again darkened the doorways of any school.

A new way of thinking about what a credit is opens up a slew of opportunities for students. Think, for example, of a credit as *mastery of the standard, competency, or requirement* rather than the time spent in a subject, class, course, or grade level with "passing" achievement.

Credit as Mastery of a Standard

All sorts of exciting possibilities open up when "credit" is defined as mastery of a standard, competency, or requirement. For example, what if failure were *not* an option (to borrow from the title of Alan Blankstein's [2004] book)? Students would work on achieving standards until they had done so. Without the possibility of failure, students take risks, put themselves "out there" to learn something. It is less disastrous not to reach mastery on a single standard than to fail a whole course or, worse, the whole year. The phrase *not yet* is useful for describing students who are working toward mastery.

The concept of "no failure" leads to some structural decisions. For example, when "mastery" or "in progress" are sufficient labels for students' work, there's little point in grades. Many innovative schools have eliminated grades. Francis W. Parker School in Massachusetts relies on portfolios and rubrics for demonstration of mastery. Portfolios are assessed as Just Beginning, Approaches, or Meets, relative to standards, and students pass from one division to another on the basis of that evaluation (Parker School, n.d.). New York City's School of the Future uses exhibitions as a way of determining promotion and graduation. Exhibitions are assessed according to rubrics as Needs Improvement, Satisfactory, Mastery, and Mastery With Distinction (School of the Future, n.d.). Wildwood School in California uses narrative assessments rather than grades (Wildwood School, n.d.). Chicago's Young Women's Leadership Charter School uses the designations High Performance, Proficient, and Not Yet instead of letter grades. Those who receive Not Yet are required to demonstrate proficiency at a later date (Young Women's Leadership Charter School, n.d.).

Eagle Rock has no grades and assesses students according to rubrics with four categories: Needs Work, Basic, Proficient, Exemplary. Only ratings of Proficient or Exemplary count as mastery and result in credit for a requirement, standard, or competency. Eagle Rock's "report cards," called Learning Experience Record Sheets, provide only three possibilities: Mastery, In Progress (to be completed within six weeks), or Not Yet. Many schools include narratives from the student, teacher, and parent, as well as work samples to illuminate the words used to describe mastery.

GPA and class rank become meaningless. In fact, sorting of any kind is meaningless, since all students are working to master the same standards. Competition for grades flees when all students are expected to succeed. In fact, students help each other out as they work to learn, understand, and display their learning. Heterogeneous grouping, even across age levels, provides scaffolding so all students can work toward mastery.

Time changes because students are not expected to make the same progress on all standards in an arbitrary number of months (nine, for example) or years (twelve, for example). Perhaps the day changes in some way. In secondary schools, the class period may morph into the project period, during which students work on several standards at one time. In both secondary and elementary schools, several standards might fit themselves together into an interdisciplinary unit or class.

Perhaps grade levels themselves become obsolete. Instead of making decisions after nine months of learning, educators might be willing to make decisions at the end of a cluster of grades. Most state standards committees wrote standards according to clusters of grades anyway: K–3, 4–8, and 9–12. Perhaps third, eighth, and twelfth grades are public reporting times on standards.

Policy makers have embraced standards as the best thing to happen to schools since, well, the Carnegie unit. They may be more inclined to rethink school schedules and traditions if they understand that changes in these will result in schools being truly standards-based. Although such schools would be very different from those they attended themselves (think factory system on an agricultural calendar), these schools would be based on the standards they promoted so hard during the latter part of last century and the first part of this.

Best of all, because subjects, courses, and classes are simply vehicles for learning and demonstrating standards, they can be constructed to beguile. Students may vie to get into classes. Which one would you choose: *For the Birds* or *Colorado Rocks* or *Social Statistics and Fantasy Baseball*?

An Example of a Curriculum Based on Mastery

What follows is more detail about how Eagle Rock is an example of a standards-related system. Eagle Rock's approach illustrates what Westerberg and Webb (1997, p. 92) called a "standards-based model." Eagle Rock expresses its graduation requirements (also known as standards or competencies) as documentations of learning. Classes are vehicles students use to work toward and document learning. Classes do not count for credit. The documentations students use to demonstrate mastery are organized to be easily recognizable under typical subject matter headings and other categories, which are specialized to Eagle Rock. Please examine Figure 6.2, the Individualized Learning Plan (ILP). You'll see the following major headings:

AIDS Awareness

Art

Career Development

Environmental Studies

ERS Orientation

ERS Transition

Food Service

Human Performance

Literature

Mathematics

Music

Performance

Personal Growth

Presentations of Learning

Societies and Culture

Technology

Wilderness Experience

World Language

Writing

You'll see subheadings under some of the subject headings, such as Civics, Geography, United States Government, United States History, and World History under Societies and Cultures.

Under each one you'll see one or more ways that students document their learning. Here is an example:

Society and Culture

Geography

___ Physical Geography Project

___ Cultural Geography Project

Students do reports, projects, demonstrations of learning, portfolios, action projects, and journals. They write essays, demonstrate skills, take quizzes, and earn certificates. Only rarely do they get credit for spending time doing something (example: two trimesters as crew leaders in the kitchen for credit in Food Service).

Documentations are judged according to rubrics that delineate what quality looks like on several characteristics at between four and six scoring points. You'll learn more about these in Chapter 8 but, basically, Eagle Rock uses generic rubrics as well as those customized to fit the performance. At the very least, students receive the rubric for their documentation before they begin to work on it. In some situations, they participate in creating the rubric; in others, they create their own rubrics. Mastery on a required documentation leads to earning a credit. *Mastery* is defined as obtaining a *Proficient* or *Exemplary* on the rubric.

Students whose documentation is judged below mastery do not fail. They do not lose a credit. They simply do not—yet—earn a credit. Some students continue to work on improving their documentation, perhaps through independent study or taking another, different class that offers

Figure 6.2 Individualized Learning Plan

STUDENT _____   INDIVIDUALIZED LEARNING PLAN _____

☐ **AIDS Awareness**
— Service Project
— Presentation of Learning

☐ **Art (2 portfolios in any combination)**
— Fine Art/Art History portfolio
— Crafts/Art History Portfolio

☐ **Career Develoment/Lifeskills**
— Interest Portfolio
— Lifeskills Portfolio
— Portfolio of Possibilities

☐ **Environmental Studies (2 issues)**
— Environmental Issue:
— Composition or Presentation
— Environmental Action project

☐ **ERS Orientation**
— Presentation: 8 + 5 = 10
— Group Work Journal Entries
— Wilderness Prep

☐ **ERS Transition**
— Food Service Skills
— Kitchen Safety Sanitation Quiz
— Keyboarding
— Student Success Skills
— Aikido

☐ **Food Service**
— Two Trimesters Crew Leader
— Prepared Meals – Last Trimester (2)

☐ **Human Performance**
— Personal Health /Fitness Portfolio
— Activities Presentation
— First Aid & CPR Certification
— Aquatic Skills

☐ **Literature**
— Literature Discussion Skills
— Partcipant (4)
— Leader (2)

☐ **Mathematics**
— Portfolios (6)

☐ **Music**
— Project – Music History
— Project – Music Theory
— Presentations (4)
— Performances (Band/Choir)

☐ **Performance**
— Public Performances (1)
— Rehearsal Periods (1)

☐ **Personal Growth**
— Portfolio I
— Portfolio II
— Presentation
— Peer Mentor

☐ **Presentations of Learning**
— Trimester ___   Trimester ___
— Trimester ___   Trimester ___
— Trimester ___   Trimester ___

☐ **Science**
— Portfolios (4)

☐ **Service Learning**
— Portfolio
— Legacy Project
— Public Service Presentation

☐ **Societies & Culture**
— Civics
— Community Action & Education Project
— Geography
  — Physical Geography Project
  — Cultural Geography Project

— United States Government
— Democracy Project
— International Issues Project
— Domestic Issues Project
— United States History
— Political Theory Project
— Power Relations Project
— Growth & Transition Project
— Technological Evolutions Project
— World History
— Political Theory Project
— Power Relations Project
— Growth & Transition Project
— Technological Evolutions Project

☐ **Technology**
— Multimedia Presentation
— Electronic Resource Portfolio

☐ **Wilderness Experience**
— Wilderness POL
— Reflection Paper
— Service Projects

☐ **World Language**
— Language:
— Portfolio Level 1
— Portfolio Level 2

☐ **Writing**
— Autobiography (POL packet)
— Creative Writing (lit class if poss.)
— Review (book/movie/CD)
— Essay of Explanation
— Essay of Explanation in Lit Class
— Persuasive Essay
— Early Career Research Project
— Late Career Research Project

NOTE: The ILP is not the IEP (or Individualized Education Plan) that is used in Special Education classes. Every student must achieve Eagle Rock's ILP requirements. What varies are the different ways students learn and demonstrate their learning.

a chance to work on that requirement. Never do Eagle Rock students have to retake the same class.

Only when a documentation reaches *Proficient* or *Exemplary* on a rubric does a student get a credit, a check-mark indicating accomplishment of a documentation. Only when all documentations are accomplished does a student receive a check in the subject area box. Only when all boxes are checked does a student petition to graduate.

Rubrics work because instructors share them and student work with each other, calibrating their concept of quality. One of the tools they use is the Tuning Protocol (see Easton, 2004d, pp. 237–244).

Figure 6.2 is, therefore, Eagle Rock's one-page curriculum. It simultaneously serves three purposes:

1. It expresses the curriculum;

2. It's a planning tool for students to use to aim toward graduation and for instructors to use to plan classes; and

3. It's a record of student mastery, a transcript.

Students carry it around with them. Some post it above their beds. Graduates-to-be laminate it and mark their accomplishments on it. They regularly check the official document in a binder on the registrar's desk to see if somehow, magically, they've gotten some of the requirements checked off. Eagle Rock believes that curriculum should be portable and in perpetual draft state; the next version will, perhaps, be pocket-size.

This one-page curriculum is elaborated on in a curriculum guide that contains a page or more for each of the subjects, specifying in more detail what is meant by the subject, what the documentations might look like, and how they will be evaluated. Even students have copies of this curriculum guide. Eagle Rock's is a transparent system.

What you have probably already noticed is that content is not specified. The Franco-Prussian War is not listed under world history, for example. Nor is biology listed under science. Although there is more detail in the curriculum guide, the guide does not get to the level of specific content. Eagle Rock staff members believe that specific content should be up to the instructor and students, as a group and individually. In this way, students can pursue their passions (and instructors can teach them), making room for courses such as those you read about in the beginning of this chapter. Very few students will get to the Franco-Prussian War, but all will get to significant events in world history during their learning time at Eagle Rock.

Here's an example of how the system works. Civics Standard 1 from the Colorado Model Content Standards (2007) says, "Students understand the purposes of government, and the basic constitutional principles of the United States republican form of government." At Eagle Rock, students document their mastery of that content standard by creating a democracy project in any number of different classes. Many students may do so by participating in Close Up, a trip to Washington, D.C., that occurs after students have studied the Declaration of Independence, the Constitution, the Bill of Rights, the Federalist Papers, and other historical papers. Close Up is sponsored by a foundation that works to promote "nonpartisan citizenship education organization. Since its founding in 1970, Close Up has worked to promote responsible and informed participation in the democratic process through a variety of educational programs" (Close Up, 2005).

After their trip, they submit a number of different pieces of documentation—from essays to charts, from research papers to oral presentations—to prove that they have mastered the standard. These are scored according to a variety of rubrics.

Students can work toward and demonstrate mastery of this standard in other ways: by serving an internship, doing independent study, or enrolling in other classes that offer this credit. For example, one course that has been repeated a few times because it turned out to be so popular with students is *Civil?izations*. In it students studied a variety of societies in order to answer the essential question: What is a civilization? They, then, focused on a society of their choice—could be the United States at its founding—to determine to what degree it was civilized.

Some instructors track content through an internal system. For example, one of the mathematics instructors kept track of what individual students were doing according to a grid that featured NCTM content and process indicators. Part of a tracking grid is shown in Table 6.2.

Writing standards are tracked through a portfolio process. Students put drafts and finals of papers into their portfolios and use a cover sheet to keep a record of what they have mastered and what they still have to work on. They reflect on their writing and their progress as a writer. Near graduation, they enjoy a one-on-one conversation with their instructor(s) about themselves as writers.

Table 6.2   Example of a Tracking Grid

Student's Name:_____

Content Standards *Processes*	*Problem Solving*	*Algebra*	*Functions*	*Geometry*
Multiple Sources of Information		X		
Communication				
Reasoning			X	
Mathematical Power			X	

Instructors work with students to accomplish as broad a content base as possible, but they are also willing to let students discover their passions and follow them. There are no guarantees in the Eagle Rock curriculum that all students will come out at the end (factory model) with exactly the same content knowledge and skills . . . and that's all right with the students, their parents, and the staff. Returning students have told staff that what they really got out of Eagle Rock were these three things: problem-solving skills, confidence in themselves as learners, and a thirst for continued learning. They suffered little—or not at all—because they didn't know about the Franco-Prussian War.

The Way the Curriculum Works

The Individualized Learning Plan is the bedrock for all other aspects of curriculum. Instructors use it to plan courses. At instructional meetings, for example, they look at the Individualized Learning Plans of students who will graduate soon. If they discover that soon-to-be-graduates need credit in something that hasn't been offered recently, perhaps world history and writing a review, they'll work together and with students to design a course that will be high interest, interdisciplinary, project based, and service-oriented . . . and offer students a chance to work on those two documentations, as well as any number of other documentations they think might be possible through the course.

In the middle of a trimester, the Director of Curriculum compiles all the course offerings for the next trimester and schedules a Gathering at which instructors can pitch their courses (see the beginning of this chapter). Students work with their advisors, consult their own Individualized Learning Plans to see what they need, and sign up for courses that will allow them to work on credit they need for graduation.

During the courses they take, students usually work on several documentations, sometimes completing them to a level of mastery (*Proficient* or *Exemplary*) and sometimes not. Only if they've reached mastery on a documentation does the instructor forward that information to the Registrar, who records it on the official Individualized Learning Plan, which is also their transcript.

You've probably noticed that the subject of grades has not entered into this discussion. Students do not get grades for their classes or for their work in classes. They either reach *Proficient* or *Exemplary* on their documentations or they don't. Thus, they get credit only when they display a level of work that is at least a B+ (*Proficient*).

You may also have noticed that the subject of grades in another sense has not been a part of this discussion. Students are not divided into grade levels, such as ninth grade, with the expectation that they need to earn a certain number of credits to move to the next grade level. Purposely ungraded, Eagle Rock focuses on students doing work that is good enough for graduation at any point in their career there and is willing to give students the time it takes to complete that work, rather than a year for some of the credits, another year for others, and so on.

This means that a mix of age levels—from 14 (if a student has been admitted earlier than usual) to 21 (if a student has continued to work on graduation beyond the typical age of graduation)—enroll in courses at Eagle Rock.

In Progress

Eagle Rock's curriculum process and documents are all considered "in progress" or in a state of "perpetual draft." Periodically, based on feedback from students and on their own experiences, faculty revise these documents. For example, prior to 2006, faculty reduced the number of documentations, refocusing on "less is more," with the intention of having students do more in-depth work on each of a few, selected documentations. They added a place to record electives, anticipating that, in its next iteration, the ILP will have students take "electives" according to a "major" or "specialty." In reality, all courses are electives because students can choose them and, within them, work on the documentations that interest them and help them graduate.

A Curriculum Caution

Mastery is an absolute. Students either reach it or not. They either get credit or not. In traditional schools, "mastery" is a variable. Students get credit for a range of performances: "A," "B," "C," and "D."

When mastery of standards is an absolute, everything else needs to be variable. All of the conditions under which young people learn—such as time, space, learning choices and styles, documentation choices—must be variables. If we truly wish students to master standards, we must be willing to vary learning conditions (Easton, 2000, p. 50; Easton, 2007, p. 391).

Some schools even stipulate the conditions under which they work best. Founders of The Boston Arts Academy made a deliberate decision not to be a charter school; they wanted to keep BAA as a public school in the Boston Public School System. However, they also wanted to be clear about the conditions that would help them educate young people— particularly students interested in the arts—well:

> The following conditions for learning were identified by [the founders] as critical for promoting schools to become laboratories for educational innovation: The ability to hire and excess staff; annual per pupil lump sum budget, ability to set working conditions, flexibility in adopting the Boston Public Schools Learning Standards and textbooks, diverse and inclusive governance structures, accountability, and being a member of a network of like-minded schools. (*Pilot Network*, n.d.)

BENEFITS OF A STANDARDS-RELATED CURRICULUM

Benefits to Teachers

Teachers who base what they teach on standards rather than required classes are invited to be creative and cross-disciplinary. Rather than hauling out the requirements for a class they've taught too frequently (or the folder that holds the materials they've always used), teachers in a truly standards-based curriculum often begin with a great idea, something they've always wanted to teach or something students have expressed interest in learning. Some may get an idea for a class by looking at standards across the curriculum, but many begin with the great idea and then look for a variety of standards that students can work on through the class.

(Please note that when I talk about "courses" or "classes," I am talking about learning experiences that in other settings might be called units.)

They follow this variation on the backwards-planning process that Wiggins and McTighe (2005) describe:

1. Determine the outcomes (what standards students will be expected to master; how students will demonstrate the standards; how teachers will know students have mastered the standards). At Eagle Rock, outcomes usually take the form of documentations.

2. Think about the rubric categories for each documentation since these are what you'll want to be sure students learn.

3. Consider the essential question (the driving force behind the learning).

4. Consider service learning or project-based learning as a structure for the course (see Chapter 7).

5. Design activities that will help students learn.

6. Gather resources.

7. Initiate the unit in some inviting way (a discrepant event, a problem to be solved, a survey of students, a community need).

It is sometimes hard for teachers who are teaching subjects or courses to understand how learning can be interdisciplinary. They feel limited to covering required content in their subject area or course. How can they fit anything else in? Teachers who are working within a standards-based system, however, can much more easily consider interdisciplinary learning, especially if they begin with a great idea. Most great ideas are naturally interdisciplinary and lend themselves to a number of different explorations. Here are some great ideas that have intrigued Eagle Rock students over the past few years and have led to interdisciplinary courses that feature standards from several different disciplines (Note: *Human Performance* means physical education and health):

Adventure Art (fine arts, art history, essay of explanation, human performance)

Shape o' the World (American history, world history, geography, essay, art, science)

Eco-Challenge (science, human performance)

Simple Solutions to Life's Enduring Questions (art portfolio, essay of explanation, mathematics, service learning)

Waiting for the Barbarians (literature, world history, performance, music theory)

8 + 5 = Sustainability (civics, essay, literature, service learning)

Over the River and Through the Woods (service learning, environmental science, human performance)

"The Idea of Order Beyond the Genius" (from "The Idea of Order at Key West" by Wallace Stevens) (essay of literary analysis, creative writing, essay of opposing ideas, literature, fine art portfolio, art history)

Keep Home Alive (essay of literary analysis, performance, hypothesis related to history, historical event, current events for U.S. and the world)

Artnatomy (science, fine art, art history)

Paradigm Shift Ahead (creative writing, literature, geography, comparing cultures, personal growth portfolio)

Women in the Wilderness (human performance, literature, essay writing, history)

(Un)Natural Disasters (science portfolio, world history, geography, essay writing)

It is challenging to create new courses or units on a regular basis, but it is also invigorating, even rejuvenating. And, of course, some classes that are especially successful with students can be repeated. Teachers who are creating courses based on standards soon learn that they do not have to know everything about the subject(s) of the course. In fact, it is better if they *don't* know everything and, like the students, are curious. Those who believe that teachers are the ones who need to have all the answers may not be comfortable developing interdisciplinary curriculum based on big ideas and standards in other disciplines.

Some teachers would argue that interdisciplinary curriculum is hard to create and manage. It is hard, but it's worthwhile in terms of learning and teaching. Schools that are moving toward more interdisciplinary work should do so slowly—one new unit at a time, for example—rather than revamping the whole curriculum at once. Like all significant change, developing interdisciplinary curriculum based on big ideas and a mix of standards should happen over time. Celebrate one unit at a time.

Faculties making the move toward more interdisciplinary work should also understand that no one perfect model exists; rather, there are a variety of models for interdisciplinary learning. Interdisciplinary learning, based on big ideas and standards, occurs when one teacher stretches the learning in her class beyond her own subject. For example, an English teacher decides that learning about the Revolutionary War is essential for appreciating a novel about that period. Elementary school teachers who teach a variety of subjects are ideally situated for implementing an interdisciplinary approach.

Interdisciplinary learning may happen best in secondary schools when two teachers decide to teach the same content at the same time (parallel curriculum)—perhaps one from a science point of view and another from a mathematics point of view. Teachers in schools with block schedules and team teaching can take advantage of these innovations to design inter-disciplinary curricula. Some schools incorporate interdisciplinary studies through a theme week during which all classes address the same, big topic. Sometimes theme weeks occur as sessions between quarters or semesters.

Benefits for Students

One of the most obvious benefits of standards-based curriculum is that it makes possible the type of course described at the beginning of this chapter and in the preceding section. Students get jazzed about learning. They race to sign up for such courses. They know their teachers will be as excited as they are.

Amanda, a current student, described seat-time literally: "Well, first of all," she said in answer to a question about seat-time, "there is absolutely no seat-time. Most of the time you are out and about doing things or having a really juicy discussion in class and it takes up all the class time."

Another benefit begs restatement. Students know what is expected—not only from a course, but from them in terms of requirements. They know they have to do work that demonstrates mastery of these requirements (standards, competencies). There is no "hidden ball trick" to the curriculum. The curriculum is transparent; in fact, students have copies of the single-sheet multipurpose ILP as well as the curriculum book.

Students know there is no one, right way to work through the curriculum. Students have lots of choices, not only about the classes they take but how they learn within classes and how they document their learning. They have a sense of ownership for the curriculum, a feeling that they can control their own learning. The result is that they become engaged in their own learning—a need that struggling (and other) students have.

According to many graduates, their diplomas mean something. They stand for real learning, not just survival. Graduates who failed before have mastered high expectations. They are proud of themselves as learners because they were held to and lived up to standards.

Some Eagle Rock students remember their previous schooling. Amanda recalled, "In my three years of public high schools I didn't learn as much as I have these past six months here. You just don't learn much when you are not doing things 'hands on' or with others. Instead of having a packet given to me and studying for tests on things I eventually forget, I focus on things that matter to me. I don't forget them." Jeremy, the graduate you met earlier, says, "The traditional system applies mostly to schools that have many students and offers a consistent, easy way to promote to higher grades or graduation." The traditional system is a management system, not a learning system. Jeremy adds, "This type of system finds and celebrates those intelligent students who are 'test takers' and fails to identify those intelligent students who are not 'test takers.'" Karolee, a staff member, commented, "Students take charge of their own learning by realizing that it's not all about tests they have to pass for someone else; it's really about their own learning." Dan, a staff member, adds, "I think it's great that we expect students to take ownership over their own learning. This can occur in a learning experience where students may be pursuing entirely different graduation requirements in the same class."

Brianna, a graduate, focused on the creativity the system allowed her:

It allows the student to be more creative in their learning, how and what they want to learn. I believe that the medical field would never have become an opportunity for me if [it weren't for] the wonderful teachers who exposed me to the human body through art, mathematics, and science classes.

Karolee claimed that the benefits of the system are that "students learn in a variety of ways, and schools and teachers recognize and provide avenues for those ways."

Still, students and staff acknowledge problems. Jeremy cited the subjectivity of a rubric as opposed to single answer multiple-choice tests. "Tests have definite answers; there are true and false, rather than new and creative answers." He also remarked that a school allowing students to document mastery of competencies is going to "graduate with the same credentials as other graduates but with less knowledge and proficiency in some areas than other graduates. As the system intends, each student learns what he or she wants and displays knowledge of all the study areas to earn graduation. But, all graduates are not exactly the same." Dan said, "Students want to stay here too long. They need to get on with their lives. They get too focused on their learning and forget to work toward graduation."

Amanda and Kirk, current students, chimed in: "It takes longer, but I learn a lot more. It's harder when you have to do the real work, not just sit there." Michael, a staff member, stated that there are still problems with the standards-based system as Eagle Rock applies it, but "it's still a giant leap in the right direction: graduation by competency or proficiency."

A FEW MORE EXAMPLES

Other schools have taken a standards-based route toward promotion or graduation; some of them are only partially there but trying. For example,

Poland Regional High School in Maine uses a "standards-based grading system. First, teachers start by establishing the standards, or the essential skills and knowledge that students must achieve in order to receive credit. Final, or semester, grades indicate the degree to which students have mastered the stated standards" (Poland Regional High School, 2007). This high school is, in fact, paying attention to the Standards for Accreditation of the New England Association of Schools and Colleges: "Teachers shall base their classroom assessment procedures on clearly stated expectations for student learning. . . . Specific learning criteria based on specific expectations for student learning shall be the basis for grading and reporting . . ." (Poland Regional High School).

Amy Biehl High School, an inner-city school in Albuquerque, New Mexico, is a member of the Coalition of Essential Schools, as is Poland. It bases its curriculum on a "thematic approach across subject areas. We teach students to apply and demonstrate skills and knowledge to analyze and address community needs. Through service, students are challenged to play meaningful roles in their communities . . ." (Amy Biehl High School, 2007). New Mission High School in Roxbury, Massachusetts, also a Coalition school, features a standards-based mathematics curriculum that focuses on mathematical modeling, mathematical proof, and problem-solving. According to an article in *Horace,* the school is still working "on balancing the breadth and depth of the mathematics program" (Gina, 2004, p. 3).

The venerable Central Park East Secondary School in New York City requires for graduation oral defense of fourteen competencies in a portfolio. These fourteen are:

1. Post-graduate plan

2. Autobiography

3. School/community service and internship

4. Ethics and social issues

5. Fine arts and aesthetics

6. Mass media

7. Practical skills

8. Geography

9. Second language/dual language

10. Science and technology

11. Mathematics

12. Literature

13. History

14. Physical challenge (Cushman, 1993, p. 5)

Schools that belong to other national reform networks are also active in advocating for meaningful alternatives to the Carnegie unit, seat-time, and grades. Check out the ATLAS Communities (n.d.), for which the Coalition was a founding partner. The philosophy called the Paideia Plan (Adler, 1982; Paideia Plan, 2006) is active in a number of schools that support interdisciplinary unit planning based on standards. Also check out schools incorporating the ideas of Expeditionary Learning Outward Bound (ELOB, n.d.). These schools are strongly engaged in project-based learning that is multidisciplinary and oriented toward self-discovery. Foxfire is another network that focuses on experiential education based on standards rather than seat-time and credits. You will probably find schools in your area or region that are working with these networks to make learning more engaging for students.

CONCLUSION

It is natural and right that school communities should ask what they want their students to know and be able to do. This chapter has addressed how school communities might answer that question, with the result being a set of personalized standards related to national, state, and district standards. School communities must also seek answers to the question, "What will we do to help students know and do what we value?" The answers to this question are addressed in the next chapter, which is focused on instruction. Finally, school communities must ask and answer this question: "How will we know students know and are able to do what we value?" The answers to this question are the basis of the third chapter in this sequence, Chapter 8.

SO WHAT

Think about a young person you know—a relative, your own child or grandchild, a neighbor, a child in your school or district. Write that child's name on a piece of paper and under it write this starter:

When _____ graduates from high school, I want to be sure he or she knows and can do the following.

Then list five (only five) critical learnings worthy of this child's time and effort in school. Reflect on what you wrote.

NOW WHAT

Curriculum reform isn't easy. In fact, the ideas in this chapter are probably both the hardest to implement and the most worthwhile (in comparison to those in other chapters). Basing curriculum on standards and being willing to change conditions for learning so that all students master essential learnings challenge any school. Use the following chart to help you analyze the barriers and boosters in your system: the forces against and for the multitude of changes that come with a truly standards-based system (see Table 6.3).

Table 6.3   Boosters and Barriers

Aspects to Consider	Boosters (Forces For)	Barriers (Forces Against)
Students following their interests		
No grades, GPA, or class rank		
Promotion/graduation according to mastery of standard		
Adapting state and district standards		
School-specific standards		
Ungradedness (clusters of grades as "numbered year-in-school") rather than decisions after each nine months of school		
No letter grades; only mastery or "not yet"		
State seat-time requirements		
College admissions		
Lecture and tests		
No failure		
Not covering the curriculum		
Less is more		
Documentations of learning		
Use of rubrics		
Mastery (what it is and how to recognize it)		
Retention in a grade		
"In progress" curriculum, and so on		
Adapting some of the conditions for learning (time, for example)		

7

"How Do You Get Them to Learn?"

Innovative Instructional Strategies Help Students Learn

At first, I thought that this would be a very short chapter because, of course, the answer to the question in the title is that no one, really, gets students to learn but the students themselves. Much has been written about motivation, both intrinsic and extrinsic, but students choose to learn. They also choose not to learn.

Nevertheless, schools can create conditions that are conducive to learning, and one way to do so is through instructional strategies. It helps me to think about instruction as the intersection between the student and the content. The triangle in Figure 7.1 represents this relationship.

Part of what a teacher does is to help negotiate the content for the students. Another way to put it is that teachers know students and they know content, and they help their students find personal meaning in the content. These negotiations are the heart of pedagogy or instruction.

Figure 7.1   The Instructional Triangle

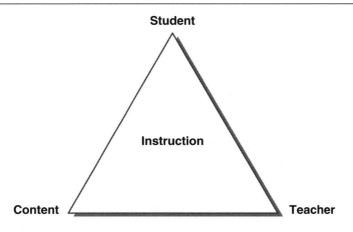

THE INSTRUCTIONAL IMPACT OF PREVIOUSLY MENTIONED STRATEGIES

I have described in previous chapters several strategies that make a difference for struggling students. These strategies are also powerful in terms of instruction. They can affect the relationship between students and content; they can be mediated by teachers.

Choice and Accountability

Isabel spoke for a lot of struggling students when she said, "If I don't have choices and I have to do something I don't like I won't put any effort into it." Haleigh claimed, "The more options I have, the more possibilities there are that there will be something I WANT TO DO!" As Danny, a student, said, "If people feel no control over a system, then they can easily 'check-out.'" Jason spoke bluntly, "They [choices] are really important to me because when I was in jail I had no choices, so now I value them."

The words *choice* and *accountability* go together. Students realize that, having made a choice, they are accountable for the results. Sevi said, "Choices require responsibility and in my experience the more responsibility I have the more responsible I become. It is important for me to see the effect my choices have so I can begin to see how my choice affects my life." Ana remarked, "Choices are opportunities to direct my own life. I think . . . knowing we have the choice in our lives to succeed or fail is essential to learning responsibility."

Choices help students learn about themselves. Only by making choices do students learn about making choices. Amanda said, "It's very important to have people around me I can talk to about the choices I have and what I need to learn about making choices." Choices help students gain confidence. Christian claimed that making choices and seeing how they work out makes him more responsible and the more responsible he is able to feel, the more he "build[s] up his confidence." At first, students are a little afraid of making choices; it is foreign to them. Cynthia, an instructor, remarked, "Some students are stumped by the fact that they have to make choices. Blooming and growth begin when students embrace the choices put before them." "Teenagers want to be independent," Heidi said, "and choices help students gain a sense of independence." A staff member, Lan, spoke up about her own learning: "I like having choice, and I like being coached or assisted with seeing what the consequences of my choices are."

Choices extend learning. Ashley said, "The more I am in control of my own choices, the further I am willing to take my own learning. I'm willing to push further and learn more." Sarah, an intern, agreed: "Once I buy in to my own choice, then I am in a better place to learn." Another intern, Jenna, claimed, "Choices are a good way to personalize education. What you've chosen becomes your personal learning path. You've elected to follow it."

Teachers like choice for themselves. As Jill, an intern, said, "I like having the choice of how to teach math. That way if one approach doesn't work, I can try to find an approach that does." Students like observing how the adults in their lives make choices and appreciate it when these adults share their processes. "I want to know what different choices teachers have," said Sia, "and why they chose to do what they do." Jimmy, another instructor, said, "Choices have allowed me to focus energy where I believe it needs to go. It increases my accountability—because I chose it. I put more energy into my choices."

What choices can teachers *choose* to offer? Meghan said, "I like to choose whether or not to be engaged, the type of assessment I'll use to prove I've learned, and what is important to learn within a subject." Coral Ann talked about learning style choices: "Deciding the ways I learn best—whether visually, orally, or through reading—choosing the ways to learn that suit me the best is very important and so is being put in an environment that honors that way of learning." In summary, teachers can offer choices in many areas:

- Choice of class or unit from among a variety of offerings
- Choice within a class of the particular aspect of the subject they are going to pursue (their passion)
- Choice of how they are going to learn (reading, interviewing, using the Internet or appropriate software, researching)
- Choice of how they are going to document learning (provide a demonstration, write a research paper, teach someone else, take a test, perform a skit, etc.)
- Choice of the categories and quality indicators for a rubric to judge their work
- Choice of how they'll work—alone or with others
- Choice regarding how they are going to make use of the expertise and advice offered by adults

- Choice of how they will get help when they need it
- Decision about how to use their time . . . and whether they'll need extra time
- Decision about where they'll work—in the library, in a classroom, outside, in a study hall, at home
- Decision about how they'll get feedback about their work
- Choice about how they'll improve their work
- Decision about how they will share or publish their work
- Choice of how they will reflect on their work and give feedback to the instructor about their work (adapted from L. B. Easton, 2002, p. 145)

Choice can be tricky. Should students have total freedom to choose? "Sometimes that works," according to Jen, an instructor, "but students usually like a framework within which to make their choices. Total freedom can be chaos." Robert, head of the school, suggests, "Some amount of choice is essential as is some amount of non-choice. Students need to understand the reality of both situations and know what to do." Michael, another staff member, said, "There should be some limit-setting in that you have to perform within this window of opportunity but providing a range of ways or means is empowering." Katie, a student, worried about having "too many choices, and no one takes advantage of options."

What if students just say "no"? According to Sia, "I like the choice to say no." To what extent should teachers intervene? Students believe that "it depends on how big and important the issue is and what kind of relationship the student and teacher have." "Ultimately," Coral Ann said, "the teacher has to let the student say no and then deal with the consequences. Otherwise the student will never learn."

Voice

You have already encountered this saying in this book: "You have no right to no opinion." This much-used aphorism goes a long way to support voice. Amanda stated, "The concept of students having voice has created a standard for our instructors. They definitely push to get participation from their students. They don't push in a bad way, though; it is a very warming and welcoming process."

Having voice means that "you are respected as a learner," said Sia.

Voice helps in cultural and personal ways, too. Brizeida said, "Having a voice is very important to me since in my culture it is something that isn't practiced, at least by women." As Lan, an instructor, said, "Having a voice is important—it helps me acknowledge who I am. Being heard, however, is even more important." Kelley stated, "Having a voice builds confidence."

Sevi addressed how a community benefits from the voices of its members: "The more I feel my input is valued the more I value the opinions of others. At ERS there are many opportunities for student voice, from hiring staff to dealing with community issues." Edwin agreed, "To me having a voice is helping, contributing to a decision that may affect my life." Beth, an instructor, added, "Allowing voice promotes a diverse community of ideas." Another instructor, Cynthia, said, "Having voice helps us understand our similarities and respect our differences."

Having voice affects learning. Ana maintains, "I don't have the tendency to become discouraged simply because I can't or won't be heard." Robert, head of school, claimed, "Absent a voice, students go passive, and that's not good for learning." Michael, a staff member, commented, "If it's clear in the classroom that my voice matters—and the teacher has to show evidence that my voice is a contribution—then my mind, body, and spirit are really engaged. I learn more and I hope I better contribute to other people's learning." Rob declared, "This is our education and, if something isn't working, we are encouraged to do what we can to fix the situation by trying to find something better." Dustin said, "Voicing my opinions has a good effect on what I do because it helps me to be able to think."

Feedback is one aspect of voice. Students are accustomed to one-way feedback; they have gotten it (sometimes in quantity) from their teachers. However, it is just as important to them to have a way to give feedback to each other and to their teachers. Students appreciate the opportunity to offer feedback to teachers about how well their learning experiences are working for them. Bern claimed, "I am more engaged because I feel my feedback makes a difference in my education." Jen, a teacher, likes the fact that feedback to staff will be heard and acted upon: "It makes students feel empowered to influence their learning experiences. Feedback is an organic process."

Feedback has an impact on teachers. As an intern, Meghan, said, "It's important to get students to tell you what they need. Seventy percent of my job is learning how to listen." Listening is important for everyone, actually. According to Katie, "It is the listening that needs to change." Amanda calls for "people who listen to listen. Not to listen to speak."

Voice is part of a learning community in a variety of ways, both formal and informal. Formal gatherings or community meetings that provide for dialogue and discussion are one way to provide voice. Classroom structures such as check-in, class meetings, questionnaires, and surveys help to provide voice. Classroom norms also help. The proposal process described earlier is an important formal mechanism for voice. As important as these formal strategies are, the informal ones are almost more important. Being approachable helps students risk saying something in a classroom. "Hanging out" or being available is another informal strategy for providing students voice.

Like choice, voice can be troublesome, especially when people have the expectation that what they say will be acted upon. As Jenna said, "Voice can lead to a sense of entitlement, too." Dustin addressed this reality: "I have a voice in everything I do, although my voice isn't always used."

It may be very hard for educators to hear feedback from their students, especially if they feel that they are in charge and students should do what they ask. Yet, if they conceptualize learning as a partnership between themselves and students, they'll recognize that two-way feedback is very important to the process.

Some people are uncomfortable with feedback. In a community that values voice, feedback is inevitable, but it doesn't have to be hurtful. People can learn to give feedback gently and so it can be heard. They can give feedback by asking "What if" questions, for example. They can personalize feedback by using "I," not "you." They can give feedback in writing or privately. Those who are uncomfortable can gradually encourage more direct forms of feedback.

Transparency

Of course, young people can have choice and voice only if they know what's going on. If they don't understand the culture or the structure of a school—including curriculum requirements and assessment practices—they are less likely to feel they can voice a concern or make a choice. They are less likely to speak up for themselves. They are more likely to fade away from a system that is opaque to them.

Power, Control, Authority

The result of choice, voice, and transparency is a feeling of power, control, and authority, which is missing in a lot of schools. Young people who have struggled are especially likely to feel powerless. Someone else has controlled their education. They feel they have no authority over their own learning.

Sevi puts it well: "My teachers' willingness to put my education in my hands helps me care about my learning, for it is mine and determined by my passions." A teacher commented, "It's very important for students to know that they are not just receptacles for learning." Ashley felt more confident about herself as a learner because, "They treat me as an equal." Jonathan commented, "Voice is power."

Passion

Amanda said it well: "Instructors who find what they do absolutely fascinating help us learn. If teachers are very excited to teach what they teach, that makes learning fun." Hae-John, a student teacher and later an intern, remarked that instruction is "taking into account the student and planning to their passions." The curriculum process described in the previous chapter is one way teachers can infuse their teaching with passion. The choices that students make is one way they can pursue their passions.

WHAT WE REALLY WANT: SELF-DIRECTED LEARNERS

Choice and accountability; voice; transparency; power, control, and authority; and passion. These are all very nice. But, to what end? The answer to that question is this: What we really want is self-directed learning. A recent regional needs assessment by the Northwest Regional Educational Laboratory (2002) states that

> "helping students become self-directed learners who take responsibility for their own academic performance" was ranked near the top of identified priorities by 75 percent of teachers, 83 percent of principals, and 83 percent of superintendents in the region. This was especially important for teachers at schools that were identified as "low-performing" under the accountability requirements of NCLB.

NWREL provides a good definition of the "self-directed learner": According to Abdullah (2001), "self-directed learners are 'responsible owners and managers of their own learning process'" (as cited in NWREL, 2002):

> Such individuals have the skills to access and process the information they need for specific purposes. Self-directed learning integrates self-management (management of the context, including social setting, resources, and actions) with self-monitoring (the process whereby learners monitor, evaluate, and regulate their cognitive learning strategies). It is important to note that being a self-directed learner is a trait or disposition we want students to develop, rather than a laundry list of observable behaviors we wish students to exhibit. (p. 1)

NWREL's (2002) report, *Developing Self-Directed Learners*, lists a number of traits of such learners:

- They are self-motivated, which can be understood as "situational reasons why students choose whether or not to engage in academic tasks." In some cases, self-directed learners must balance extrinsic factors with intrinsic factors.
- They have a goal orientation.
- They evidence some self-efficacy.
- Their locus of control is internal (related to factors they can control).
- They engage in metacognition.
- They are self-regulated.

One of the instructional strategies NWREL lists as effective in encouraging self-directed learners has already been described: student choice and responsibility. The other, project learning and collaboration on results, is one of the strategies described below.

The National Research Council (NRC), in *How People Learn: Brain, Mind, Experience, and School,* describes self-directed learners as those who (1) work on their learning even when there is no external pressure to perform, (2) "seek and create novel challenges, and (3) have an innate need to solve problems" (NRC, 2000).

Instructional Strategies That Encourage Self-Direction

A Constructivist Theory and Related Strategies

Constructivism is a theory of learning, not an instructional strategy. It addresses how learners process information. It most directly contrasts with the behaviorist "view of the learner as a passive recipient whose learning is automatically shaped by practice and reinforcements" (Mayer, 1998, p. 360). Most educators are familiar with stimulus-response (S-R). According to the behaviorist theory, the learner is trained through rewards and punishments to give correct responses. According to constructivist theory, on the other hand, the learner is "an active processor of information" (Mayer, 1998, p. 360).

Briefly, constructivism as a theory of pedagogy "assumes all knowledge is constructed from previous knowledge" (NRC, 2000, p. 10). Interestingly, previous knowledge can be obtained in a variety of ways, from lecture to direct experience. Also, previous knowledge can be wrong. Part of teaching according to constructivist theory involves paying "attention to the incomplete understandings, the false beliefs, and the naïve renditions of concepts that learners bring with them to a given subject" (p. 10). In fact, "if students' initial ideas and beliefs are ignored, the understandings they develop can be very different from what the teacher intends" (p. 10).

The children's book *Fish Is Fish* (Lionni, 1970) describes how a fish understands the world it cannot see from under the water. The fish enlists the help of a tadpole who becomes a frog. As a frog, it returns to the pond periodically to describe what it has seen. The fish interprets the frog's descriptions according to what it knows from under the water. For example, the fish conceptualizes birds as fish with wings. The frog unwittingly helps the fish create false beliefs about the world outside the pond. If there were any fish teachers around, they would need to begin with the fish's initial understandings of that world in order to help the fish correct them.

Understanding how the brain works is fundamental to understanding cognitive theory. Caine and Caine (1991) are among the many educators and researchers who have explored brain-based learning (others include Fogarty, Hart, Jensen, Kovalik, Sousa, Sylwester, and Wolfe). Caine and Caine describe what the brain can do, as follows: It has

- "the ability to detect patterns and to make approximations;
- "phenomenal capacity for various types of memory;
- "the ability to self-correct and learn from experience by way of analysis of external data and self-reflection and
- "an inexhaustible capacity to create." (Caine & Caine, 1991, p. 3)

Brooks and Brooks (1993) have developed cognitive and constructivist theories and brain-based learning into a guide for classrooms. Here is how they contrast traditional classrooms with those adhering to a constructivist theory:

Table 7.1   A Look at School Environments

Traditional Classrooms	*Constructivist Classrooms*
Curriculum is presented part to whole with emphasis on basic skills.	Curriculum is presented whole to part with emphasis on big concepts.
Strict adherence to fixed curriculum is highly valued.	Pursuit of student questions is highly valued.
Curricular activities rely heavily on textbooks and workbooks.	Curricular activities rely heavily on primary sources of data and manipulative materials.
Students are viewed as "blank slates" onto which information is etched by the teacher.	Students are viewed as thinkers with emerging theories about the world.
Teachers generally behave in a didactic manner, disseminating information to students.	Teachers generally behave in an interactive manner, mediating the environment for students.
Teachers seek the correct answer to validate student learning.	Teachers seek students' points of view in order to understand students' present conceptions for use in subsequent lessons.
Assessment of student learning is viewed as separate from teaching and occurs almost entirely through testing.	Assessment of student learning is interwoven with teaching and occurs through teacher observations of students at work and through student exhibitions.
Students primarily work alone.	Students primarily work in groups.

SOURCE: Figure 2.1 (p. 17), "A Look at School Environments," *In Search of Understanding: The Case for Constructivist Classrooms,* by J. G. Brooks & M. G. Brooks, 1993, 1999. Alexandria, VA: ASCD. Used with permission. The Association for Supervision and Curriculum Development is a worldwide community of educators advocating sound policies and sharing best practices to achieve the success of each learner. To learn more, visit ASCD at www.ascd.org.

Perhaps you detect some similarities between what students and staff said in the first part of this chapter and what Brooks and Brooks describe as a constructivist classroom. Brooks and Brooks also describe constructivist teachers (see Table 7.2).

Again, I'm imagining that, as you read these twelve descriptions of teacher actions, you thought about earlier chapters and students' comments from the first part of this chapter.

Table 7.2   Constructivist Teachers

---

1. Constructivist teachers encourage and accept student autonomy and initiative.

2. Constructivist teachers use raw data and primary sources, along with manipulative, interactive, and physical materials.

3. When framing tasks, constructivist teachers use cognitive terminology such as "classify," "analyze," "predict," and "create."

4. Constructivist teachers allow student responses to drive lessons, shift instructional strategies, and alter content.

5. Constructivist teachers inquire about students' understandings of concepts before sharing their own understandings of those concepts.

6. Constructivist teachers encourage students to engage in dialogue, both with the teacher and with one another.

7. Constructivist teachers encourage student inquiry by asking thoughtful, open-ended questions and encouraging students to ask questions of each other.

8. Constructivist teachers seek elaboration of students' initial responses.

9. Constructivist teachers engage students in experiences that might engender contradictions to their initial hypotheses and then encourage discussion.

10. Constructivist teachers allow wait time after posing questions.

11. Constructivist teachers provide time for students to construct relationships and create metaphors.

12. Constructivist teachers nurture students' natural curiosity through frequent use of the learning cycle method.

SOURCE: From chapter 9, *In Search of Understanding: The Case for Constructivist Classrooms*, by J. G. Brooks & M. G. Brooks, 1993, 1999. Alexandria, VA: ASCD. Used with permission. The Association for Supervision and Curriculum Development is a worldwide community of educators advocating sound policies and sharing best practices to achieve the success of each learner. To learn more, visit ASCD at www.ascd.org.

I find the following instructional planning guide by Gagnon and Collay (2006) helpful in designing learning based on the theories of constructivism and brain-based learning. They recommend use of the following process by the teacher, who:

1. "Designs a Situation that describes the purpose, determines a topic, and decides an assessment for student learning;

2. "Organizes Groups of students, materials, and furniture to facilitate meaning making;

3. "Builds a Bridge between what students already know and what they are expected to learn by describing students' developmental level, socioeconomic circumstances, and cultural background, surfaces their preconceptions, and makes connections to their lives;

4. "Crafts a Task for students to accomplish that anticipates questions from students as they engage in tasks, considers responses to these questions so that students will sustain thinking, and describes how students are learning by making social meaning during tasks;

5. "Arranges an Exhibit for students to demonstrate the results of their collaborative thinking by producing artifacts as a result of their learning, making presentations of these artifacts, and offering explanations about how they made social meaning; and

6. "Invites Reflection by students on their process of thinking during the learning episode through feelings in their emotional and physical responses, images in their sensory representations, and languages in their consideration of shared and common meanings." (pp. 4–6)

These six steps—Situation, Groups, Bridge, Task, Exhibit, Reflection—help teachers design a unit or class based on a constructivist theory of knowledge.

Experiential Education

Experiential education offers another pathway into learning for struggling students. Although it is often associated with outdoors or wilderness education—indeed with therapeutic outdoors education—experiential learning offers important considerations for school-based learning. The Association for Experiential Education offers a number of resources and hosts national and international conferences that are attended by classroom teachers as well as wilderness instructors.

Experiential education, as defined by Stevens and Richards (1992), is

the process of actively engaging students in an experience that will have real consequences. Students make discoveries and experiment with knowledge themselves instead of hearing or reading about the experiences of others. Students also reflect on their experiences, thus developing new skills, new attitudes, and new theories or ways of thinking. (n.p.)

Experiential education has been around awhile.

John Dewey (1938) was an early promoter of the idea of learning through direct experience, by action and reflection. This type of learning differs from much traditional education in that teachers first immerse students in action and then ask them to reflect on the experience. In traditional classrooms, teachers begin by setting knowledge (including analysis and synthesis) before students. They hope students will later find ways to apply the knowledge in action. (Stevens & Richards, 1992, n.p.)

There are two keys to experiential education in schools. The first is the experience itself, which usually happens without any introduction, explanation, lecture, or background reading (except for safety purposes). It just happens. It is not always a highly physical activity, such as squeezing through a web of rope on a challenge course. It can be witnessing the debate at a school board meeting, putting together a playground-sized puzzle of the countries of the world, watching birds in the forest, or noticing the rust-colored trees blighted by pine beetles. It can be a data set that results from surveys. It can be witnessing a curious phenomenon in the science lab. It can be working in a homeless shelter. It can even be a game, role-playing situation, or simulation. The important thing is that it's active and real or life-like.

Whatever the experience is, it must be followed by reflection to have any impact. Students reflect personally (perhaps in writing) and then share their reflections. Close behind reflection comes the big question that leads to learning: "Why did that happen?"

Sometimes schools can take advantage of their settings to offer experiential learning opportunities. The School for the Physical City in Manhattan did just that. Amy Biehl High School in Albuquerque, New Mexico, claims that downtown is the school's classroom. Students experience downtown in all of its variety, from museums to cultural centers, from the BioPark to the dance company (Amy Biehl High School, 2007).

At the High School for the Recording Arts in St. Paul, Minnesota, students engage in a real-life experience that leads to significant learning; they run two businesses, Another Level Records and Another Level Entertainment. Students also produce a weekly radio program, "The Fo-Show" (High School for the Recording Arts, 2007). The Met schools, in Providence, Rhode Island, and other urban locations, base learning on internships—a solid example of experiential education (The Met, 2006).

The teacher who wants to use experiential education as a way to capture the interest of struggling students can use many of the planning and teaching and learning strategies that were described in the previous section.

Project–Based Learning

Another instructional strategy that excites students about learning is project-based or problem-based learning. Both of these instructional strategies have links to constructivist theory and experiential education. Teachers at Eagle Rock, particularly Janet Johnson, science teacher, helped to generate a set of characteristics of project-based learning:

- Its focus is a product or outcome toward which the whole class is working—the reason behind the work.
- The product or outcome is worthwhile; it is often, therefore, service-oriented.
- The learning is inquiry-based, related to the problem or to an essential question.
- Project-based learning is naturally interdisciplinary learning; the learning focuses on connections.
- Project-based learning is complex and real; no easy solutions or one-sentence answers.
- Project-based learning is hands-on and experiential.
- Students work in small groups and also have individual learning opportunities. They share their learning with the whole group or other groups.
- They are engaged in the social construction of meaning. No single member of the group has all the information or skills; all of them have some information and some skills, which they offer to the whole group.
- Project-based learning is engaging; it requires planning and decision making on the part of the students, preplanning by the teacher.
- Project-based learning occurs on the application level—consequences, implications, ramifications.
- Project-based learning is beyond content for content's sake.
- Teachers are involved as equal partners in the learning or as coaches.

Many of Janet's classes, such as *For the Birds*, are project-based. Others have included *Gluttons for Punishment* (the project was the science of nutrition and weight control); *Mind, Body, & Spirit* (the project was human physiology, mind-body connection); and *Harmonic Motion* (the project was music and movement).

Service Learning

Marge Piercy's poem,[1] "To Be of Use," helps us remember why service learning is important. She announces:

The people I love the best
Jump into work head first. . . .

In the middle of the poem, she exults:

I love people who harness themselves, an ox to a heavy cart,
Who pull like water buffalo, with massive patience,
Who strain in the mud and the muck to move things forward,
Who do what has to be done, again and again.

At the end of the poem, her words sing:

The pitcher cries for water to carry
And a person for work that is real.

Everyone needs to be of use, as Marge Piercy suggests, and struggling students are no different. They need to feel valued, useful, and important. Perhaps when they asked to do meaningful work, students were told that they were too young, to wait until they were older. Service learning addresses the need to be useful through a variety of serving to learn and learning to serve approaches.

The National Youth Leadership Council defines service learning well:

Picking up trash on a riverbank is *service.* Studying water samples under a microscope is *learning.*

When science students collect and analyze water samples, document their results, and present findings to a local pollution control agency . . . that is *service-learning.*

Service-learning is a teaching method that enriches learning by engaging students in meaningful service to their schools and communities. Young people apply academic skills to solving real-world issues, linking established learning objectives with genuine needs. They lead the process, with adults as partners, applying critical thinking and problem-solving skills to concerns such as hunger, pollution, and diversity. (National Youth Leadership Council, 2007)

Service learning embodies many of the concepts of constructivism, experiential education, and project-based learning . . . with an added focus on learning how to serve and serving others.

Each student at Eagle Rock spends nearly 500 hours a year engaged in some form of service. They are not alone. Several states require service for graduation, and many schools incorporate service into their curriculum or schedule. At Amy Biehl High School in downtown Albuquerque, students complete a variety of service projects each year, leading up to a yearlong, self-designed project their senior year. In fact, at Amy Biehl, students proceed through a sequence of service-related activities leading up to their final project. In ninth grade they engage in the Foundations of Project Citizen; in 10th grade, service is embedded in the curriculum; in 11th grade, students develop a proposal for their senior project; and, finally, in 12th grade, students do their senior project, spending at least six hours per week on it (Amy Biehl High School, 2007).

At Leadership High School in San Francisco students perform 35 hours of community service each year (Leadership High School, 2003). Wednesday afternoons at the Urban Academy in New York City are devoted to community service (Urban Academy, n.d.). The big service project at the Young Women's Leadership Charter School of Chicago is its Chicago River Project. Teachers at YWLCS develop river-based curricula and students become interested in the Chicago River Watershed, "The Everglades of the North." The school works to improve the river (Young Women's Leadership Charter School, n.d.).

Eagle Rock features four types of service learning:

1. Eagleserve

Three times a year—at the beginning of each trimester—staff and students alike perform service together outside Eagle Rock. For two-and-a-half or three days, the entire ERS community works together to serve the greater community. Some examples of EagleServe projects include

- Cleaning up old tin cans from a dump at the Rocky Ridge Music Center
- Painting the Estes Park Museum
- Setting up for and cleaning up after the Scottish/Irish Festival
- Cleaning up the grounds of the MacGregor Ranch Historic Landmark

2. On-Campus service

Students return to their own community at Eagle Rock through on-campus service. Throughout the year, they perform the following:

- Kitchen Patrol (KP): preparing, serving, and cleaning up after meals
- Chores: crews keep the grounds neat and the buildings clean, setting their own tasks and times to accomplish them
- House Clean-Up: house (dormitory) members clean up their own houses during lunch times each day
- Evening Clean-Up: house teams on a rotating basis clean up the major buildings (library, Lodge, gym) at the end of the day
- Specials: students sign up to do special building or grounds clean-up for 45 minutes a day during a time called "Specials"

3. Integrated service learning

Interdisciplinary classes focus on learning through doing service. Students learn academic content while they are doing service for others. Here are some examples:

- Building a playground for Estes Park and learning mathematics and science
- Building a fishing pier for the handicapped for Lake Estes and learning mathematics, science, and work skills
- Building a playground for the town of Lyons and learning civics (through interviewing citizens and officials about the playground) and mathematics and science
- Helping Spanish-speaking students learn their lessons at the local elementary school; refining their own reading and writing skills
- Reading stories to elementary school students; refining their own reading and writing skills
- Collecting data on birds for Cornell University; learning science and environmental science
- Painting a mural in Estes Park and learning history, geography, and art
- Interviewing elders in the community and presenting their stories; learning history, speaking and listening, and writing skills

4. Special projects

Some projects occur on a regular basis. Every holiday season, Eagle Rock students and staff take the holidays to the Pine Ridge Reservation. Beforehand, they have baked cookies, collected food and other goods, and decorated a tree. They have a continuing relationship with families on the reservation and have learned a great deal about their culture and history.

Other projects occur as needed. For example, one wet spring, Estes Park flooded and Harmony House (a home for the families of women who have been abused) was threatened. Eagle Rock spent the night sandbagging the buildings.

The most important type of service in terms of this chapter is the third use: integration of service into academics. Integrated service learning classes usually feature the following components:

1. Student decision making regarding the project; inventorying need, planning and organizing, making or obtaining materials, staffing the project, and training staff—as needed.

2. The activity itself.

3. Reflection on the activity, both individually and as a group.

4. Celebration.

Students are enthusiastic about service. Ashley commented that the highlight of service is, "Learning new things from the people I work with!" Brizeida agreed: "Service learning affects me because it is how I open my mind to learn about a variety of things."

Many like, as Bern did, "the hands-on relationship between you and the project at hand." Haleigh commented, "It's more hands-on and engaging. Also it's different from classes and interesting. It keeps me from being bored. I used to become disengaged and get bored. When I do service projects, I give learning a chance."

For many, service brings the real world into learning. Ryan exulted, "Service has a BIG BIG effect on me. It helps me connect learning to real-world stuff."

For some, altruism is a new experience. Isabel said, "We give and receive. We give our time and effort and we receive the pleasure of knowing we helped someone and the project most likely taught us more than just academics." Amanda stated, "It reminds me some days of how good it is to help other people."

Service helps self-conscious adolescents see something bigger than themselves. Sarah commented, "It opens our eyes to how learning is important to the whole, bigger world."

Head of school, Robert, summarizes the effect of service learning nicely: "When combined with reflection, service learning offers a remarkable opportunity to blend theory and practice. This can help sharpen the mind, broaden awareness, enhance effectiveness and anchor skills. It's a no-brainer!"

Learning Based on Essential Questions

Essential questions lead to authentic work. Students are quick to discern the differences between teacher questions (to which the teacher already knows the answer) and essential questions. Essential questions are big questions without easy answers. The teacher becomes as engaged in seeking answers to the big question as students do; the teacher serves as coach, helping students find resources, shape their hypotheses, and present their learning—often in exhibitions (see Chapter 8).

Grant Wiggins, who worked with the Coalition of Essential Schools in its early years, describes authentic work as work that lets students be real workers: "They can always answer certain questions—about the task's purpose, about the resources needed to carry it out, about what it means to do the task well. They can grasp what is essential about the task, set priorities, make intelligent judgments" (as cited in Cushman, 1989, p. 1). In typical "school work," students seldom know why they're doing the work, other than to get a grade or please the teacher.

As an instructional strategy, asking essential questions opens up all sorts of learning opportunities and is likely to lead to interdisciplinary learning. One famous question asked at Central Park East Secondary School in New York City—"Whose country is it, anyway?"—led to explorations in history, economics, sociology, the arts; the explorations culminated in oral and written presentations. At Eagle Rock, the course *Civil?izations* was based on the essential question, "How civilized are/were our civilizations?" and students explored historical and contemporary civilizations in all of their aspects, including the arts and literature, science, politics, and history. Results were surprising to both the teacher, James, and the students.

An essential question about change led primarily to explorations in science and social studies. Although this question was developed for a five-week course, pursuit of answers could have extended over an entire year. Essential questions can even be about questions, as in this question about AIDS: "What are the questions we need to ask about AIDS?" (Cushman, 1989, p. 7). The question that spurred learning in a course called *(Un)Natural Disasters* was, "Are natural disasters natural?" In "Riverwatch," students pursued the essential question, "What makes a river healthy?"

At Francis W. Parker School in Massachusetts, an essential question each year guides coursework. Here are a few: What is community? (1995–1996); What is balance? (1997–1998); Where are the patterns? (1998–1999); What really matters? (2000–2001); What is unique? What is universal? (2004–2005) (Parker School, n.d.).

Wiggins calls essential questions

> "entry points" to larger questions that can go to the heart of a discipline. Because they take shape as projects, case studies, or simulations, they get students under way quickly, making inquiries that lead to the essential facts and theories the course will cover. And they evoke these abstract and complex issues in a concrete setting with which students are already familiar. (Cushman, 1989, p. 5)

Essential questions are helpful entry points for the other types of instructional strategies discussed in this section. An essential question can emanate from an experience, guide project-based learning, or serve as the basis for service learning.

Critical Attributes of Any Instructional Strategy

No matter which instructional strategies you use—those closely related to a constructivist theory, experiential learning, project-based learning, service learning, or essential questions . . . or your own combination of these— you'll want to be sure to pay attention to the following critical attributes of instruction.

Students as Teachers, Teachers as Students

No matter what strategy teachers use to connect learning and learners, as often as possible students should be teachers. Teachers should also be students—learning about students, their own classrooms, their schools, and their own teaching.

Eagle Rock students teach in a variety of ways. As members of a learning community, they help each other learn. Classrooms feature circular tables so that there is no "back of the classroom" that excuses students from learning. There is also no "front of the classroom" where expertise resides. Students take responsibility for the learning of everyone in a class, sometimes becoming teachers themselves to help others learn.

Eagle Rock students suggest classes to instructors, sometimes working with those instructors to plan classes and even coteaching with them.

They sometimes teach their own classes under supervision from instructors. Jerry, a graduate who went to Thailand and Vietnam on a service-learning scholarship while an Eagle Rock student, returned to campus ready to share what he had learned. He worked with the social studies instructor to create a class that would help others experience living in another culture. Bern—soon-to-graduate—said, "I have also been involved in planning a class that I will coteach. I have helped teach another class. People, especially students, learn best when they are asked to teach."

Seeing teachers as learners also helps students learn. Amanda, for example, says, "Most important, teachers learn from us, and that's one of the reason why they are so good, because they take what they can to learn from the students."

Teaching highlights what students are capable of sharing, not what they lack. Teaching enables learning. Learning enables teaching.

Not Having All the Answers

Students as teachers. Teachers as students. These scenarios suggest that teachers might not always have all the right answers. That's a scary place for teachers who are used to being the experts, the "sages on the stage," the ones who know the right answers (or have them in the back of the teacher's edition of the textbook). Some teachers hesitate to experiment with curriculum and instruction, such as project-based learning, because they are worried that they might not know enough about the subject to "teach" it, or they might get stumped by a question that comes up unexpectedly.

The most freeing statement a teacher can make, freeing to the teacher as well as to students, is, "You know, I don't know the answer to that," followed by this invitation: "Why don't we work together to try to find out?"

Alex described the situation well: "Teachers here make you figure out how to solve problems. In my other high school they made us memorize the solutions to the problems." Christian knows the current jargon: "It's all about problems and unpacking them."

Sia spoke of the effect of teachers who don't know everything: "It's really important to me that teachers show me more of their own learning, how they learn." Amanda claimed, "I like it when teachers are doing most of the work with us."

Rather than as a "sage on the stage," teachers who want to help struggling students might think of themselves as coaches or facilitators of learning.

Flexibility and Persistence

Amanda continued, "Another thing that our teachers are good at is making sure that their students understand what is being said in class; if we don't understand, they will show us a different way to understand until we do. They have a lot of patience and compassion toward their students."

No matter which instructional strategies teachers use, they should mix in a healthy dose of flexibility and persistence. Edwin, a new student, described this aspect of instruction particularly well: "They do not stop until we say we got it. Instead of tests, we have revisions. Revisions really help us get to learn a certain subject." Or, as Ashley said, "They teach it 'til I know I know it!" If they're really good, teachers will "show different sides of the same idea," according to Lan, a staff member. Rob conceded, "Not everyone learns best through alternative teaching, but teachers here are even willing to teach 'the regular way,' if that's what we need."

Dialogue and Discussion

Walk into any school after the warning bell for the start of school has rung. The noise is awesome. Kids, hanging out, are engaged in conversation. They like to talk. Classes offer plenty of discussion opportunities, but few that are truly open. The typical classroom discussion sometimes seems like serial one-way inquisitions. If you were to track the interactions in such a discussion, they would look like this:

Teacher asks a question.

One student responds with right answer.

Teacher asks another question.

Another student responds with right answer.

Repeat.

Brooks and Brooks (1993) call this the "Gatling gun approach to asking and answering questions" (p. 115). In the interest of moving along (covering the curriculum) teachers may advance the topic by calling on students who are most likely to have the right answer. Sometimes those are the students who get their hands up first. What a relief to other students, especially those who have no clue about the answer! For everybody else, the competition to be called on is not worth the effort, so they tune out as soon as they are sure they will not be called upon.

Students are disdainful of this kind of "discussion." "It's a matter of guessing what the teacher wants," Sia declared. "Why bother? If you wait long enough, the teacher will answer her own questions."

Students want real discussion. They want dialogue. They want a "hanging-out," open type of discussion, even a conversation. Discussion and dialogue are counterparts, according to Peter Senge (1990), who wrote in *The Fifth Discipline*, "In a discussion, different views are presented and defended, and . . . this may provide a useful analysis of the whole situation. In dialogue, different views are presented as a means toward discovering a new view" (p. 247). Garmston and Wellman (1999) describe the phenomenon of "group talk" as a shared way of learning (p. 51). They describe dialogue as a way to get to shared understanding, while discussion is a way to get to a decision. Dialogue is convivial; discussion resembles a debate.

Whether it's dialogue, discussion, or plain old conversation, students can learn through conversing—exchanging ideas, opinions, feelings, information, examples, and stories. Constructivists refer to this phenomenon as the social aspect of learning. People make meaning with the help of others. Lev Vygotsky wrote extensively about how "robust knowledge and understanding are socially constructed through talk, activity, and interaction around meaningful problems and tools" (National Research Council, 2000, p. 184). Provocative questions, without single answers, and discussion among all members of a group lead to learning.

Michael, a staff member, praises "scaffolding" as one aspect of social constructivism. Scaffolding is related to Vygotsky's concept of the Zone of Proximal Development, which is the distance between what a child currently knows and what the child learns with the help of others. Learning happens just beyond what students know on their own; scaffolding can help children take the next step, just as real scaffolding helps builders add the next floor of a building.

Scaffolding happens when individuals with different backgrounds, experiences, skills, and knowledge contribute to a discussion, dialogue, or conversation. Others learn from them, and they learn from others. They have scaffolded learning for each other. Teachers can intentionally create mixed groups of students so that each student has something to contribute (an aspect of the cooperative learning); each student's contribution is necessary for the success of whole group's work. Teachers can also intentionally create a scaffolded project that helps students gain new knowledge or skills as they work. Think of the steps of an "I-Search" type of research paper (Macrorie, 1988). In an "I-Search," students decide to research topics of personal interest. As they research the topic, they keep a log of their research processes (their actions, thoughts, feelings, dead-ends, direction changes, etc.). In their final report, students weave entries from their log in with the results of their research. In a sense, they have created their own scaffolding through keeping a log, a process of metacognition that affirmed what they were doing or pointed them in different directions. Teachers can also work individually with students to scaffold their learning through reflecting what students say, checking for understanding, and probing with questions.

Imagine, then, an open discussion, based perhaps on a student's authentic question about a topic. It may even be based on a question the teacher genuinely has—and has no one right answer for. The teacher sits with the students and listens, interjecting only on occasion, letting students discover for themselves what they know and build upon each other's knowledge. Often, teachers discover that points they might have made (or content covered) are brought up by students themselves . . . and are much more meaningful coming from them.

Discussions like these are not free-for-alls, nor are they "free time." They are one of a teacher's set of instructional strategies for helping students build understanding and knowledge. Obviously, deep discussions work well with a constructivist-based instructional strategy, but they also work well with experiential learning, project-based learning, and service learning. Essential questions are often the foundation of such discussion.

Students may need to be helped to engage within the classroom in what they perform so effortlessly in the hallways and cafeteria. They may not trust this "newfangled" type of discussion, having experienced the Gatling gun for so many years. They may wait for the teacher to start the process or ask the first question. They may disregard what other students say. If the question is provocative enough and if the teacher either sits outside the circle at first or remains a listener throughout, students may come to trust the process. If they are already engaged in their own learning and the question is one they brought up, then success is almost guaranteed, especially if the teacher says, "I don't know. Let's talk about it."

Learning Differences and Personalization

Finally, no matter what instructional strategy a teacher employs, the teacher must know enough about individual learning styles to help each student learn. Here are a few lenses for looking at how students learn:

- Gardner's (1993) multiple intelligences: Verbal-linguistic, Logical-mathematical, Spatial, Bodily-kinesthetic, Musical, Interpersonal, Intrapersonal, Naturalist
- McCarthy's (1990) 4MAT System: Four major learning styles (Sensing/Feeling, Watching, Thinking, Doing)
- Sensory preferences—visual, auditory, kinesthetic, or tactile (VAK; or, with reading/writing added, VARK) (VARK, 2006).
- Goleman's (1995) emotional intelligences
- Sternberg's (1994) thinking styles (Mental Self-Government)

- Carbo's (1987) Reading Inventory
- Dunn's (1990) Learning Style Model (five strands: environmental, emotional, sociological, physiological, psychological)

One of the most thorough, historically proven, and useful style descriptions is the Myers-Briggs Type Inventory (MBTI). One of the most useful books for using the MBTI in instruction is *Differentiation Through Personality Types: A Framework for Instruction, Assessment, and Classroom Management* (Kise, 2006).

Most of the approaches to learning styles feature inventories on the Internet that can be taken by teachers and students. It probably doesn't matter too much which learning style inventory you and your students take; what's important is that you talk with each other about how you learn. As you plan instruction, keep in mind what you know about the learners in your class. You are more likely to plan for a variety of learning styles if you follow one of the instructional strategies described in this chapter—a constructivist-based strategy, experiential learning, project-based learning, service learning, or using essential questions—rather than a more traditional approach to instruction. Offering a variety of choices in terms of how to learn and how to present learning will help you accommodate a variety of learning styles.

Finally, be sure to open yourself to feedback from students. If they know something about their own learning styles and have an invitation from you to share their progress as learners, they'll feel comfortable talking to you about difficulties they may be having.

Eagle Rock students appreciate how well teachers accommodate to a variety of learning styles. Amanda claimed,

> The instructors know a lot about the different types of people and they apply that to be flexible to teach different ways to different types of people. Most of my instructors really get to know me on a personal level, therefore, it is a lot more rewarding to watch my growth from my viewpoint and to see it through the eyes of an outsider.

An instructor, Cynthia, added "I believe we help students to be empowered by their learning and realize that every learning style/strategy is valid."

Brizeida commented, "Teaching visually helps because I know what's going on and what I should expect. Also hands-on and field trips because I need to experience first in order to learn."

CONCLUSION

This chapter was supposed to be short because, after all, you can't make students learn unless they want to. It got longer as I thought about instructional strategies that would create learning conditions that would help students learn. That would draw students into learning. No, that would entice students into learning. Beguile. Tempt. Lure. Inveigle. Whatever it takes.

SO WHAT

How do you learn? Think and write about what your mind does, what you do physically, how you arrange your environment, whether or not you prefer working alone, whether you're an a.m. or p.m. person, and so on.

NOW WHAT

Work with your colleagues to answer these questions about learners you all know.

To what extent do our learners

1. Have choices in learning?

2. Feel personally accountable for their own learning?

3. Have a voice in school—various ways to impact the school and classrooms?

4. Follow their own passions and interests in learning?

5. See their teachers as passionate about certain subjects as well as their own learning?

6. Know the curriculum (what they are expected to learn) and assessment (how they are expected to demonstrate learning)?

7. Feel some power, control, and authority over their own learning?

8. Act as if they are self-directed learners?

9. Learn from experiences and reflection?

10. Learn from doing projects or solving problems together?

11. Learn from doing service as part of academic learning?

12. See themselves as meaning builders?

13. Have opportunities to teach?

14. Experience learning conditions as flexible?

15. Know their teachers will persist until they learn?

16. Participate in vibrant dialogue?

17. Help teachers learn?

18. Learn from each other?

19. Help each other learn?

20. Know their own learning styles and let teachers know when they are not learning?

Now answer this question with regard to each question above: To what extent does our school support students so that they (Items 1–20)? Example: To what extent does our school support students so that they have choices in learning?

NOTE

1. "To Be of Use," from *Circles on the Water* by Marge Piercy, copyright © 1982 by Marge Piercy. Used by permission from Alfred A. Knopf, a division of Random House, Inc.

8

"How Do You Know They've Learned?"

Learning From Assessing Learning

Dear Reader,

Thank you for agreeing to participate as a panel member for four Presentations of Learning that will be held at Eagle Rock School and Professional Development Center on December 4, 2002. Enclosed are packets from each of the students expected to make a Presentation of Learning on that day. Students have sent you their packets in order to introduce themselves before you meet them in person.

Please take a few minutes to read their packets and use the orange scoring sheets to give them feedback. Enclosed with these packets are a variety of materials that will help you prepare for the Presentations of Learning themselves. Please do not hesitate to contact me if you need additional information.

Yours,
Director of Curriculum
Director of Professional Development

You pull out the first packet and start with the title page:

My Path, My Journey
Presented in
Fulfillment of the
Requirements of Learning
Eagle Rock School
ER-28
Sevi D. Foreman
ER-28
November 15, 2002

ER? ER? ER? You dig through the bulky package containing the four packets and additional information and discover a glossary. Oh, ER stands for Eagle Rock (of course), and the number refers to the trimester when the student entered. Ah, ER-28. That means that this is Sevi's first Presentation of Learning.

You read the cover letter:

November 15, 2002

Dear Panel Members,

First of all, thank you for taking the time to read my Presentation of Learning packet. In this packet I will be telling you a little about what I have learned and experienced at Eagle Rock so far, where I came from, and a few other things about myself. Also I will talk about some of my goals for Eagle Rock, myself, and the career I am working toward. I will say a little about what I believe in and also what I used to be.

Once again thank you for taking the time to read this. I hope you enjoy what I have written.

Sincerely
Sevi D. Foreman

It's a very correct letter, though without a signature. It seems a little like a stock letter, actually. (Later you learn that new students, many of whom have never written a cover letter, are given a variety of opening sentences. Some use all of them in one letter; some use only a few. As they become more veteran, they enjoy writing a very personalized letter and avoid stock openings.)

Next is a page without a title.

I am fifteen years old. I have lived in San Diego, California and now live at Eagle Rock. I was born on August 18, 1987, in Columbia. I was adopted at the age of six months and brought to the United States. Both of my parents are in the art business. My mom was a painter, but now she teaches painters and my Dad is a sculptor. He is now starting to write books for the first time in his life because his sculpting was not as fulfilling.

For the first three years of my life I lived in upstate New York on an old farm my parents had gotten shortly after they were first married. It is my favorite place to be because of how peaceful it is. We had to sell off a lot of land because money situations made it hard to hold onto it, but holding onto it is worth it.

When I turned three we went to San Diego because my parents couldn't make money where we were. I hated SD from the second we got there, and I still hate living there. We never owned a house in SD; we always rented. We first lived in a suburb and then we moved into the city itself. We had to move again from the house we were renting into an apartment.

This was the worst time because my parents were almost always yelling and fighting, and I used to get scared they'd divorce. They never did and I'm grateful. We had a lot of money problems back then and a lot of family problems.

We were in the apartment until I got into the seventh grade. Then things started to get better for the family. My Dad started working on rebuilding his career and my Mom started making more money. I still think she does not get the credit she deserves. We moved into the house we are in now and even though it's a little hard to hang on to, we still have to be careful. We are in a much better situation.

Seventh grade was not so great for me. Though we were out of the apartment and my parents were getting along again, I was already starting to take the wrong path. In elementary school I was a loner and had only one friend. Eric is still my friend and is like a brother. Now I was at a new school and all of a sudden I was making friends left and right. This first group of friends I made would later become what some would call my enemies because over about a year their ideas became much different from mine. So I made some more friends who I would find out were the wrong friends to hang with, and they would only lead me into a lot of trouble.

Then I found the love of my life, my guardian angel, my savior, my sanctuary. I got a guitar for my birthday and immediately started playing. It's all I ever wanted to do. When friends were over they would get upset because all I would do is play. Music and the guitar saved my life in many ways. One is helping me learn to express my emotions. I was always going in and out of depressions and almost always angry. However, I never showed it and locked my emotions inside of me so I did not have to deal with it then. The guitar and my song writing helped me stay sane through these times. I had so many emotions built up from over the years that I still went to other things such as drugs and alcohol, so I did not have to deal with them. I still felt I needed to find other ways to escape reality that were not as healthy or productive as my music.

I have been playing for a year and a half now and it is what I want to do when I get older. I want to have my music heard, and it would be nice to make a living doing something I love instead of something I have no interest in. Yet, I don't care about being rich and famous. I just want to be able to support myself playing music.

I came to Eagle Rock because I knew that I would not succeed staying in SD and needed a change of lifestyle. Another goal I have is to get a college education. The place I want to go is Cal Arts. I need a diploma to do this and I think that at Eagle Rock I can.

One thing I was worried about was what am I going to do to stay out of trouble on breaks. I realized it's easier than I thought. My plan is to set goals for myself that are extremely time consuming. For my first break I have three goals. First I want to write enough songs to have three albums (an instrumental and two albums with lyrics). Secondly, I want to record at least two of those albums. My third goal to make some money by getting a job as a guitar teacher.

So far I love Eagle Rock and feel it is the right place for me. I know if I work hard I can succeed here. I am extremely excited about all the experiences I am going to have here and all the things I will have the chance to learn.

I feel that I will really grow as a musician too, and I am real excited about that. I have already have had some jams with other musicians on campus and have an awesome experience with that.

Phew! Wow, that's an honest paper. You skim it again. A few mistakes but very readable. This is a smart kid. And it's his first trimester! You are more impressed. (You learn later that this is truly an extraordinary paper for a new student; many new students have written no more than a single paragraph and have never read a book before coming to Eagle Rock.) And then you get worried. What about breaks and all those goals? Will he survive back in SD? Will he survive at Eagle Rock? On the next page is a résumé:

Sevi D. Foreman
Street Address
City, State ZIP
Phone Number

Objectives:	Graduate from High School Attend Cal Arts College Become a professional musician and start my own recording company
Education:	Nine years Public School Education: XXX Elementary XXX High School Eagle Rock School
Honors:	
Activities:	
Work Experience:	Guitar Teacher 8 months
Technology Skills:	Microsoft Word Apple Works
Service:	Continuation High School—Feeding Homeless ERS: Service Specials ERS: Mentoring

References:

Name	Name
Address	Address
City, State ZIP	City, State ZIP
Phone	Phone

Well, you think, it's good to start them early on writing a résumé. You turn the page.

Record of Service Projects

Title of Learning Experience	Instructional Specialist	Length
TRIMESTER 28		
New Student Service	Jeff, Jacques	Two weeks
Wilderness Service	Jesse, Courtney	Two days
Service Specials	Becky	Five weeks

Record of Classroom Learning Experiences

Title of Learning Experience	Instructional Specialist	Length
TRIMESTER 28		
Show Me the Love	Philbert	Two weeks
ERS 101	Robert	Two weeks
Wilderness Prep	Jeff, Jacques	Two weeks
Wilderness Experience	Jesse, Courtney	25 days
ERS 201	Chris	Six weeks
Kitchen, LRC	Tim, Richard	Five weeks
HPC	Jon, Colleen	Five weeks

Record of Books Read

Title of Book	Author
Sidhartha	Hermann Hesse
Who Killed Kurt Cobain?	Ian Halperin and Max Wallace

Record of Eagle Rock Ambassador Activities

Description of Activity	Length
Mentoring Prospective Students	Eight days

What are these learning experiences? ERS 101? ERS 201? What's this "Show Me the Love" class? What about the wilderness trip? You check the glossary and discover that the ERS 101 and "Show Me the Love" classes help prepare students personally and socially to go on the wilderness trip. Students learn something called 8 + 5 = 10 in ERS 101. ERS 201 and Kitchen, LRC, and HPC help students transition from the wilderness trip to their first academic classes the next trimester. The LRC relates to the Learning Resource Center—why don't they just call it the library? And the HPC is the Human Performance Center, what you remember as plain old "gym"! You turn the page and find a short paragraph:

Moral and Ethical Code

I strongly believe in acceptance. I think it is wrong to judge others. I am against fundamentalism. I don't think it is wrong to believe in something strongly, but I do think it is wrong to say that there is no other way, and to put down those who do not follow your beliefs.

Amazing. You sure didn't know your moral and ethical code when you were fifteen. Oh, you probably had one, but nobody asked you to say it, much less write it down. This one is a good start, actually. On the next page you find pairs of sentences.

I Used To Be . . . But Now I Am

I used to be violent in some situations,
But now I try to handle things peacefully and the thought of fighting doesn't even come up.

I used to think that school was pointless,
But now I want to learn as much as I can and want to succeed.

I used to be unable to be happy,
But now I am learning ways to feel good about life and myself.

I used to think I was unwanted,
But now I know otherwise.

I used to hate the thought of school,
But now I think of it as an opportunity and realize that every school is different.

I used to think that teachers taught nothing and only disciplined students,
But now I know that there are teachers who care and want to teach and not be the same as police.

I used to be unaware of how much we take for granted,
But now I realize that there are so many things that I am blessed with.

I used to feel life was pointless,
But now I know how much it offers.

I used to feel I was worthless and would never be successful,
But now I have new hope.

I used to look at the glass as half empty,
But now I know it is half full.

You sit a moment, silently. Such a simple framework: "I Used to Be . . . But Now I Am." How much it reveals, how deeply it probes. You understand a lot more about this young person than you did before you started to read the packet. You think of several questions you'd like to ask, based on what you've read. You find one of the orange sheets and begin to fill it out.

TWO WAYS OF EVALUATING LEARNING

You have just read the packet a real Eagle Rock student prepared for his first Presentation of Learning (POL). In the Conclusion, you'll get a chance to read part of the packet this student prepared for his next-to-last Presentation of Learning.

Presentations of Learning are one way of evaluating learning. They may have different monikers—exhibition, defense of learning, performance, or demonstration—but they are an important part of the learning process in a variety of schools, some with students as young as second grade or as old as graduate students.

For example, at Amy Biehl High School in downtown Albuquerque, twice a year students give public presentations on topics they have researched (Amy Biehl High School, 2007). Alverno College in Milwaukee requires students to perform what they have learned, both within a class and integrated from several courses; faculty and others are trained to observe and judge a student's performance and give feedback. This practice is known as "assessment as learning" (Alverno College, n.d.).

At Boston Arts Academy, students combine service with a presentation of their learning through preparing and presenting a grant proposal that brings art into the community (Boston Arts Academy, n.d.). At Humanities Preparatory Academy in New York City, students do performance-based tasks (PBATs) as graduation requirements in English literature and language arts, history and social studies, math, and science (Humanities Preparatory Academy, n.d.).

Quest High School in Texas has students complete a semester-long Senior Exhibition in order to graduate. It is proof of mastery of public speaking, the use of technology, and in-depth research on a modern-day social issue, including a social action plan (Quest High School, n.d.). New York's School of the Future students complete and pass three exhibitions and one portfolio defense in order to graduate (School of the Future, n.d.). At Francis W. Parker School in Massachusetts, students do a capstone project based on their interests and sometimes related to a workplace internship; they present this project as part of their graduation exhibitions. Before reaching graduation, however, students have already presented "Gateway Exhibitions" in order to move from one division to another. The graduation exhibition is the final Gateway Exhibition (Parker School, n.d.).

Parker's practice of having students do several exhibitions before the final one is appropriate. Sometimes exhibitions are one-shot deals, but students need to have more than one chance to exhibit their learning, each time getting feedback so that they can improve.

The second form of evaluating learning explored in this chapter is the documentation of learning for credit. You were introduced to this form of assessment when you read about standards and curriculum in Chapter 6. You'll read more about documentations later in this chapter, too.

A Brief Discussion of Educative Assessment

Both types of assessment—exhibitions and documentations of learning—are essentially "educative assessments." Grant Wiggins (1998) coined the term in his book *Educative Assessment: Designing Assessments to Inform and Improve Student Performance*. Exhibitions and documentations of learning are educative because they go beyond proving learning to *improving* learning, for both students and adults in a school.

Performance assessments themselves go back to the English system of giving oral exams. Back, even, to the Bible. "In Judgments 12, Verses 5 and 6, the Gilead guards gave a performance test to members of Ephraim's tribe when they wanted to cross the Jordan River. Told to pronounce 'Shibboleth' they failed to pronounce the 'h,' gave themselves away, and were killed even after denying membership in the tribe" (Easton, 1991, pp. 100–101). Doubtless, someone learned from that assessment.

Performance assessments became especially popular during the latter part of the last century, an antidote to the plague of norm-referenced, standardized tests that featured multiple-choice answers. These, and similar criterion-referenced tests, had driven curriculum and instruction since early in the century, leading to "information [that] comes in bite-sized pieces from teacher-sized dispensers placed in course-sized compartments" (Gendler, 1989, p. 9). Testing was having a dire influence on learning (especially of higher order thinking skills) and educators figured that, as long as it was going to have an effect, this effect should lead to better learning. Resnick and Resnick (1985, pp. 5–20) expressed the influence of assessment on curriculum and instruction thus: WYTIWYG and WYDTIWYDG

(What You Test Is What You Get and What You Don't Test Is What You Don't Get).

Performance assessments were already commonplace in

> the arts, in tests of athletic ability, in vocational assessment (especially work sample tests), in tests of physical dexterity, in evaluations of on-the-job performance (including measures of teacher effectiveness), in tests of oral language, in foreign language tests, and in other fields such as law where bar exams require essays. (Easton, 1991, p. 100)

It was in the 1970s, when they migrated to the K–12 writing curriculum in the form of the writing assessment process, that performance assessments began to be seen as useful across the curriculum. The scoring process—involving an anchoring task and use of anchors and a rubric—made writing assessment less "subjective" (Cooper, 1977, pp. 3–31). From that point on, writing could be evaluated directly through writing samples, rather than indirectly through selection of a correct answer on a multiple-choice test. Educators in other disciplines, including mathematics, science, reading, and social studies, began to look at how they could use performance assessments to learn more directly what students were capable of and to have a better effect on learning.

Performance assessments are much better than many other kinds of assessments in terms of measuring what students actually know and can do. What makes them even better, according to Wiggins, is their educative use as learning tools for both students and teachers. Eagle Rock students claim that preparing for their Presentations of Learning helps them solidify their learning. They synthesize their learning during the trimester, looking for themes, personal meaning, and application. They reflect on themselves as learners. They connect current learning with previous learning.

After they have given their Presentations of Learning, they meet in advisory groups to review the feedback panel members have given them on both their packets and their actual presentations according to rubrics that they, themselves, have created. They formulate goals for the next trimester's learning on the basis of this feedback.

Their instructors have attended POLs given by their students, listening intently to what the students discuss: What I learned. What I didn't learn. What made it hard or easy for me to learn. What I wish I could have done in this class. How this class affected me. How it will affect my future. How I can or cannot use my learning from this class. Instructors spend part of the last staff meeting of the trimester sharing what they have learned from POLs with each other. Discussions continue into the next trimester as teachers refine their teaching strategies, adjust curriculum, and reshape in-class assessment.

Rick Stiggins of the Assessment Training Institute in Portland, Oregon, addresses the educative role of assessment from the point of view of students. In an interview with Dennis Sparks, Executive Director of the National Staff Development Council, Stiggins says,

> When students are involved in the assessment process . . . they can come to see themselves as competent learners. We need to involve students by making the targets clear to them and having them help design assessments that reflect those targets. Then we involve them again in the process of keeping track over time of their learning so they can watch themselves improving. That's where motivation comes from. (Sparks, 1999, p. 55)

Stiggins addresses the needs of struggling students, especially:

> Kids who have given up on learning are at the low end. If we can involve them in the assessment process to give them renewed confidence and motivation, they're likely to try harder and to succeed. The kids who had previously given up on themselves have rekindled interest and get renewed confidence when involved in high quality formative assessment. (Sparks, 1999, p. 55)

THE PRESENTATION OF LEARNING

The Basics of POLs

Three times a year, at the end of every trimester, every student at Eagle Rock makes a Presentation of Learning (POL). These exhibitions are overarching, stimulating reflection, synthesis, and analysis. They are also developmental; each one is videotaped every trimester, so that there is a "running record" of these presentations. They are very public, so they embody some accountability to the public. In addition to analyzing their own learning as they prepare their POLs, students learn from each other as they witness POLs—not only about the content presented but also about presentation skills and how people learn. The learning for staff members is just as profound. A visitor once commented that it seemed rather a waste of time to spend a whole week on POLs; several staff members responded that POL weeks provide the most powerful learning all year.

POLs are not about getting credit in classes. As you read in Chapter 6, students get credit toward graduation through documentations of their learning. By the time they make their Presentations of Learning, they have either gotten credit . . . or not (not yet, that is). You'll read more about documentations below.

Students have a half hour during which they make their presentation (15 minutes) and answer questions (15 minutes) from the panel and audience composed of their peers, staff, visitors, and sometimes family members who are able to attend. The POLs are timed so that they start and end at the same time in four different locations. If the presentations are too short, the question-answer session will be longer (which students may want to avoid). If the presentations are too long, they will be cut off. Needless to say, students hone their timing.

Other than two requirements—that they demonstrate personal growth and academic learning—students customize their POLs as much as they like. Panel members and audiences have been treated to dances, dramatic monologues, and computer presentations. They have been taken on a tour of a student's art. They have participated in skits or watched as other students role-play a scenario with the presenter. Panelists have been asked to do work, including the solving of mathematics problems.

After they have made their presentations (15 minutes exactly, if possible), students participate in a question-and-answer session, beginning with a transition question from the staff member on the panel that is then followed by panel members' questions. A few minutes are reserved at the end for the audience to ask questions.

The types of questions students are asked are quite different. The panel members, who know the students only through their packets, ask questions that bring an outside, world standard to the process; the people who know the students well ask much more personal, probing questions. In either case, presenters need to be prepared for a variety of questions. Panel members are told that they are free to ask any questions they would like, and that if they ask a rather too-personal question, students know they can request a substitute question. Very few students do so, however.

Preparing for POLs

Preparing a Packet to Introduce Themselves

About six weeks before the end of the trimester, students complete their POL packets (according to the head of school, they were to begin working on them as soon as last trimester's POLs were over!). These will be sent— as was the packet that introduced this chapter—to panel members as a way for students to introduce themselves. Packets have the following sections in them: a cover letter; an autobiography; a résumé; a list of learning experiences, service projects, books read, and ambassador activities; a moral and ethical code; and a list of "I Used to Be . . . But Now I Am . . . " statements. For new students, the autobiography begins before Eagle Rock; for veteran students, the autobiography summarizes the years before Eagle Rock, in order to allow space for concentrating on personal and academic growth after enrolling at Eagle Rock School (ERS).

New students receive considerable help on putting together their first packets, doing so as part of ERS 201, the transition class that follows their wilderness experience. Veteran students work on their own and with each other to prepare their packets. Both new and veteran students share packet development with their advisors, one of whom has to "sign off" on each advisee's packet. A wonderful retired teacher spends a week at Eagle Rock helping all students polish their packets, sitting with them as they read what they have written and helping them think like readers as they revise.

Potential panel members have received letters inviting them to POLs, and have agreed to come on scheduled dates for a whole or half day. Packets for the students whose POLs panel members will witness are mailed about three weeks before the POLs themselves. Packets contain a number of ancillary materials, such as a glossary of ERS jargon, a copy of 8 + 5 = 10, and a description of the curriculum. As they are reading the packets, panel members complete a rubric (see below) that will provide students feedback on the professionalism of their packets.

Preparing for the POL Itself

Students use advisory time to plan and practice their POLs. During this time, they are encouraged—but not required—to formulate a controlling metaphor for their POLs; the more veteran they are, the more they are able to succeed at this task. They are also encouraged to use the language of 8 + 5 = 10. They are encouraged to talk about themselves as learners and to describe not only what they did, but what they learned and how that learning applies to them and relates to other learning they have done and will do.

They are coached in public speaking and often spend time in advisories viewing videotapes of previous POLs (often to much laughter). They are encouraged to have a beginning, middle, and end (a novel idea for some students). Endings are particularly difficult as Eagle Rock students struggle to come up with something better than, "Well, that's it" when the time-keeper nods at them. They are also encouraged to have an advance organizer (laying out for them and their panel and audience what they will discuss and in what order).

New students spend time in their ERS 201 class preparing for and practicing their POLs, but veterans do this work out of class (or in advisories).

Advisors often share a set of questions to prompt thinking about what to present:

1. What kind of student am I?

2. How do I learn best?

3. What do I need to work on to improve my learning during the next trimester?

4. How do I feel about myself and my learning?

5. How did I grow this trimester?

6. Are there some special and terrific things I learned this trimester?

7. How do I assess my academic and personal growth this trimester?

8. What didn't I like about myself or my learning this trimester?

9. What did I learn about learning this trimester?

10. What do I wish I knew?

POL Week

You can feel the energy of POL week. Partly it's relief at having completed another trimester with no "axe murders," as the head of school notes. Partly it's the excitement of a week of celebrating learning through POLs. Partly it's about seeing some students make their graduation POLs and having a graduate come back to give a POL on life after Eagle Rock. Partly it's the anticipation of going home on break, felt by both students and staff members.

Orientation for Panel Members

Panel members are given a 20-minute orientation to POLs and their responsibilities before POL sessions start. This, in addition to the packet of materials they received, helps them prepare for what they are about to witness. Nevertheless, they are always unprepared for

- How honest the students are
- How much they help each other out
- How interwoven personal and academic growth are
- How insightful students are
- How fragile they are
- How smart, skilled, intelligent, and wise students are

During a debriefing after a set of POLs (morning or afternoon), panel members share these and other reactions and give staff members ideas on how to improve the experience for students and for them.

Logistics

Many people are curious about just how Eagle Rock manages to do Presentations of Learning three times a year. Skip this section if you're not interested in logistics.

POLs are scheduled during the last week of a trimester, like this:

Monday	Veteran POLs (which new students observe to get a handle of what a POL looks like)
Tuesday	Continuation of veteran POLs; some new student POLs
Wednesday	New student POLs
Thursday	Graduate POLs

Friday   Continuation of graduate POLs (depending upon number
              of graduates)

              Returning graduate POLs (usually a surprise)

              Graduation

Scheduling the POLs is complex but doable. In order to allow for all students to present, POLs are given simultaneously in four sites, and there are morning and afternoon sets of four POLs in those four sites. Table 8.1 shows a typical schedule for *one location* on a *Monday morning.*

Table 8.1   A Typical POL Schedule for One Location on Monday Morning

Location One

Presenting:	Student Response*	Staff Response
9:20 Tatiana 10:00 Ashley 10:40 Christian 11:20 Jonathan	PDC Greeter: Amanda IRH: Christine IRW: Brizeida Video: Adriana Time: Dustin PA: Jason Tech: Ryan & Steve Evaluators: Ana, Katie, Tahnée	Supervisor: Lan Assistant: Adrienne *PANEL*** Debbie H. Diane R. Larry P. Nancy B. Staff Member: Jeff L.

NOTES: * Students have assigned roles that vary for each time slot (a.m. and p.m. over the number of days POLs are scheduled, including graduate POLs). PDC Greeter = the person who greets the panel in the main campus building, the Professional Development Center. IRH = In-Room Host, the person who makes sure the room is set up for the presenters, the audience, and the panel and greets panel members as they arrive. The IRH also introduces the panel and each presenter. IRW = In-Room Water person, which is pretty self-explanatory. PA = Presentation Assistant. This person helps the presenter in any way possible, including setting up and taking down props. Often presenters are helped by a cadre of their peers as well as the PA. The timekeeper has a very important role, announcing the beginning of each part of the POL, letting the presenter know according to prearranged signals how much time has passed, and cutting off the presenter if necessary. The roles of the video person and the tech person are probably self-explanatory. The evaluators use a narrative evaluation form that is given to the presenter along with those from the panel. In other words, all evaluations (those from students and those from panel members) are given to students after POLs, in fact, at Advisories held later in the week.

** The panel members are local, regional, national, and even international. Eagle Rock does not pay expenses or offer a stipend for their work, but visitors often ask to be invited back to the school to serve as panel members. Some are educators, but most are from all walks of life. Some are retired, some students at nearby universities and colleges, some former Eagle Rock students and graduates.

The Rubrics

Like the curriculum, Eagle Rock rubrics are in a state of "perpetual draft." The latest iterations are a result of student work with staff on a POL committee. Students objected to both the six-point Likert scale and the specific descriptors that accompanied the scale in the "old rubric," even though the directions for these rubrics began with, "Make this rubric your own." The directions are for panel members, students said, and they decided that the directions should apply to them, too, especially for the rubric used for the presentation itself. So they invented a form and a process that allowed them to custom-craft rubrics, as well as their POLs.

The previous and the current rubric for the packet have the same categories, but the current rubric has descriptors created by the student and pertinent to what the student is trying to accomplish with the POL. The current rubric also has no scale; instead, panel members are asked to estimate how close the student has come to proficiency on the categories.

Figure 8.1 is the rubric for the POL packets, a rubric that has not changed. Figure 8.2 is the old rubric for the POLs. Figure 8.3 is the current rubric for the POLs.

The old rubric tried to be all things to all people. It was a primary trait or holistic rubric (panel members could skip the Likert scale items and go directly to General Comments and Overall Holistic Score). It was also an analytic trait rubric, with traits related to Academic Growth, Personal Growth, and Presentation Style. However, rather than describe the traits at each scoring level (1–6), this rubric simply described what a 6 would be and left it up to the panel members to decide how close to a 6 each trait had been demonstrated.

The rubric that the student and staff committee designed had been in use for eight trimesters at the time of the writing of this book. Students work with their advisors in advance to create a theme and up to four Major Learning boxes. In other words, *in advance of their POLs,* students write their theme and describe up to four major learnings for the panel members. They are in charge of making copies of their customized rubrics for their panel members, handing them to panelists as they greet them and shake their hands. What do you think? Which do you prefer?

The School of the Future in New York City publishes the rubrics it uses for portfolio defense on its Web site, in addition to curriculum maps and course catalogs.

Teachers in schools that do not sponsor exhibitions of some kind have found that they can do them at the end of a quarter or semester with their own students. Sometimes, teachers arrange for demonstrations of learning for grade-level groups. Sometimes, teachers of the same subject have their students do exhibitions based on what they have learned in that subject. These are often at night in order to make it possible for parents and other community members to attend.

Figure 8.1   Presentation of Learning Rubric for the Presentation Packet

Student _____   Panel Member _____   Date _____

Directions: Make this rubric your own. Read the proficiency descriptors and decide how close the student has come to proficiency. If it helps you to circle numbers, circle them. If you'd rather write comments, please do that. Or, do both. If you want to circle numbers, a "6" means that the student completely achieves the proficiency descriptor and a "1" means the student has not at all achieved proficiency. You may provide an overall (holistic) quality rating (X out of 20) at the end of this rubric.

Category	*Proficiency Descriptors*	*Scale (Optional)*	*Comments*
Content: Students are required to have these sections in this order: title page; letter to panelists; autobiography; resume; list of service projects; learning experiences; ambassador activities; moral and ethical code; "I Used to Be . . . But Now I Am." They may have extra sections.	All required parts are included.	6 5 4 3 2 1	
	All parts are in order.	6 5 4 3 2 1	
Effectiveness:			
Clarity:	Information is clearly communicated through detail and elaboration. The packet has depth.	6 5 4 3 2 1	
	Information is specific.	6 5 4 3 2 1	
Organization:	Organization of information is very effective in helping the reader understand the material; an effective logic is discernible. Paragraphing or heads and subheads are used.	6 5 4 3 2 1	
Readability:	The packet is virtually error-free and highly readable.	6 5 4 3 2 1	
Audience & Voice:	A clear picture of the student emerges from the packet. The student's personality and voice are strong.	6 5 4 3 2 1	
	The student clearly has a desire to communicate to the reader and uses content and format effectively to do so.	6 5 4 3 2 1	
Additional Comments:			

Overall (Holistic)
Quality Rating for
This Packet
_____/ 20

Figure 8.2 Presentation of Learning Rubric for the Presentation Itself

---

Student _____ Panel Member _____ Date _____

Directions: Make this rubric your own. Read the proficiency descriptors and decide how close the student has come to proficiency. If it helps you to circle numbers, circle them. If you'd rather write comments, please do that. Or, do both. If you want to circle numbers, a "6" means that the student completely achieves the proficiency descriptor and a "1" means the student has not at all achieved proficiency. You may provide an overall (holistic) quality rating (X out of 20) at the end of this rubric.

Category	Proficiency Descriptors	Scale (Optional)	Comments
Academic Growth:			
Content and Range	Academic learning is discussed in depth.	6 5 4 3 2 1	
	Academic and personal growth are woven together in an integrated presentation.	6 5 4 3 2 1	
	An extensive range of academic experiences is presented.	6 5 4 3 2 1	
	Academic experiences are connected in some way.	6 5 4 3 2 1	
Documentation of Learning	Learning is clearly and compellingly documented through relevant examples, demonstrations, exhibitions, projects, diagrams, charts, etc.	6 5 4 3 2 1	
Application	Application of learning is elaborated on through reference to past or future learning, with specific examples and references to other learning situations. Significance of learning is addressed.	6 5 4 3 2 1	

Category	Proficiency Descriptors	Scale (Optional)	Comments
Personal Growth:			
Content	Identification and understanding of personal growth are well articulated, elaborated upon, and documented.	6 5 4 3 2 1	
Application	Reflection is evident in identification of goals. Specific information is provided on how the learner has used or plans to use learning in other areas.	6 5 4 3 2 1	
Presentation Style:			
8 + 5 = 10	Relationship of 8 + 5 = 10 is creatively woven into the entire presentation.	6 5 4 3 2 1	
	Vocabulary of 8 + 5 = 10 is used.	6 5 4 3 2 1	

(Continued)

Figure 8.2 (Continued)

Category	Proficiency Descriptors	Scale (Optional)	Comments
Materials	Materials are creative, organized, correct, and used effectively.	6 5 4 3 2 1	
Delivery	This is a polished presentation in every way; it is within the time limit; presenter is poised and at ease in front of audience.	6 5 4 3 2 1	
Organization	Sections are organized in a logical, cohesive, even creative way; ideas are related to each other; there may be a theme.	6 5 4 3 2 1	
	Introduction and conclusion are powerful and effective.	6 5 4 3 2 1	
	The presenter clearly has the audience's need to understand in mind and helps with an advance organizer.	6 5 4 3 2 1	
Q & A	The presenter listens well to questions, answers fully, and checks on answer.	6 5 4 3 2 1	

<u>General Comments:</u>

Overall (Holistic) Score:

_____/20

DOCUMENTATIONS OF LEARNING

The second form of educative assessment used at Eagle Rock is the documentation of learning. You already know from Chapter 6 that standards (competencies or requirements for graduation) are Eagle Rock's unit of credit, rather than seat-time and grades. You know that documentations of learning are the way students prove that they have reached mastery on a requirement.

Documentations take a variety of forms, leaving considerable room for student choice and invention. Here are some typical forms:

Various types of portfolios: mastery, developmental, working, of possibilities, reading

Oral forms: presentation, Gathering, dramatization, skit, monologue, scenario, interview, panel presentation

Written forms: research paper, report, composition, poem, dramatization, plan, action plan, written statement, précis

Figure 8.3   Presentation of Learning Rubric

Presentation of Learning Rubric (Current)

Student Presenter's Name _____ Presenter's Incoming ER# _____ Location of POL _____

Panelist's Name _____ Advisor Signature _____ Advisor Name (printed) _____

Directions: Presenters will have completed the "Overall Theme of Presentation" and "Major Learning" sections of this rubric. Panel members, you are to circle the box that best describes how the presenter expressed the significant learning during his or her trimester. In addition, please add constructive comments in the spirit of expressing what you liked and what you think the presenter could improve upon for the future.

Overall Theme of Presentation:

Theme wasn't mentioned.	Theme was introduced.	Theme was introduced and referred to during the presentation.	Theme was integrated into parts of the presentation and served to highlight major learnings.	Theme was integrated into the entire presentation and served to highlight major learnings.

Comments:

Major Learning #1:

Student expressed what he or she did.	Student said what he or she learned without providing evidence.	Student provided general evidence of what he or she learned.	Student provided evidence of what he or she learned by making connections to at least one of the following: academic learning, personal growth, and/or aspects of $8 + 5 = 10$.	Student provided evidence of what he or she learned, integrating academic, personal growth, and aspects of $8 + 5 = 10$ while connecting it to his or her other major learnings, life, and future.

Comments:

(Continued)

(Continued)

Major Learning #2:

Student expressed what he or she did.	Student said what he or she learned without providing evidence.	Student provided general evidence of what he or she learned.	Student provided evidence of what he or she learned by making connections to at least one of the following: academic learning, personal growth, and/or aspects of $8 + 5 = 10$.	Student provided evidence of what he or she learned, integrating academic, personal growth, and aspects of $8 + 5 = 10$ while connecting it to his or her other major learnings, life, and future.

Comments:

Major Learning #3:

Student expressed what he or she did.	Student said what he or she learned without providing evidence.	Student provided general evidence of what he or she learned.	Student provided evidence of what he or she learned by making connections to at least one of the following: academic learning, personal growth, and/or aspects of $8 + 5 = 10$.	Student provided evidence of what he or she learned, integrating academic, personal growth, and aspects of $8 + 5 = 10$ while connecting it to his or her other major learnings, life, and future.

Comments:

Major Learning #4:

Student expressed what he or she did.	Student said what he or she learned without providing evidence.	Student provided general evidence of what he or she learned.	Student provided evidence of what he or she learned by making connections to at least one of the following: academic learning, personal growth, and/or aspects of $8 + 5 = 10$.	Student provided evidence of what he or she learned, integrating academic, personal growth, and aspects of $8 + 5 = 10$ while connecting it to his or her other major learnings, life, and future.

Comments:

Summary Comments (overall impressions, presentation style, suggestions for improvement, etc.):

Combined oral and written: project, demonstration, videotape, multimedia, critique/defense, project design, review of performance, self-assessment, reflection, reading, listening, or speaking demonstration of a language

Other: finished art piece (visual, dramatic, musical), sketchbook, journal, test results, others' assessment of performance or work habits or attitudes, evidence of skills in other work (checklist), letters/notes from adults or peers verifying learning, exemplary record of something over time, use of a planner or organizational device, sign-off sheet, calendar record, physical demonstration of skills, performance scores over time

Any of these forms could simply be a class assignment or a project. Two aspects of these documentations elevate them from assignments or projects to assessments:

1. The fact that the assignment or project is going to be taken seriously as possible evidence of mastery. Students do not receive grades or points for assignments. If an assignment is to be considered as evidence of mastery, they will learn whether it meets the criteria for mastery, according to a rubric. It must have been judged Proficient or Exemplary on a rubric in order to represent mastery. Only then will it be recorded on the student's transcript as a credit toward graduation.

2. Being evaluated according to a rubric.

Critical Elements of Rubrics

Many assignments already have rubrics. If the assignment is good enough according to the rubric (Proficient or Exemplary), it is elevated to the status of a documentation of mastery of a graduation requirement (a standard or competency). The key is the rubric. Some rubrics are holistic (asking evaluators to look at the relative success of the overall product/ outcome); some are primary trait (asking evaluators to look at the relative success of the overall product/outcome according to some key aspect, such as defending an argument); others are analytic trait (asking evaluators to rate various aspects of a product such as organization and voice).

Some rubrics can be generic, used across the curriculum in all subject areas (such as those for writing). Others can be custom-crafted for each unique class and the products or outcomes that are likely to be used to determine mastery. Many are designed by teachers and students working together. Some are designed by students to match what they are trying to learn and represent in their documentations.

The best rubrics have either a four- or six-point scale and—unlike the POL rubrics—describe a product or outcome according to each of those numbers. Table 8.2 shows another way to look at rubric quality: It is a rubric for rubrics.

Table 8.2   A Rubric for Rubrics

Scale Descriptors ↘	Does Not Meet Standards	Satisfactory	Proficient	Exemplary
Observability, Precision, and Level of Detail	Descriptors are vague, general; they require a lot of imagination. Details are sparse.	Descriptors are somewhat specific; observer can imagine them. Descriptors have some specificity about them, but not much. Details are beyond. Level 1 in some instances but still not deep enough consistently enough.	Descriptors are specific; observer can determine what they look like in action. Descriptors are specific; words describe mostly what will be seen, heard. Details are almost consistently deep and descriptive.	Descriptors are very specific; we know what they look like, sound like, etc., in action. Descriptors are very precise about exactly what something looks like/is. Details are consistently deep and descriptive.
Distinction	There is almost no distinction between scoring levels.	There is some distinction between some but not all of the scoring levels.	Most of the descriptors from level to level represent an increase in skill, ability, etc.	All of the descriptors describe genuine differences from level to level.
Value	Descriptors do not fit the outcome or product. They provide little or no help to teachers who are scoring the work.	Descriptors— at least some of them— provide some help to scorers; they get at some essential aspects of the product or outcome.	Most of the descriptors provide value to scorers by identifying some of the critical attributes of the product or outcome.	All of the descriptors provide value to scorers by being precise about what counts (critical attributes) for the product or outcome.

Calibration

What makes rubrics work is calibration, regular examination of student work using a process such as the tuning protocol (Easton, 1999, 2002; L. B. Easton, 2004d). Calibration is a process of aligning judgment of performance, product, or outcome. Grading is usually a very solitary process, the teacher alone in the classroom wondering if Work Sample 1 is good enough for an "A." Teachers wonder, alone, how other teachers might evaluate student work.

The process of examining student work often requires study of the accompanying rubric and deliberation about how well the performance indicators (quality descriptions and rankings) align with the work. Examining student work often means inquiring into whether or not the work meets mastery, as it would be defined at that school (and at any school).

Implications for Professional Learning

Implicit in the previous paragraph is that using documentation as a way to decide whether or not a student has achieved mastery on some piece of work requires using a rubric and comparing the student's work to that rubric. Typical school norms do not foster that kind of activity. In fact, teachers in some schools do not visit each other's classrooms unless to borrow something, certainly not to observe and give feedback or to learn. And, teachers do not share their students' work, unless they absolutely have to, certainly not for their own or their colleagues' learning.

Gradually these norms are changing, and classroom walk-throughs by principals, even teachers, are becoming more accepted (Downey, Steffy, English, Frase, & Poston, 2004). Gradually, schools are becoming Professional Learning Communities (PLCs)—even WSLCs (see Chapter 3)—and peer-to-peer professional learning is becoming more common. One book on professional learning communities directly addresses the need for faculty to work together when students are not learning: *Whatever It Takes: How Professional Learning Communities Respond When Kids Don't Learn* (DuFour, DuFour, Eaker, & Karhanek, 2004).

Other professional learning activities that involve looking at student work include Standards in Practice (which looks at teacher practice first, in terms of the assignments teachers give and the results of those assignments) and lesson study. Various kinds of tuning protocols—such as the descriptive review—can also be used to examine student work and rubrics (Easton, 2004d).

WHAT HAPPENS WHEN ASSESSMENTS SHOW THAT STUDENTS HAVEN'T LEARNED?

This is the third of the three classic questions that must be asked about learning, and it is the least often addressed. The other two questions are, "What do we want students to know and be able to do?" (the subject of Chapter 6) and, "How will we know that students know and are able to do what we want?" (the subject of this chapter). Alan Blankstein (2004) addressed this question in *Failure Is Not an Option: Six Principles That Guide*

Student Achievement in High-Performing Schools. His answers are six principles for how schools are run that, in practice, prevent students from falling through the cracks:

1. Principle 1: Common Mission, Vision, Values, Goals (p. 65)

2. Principle 2: Ensuring Achievement for All Students: Systems for Prevention and Intervention (p. 97)

3. Principle 3: Collaborative Teaming Focused on Teaching and Learning (p. 127)

4. Principle 4: Using Data to Guide Decision Making and Continuous Improvement (p. 141)

5. Principle 5: Gaining Active Engagement From Family and Community (p. 167)

6. Principle 6: Building Sustainable Leaders (p. 189)

Each of these principles is essentially a mandate for broad cultural change, for creating a culture in which students can thrive and succeed. The nine chapters in this book are also a mandate for cultural change, ways a school can *be there* for students, especially struggling students. The next chapter looks more closely at this cultural change in terms of the whole student.

Pyramids of Intervention

One way schools address Principle 2 is by creating pyramids of support. For example, Illinois's Adlai Stevenson High School's "Pyramid of Intervention" has several levels of support, beginning with Targeted Early Prevention & Strategies, which leads to Systemwide Intervention, which leads to Targeted Intervention, which leads to Intensive Intervention (DuFour et al., 2004). Within these levels are some great strategies:

1. Counselor Watch

2. Summer Classes

3. Good Friends Program

4. Faculty Advisor and Upper-Class Mentoring

5. Progress Reports After Three Weeks

6. Mandatory Tutoring

7. Guided Study Hall

8. Mentor Program With Parent Support Group

9. Student Support Groups (pp. 209–210)

The vignette written by Ted Hall (see Chapter 3) describes how Yarmouth High School in Maine implemented a Pyramid of Intervention.

A Culture and Practices That Prevent Failure

At Eagle Rock, the whole culture and all of the practices that emanate from it combine to help students avoid failure. This book is oriented toward what schools can do to help students succeed, to help them avoid failure in the first place—for struggling students it's often additional failure we want to prevent. Of all of the strategies and practices, curriculum, and instructional techniques that are offered in this book, this one is, perhaps, the most powerful: Relationships.

Students need people around them to support them. They want to talk with someone they trust; they want people to talk with them. They want to tell their teachers what's happening to them and why; they want to suggest new strategies to their teachers. They want to be "called"— lovingly— on their slacking. They want teachers to push their limits. They don't want to be ignored. They don't want people to turn away from them, thinking that they'll eventually drop out anyway or that someone else can take care of the problem. They need patience and perseverance. And, of course, as young people, they'll seem to resist all of these invitations and prompts leading to success and perhaps vociferously. They're testing you! Are you going to stay with them?

They like to be in a school that focuses on everyone's success, not just those who are going to succeed anyway. They like being identified as learners, just like everyone else. They require respect.

Some say, "I don't need any help," but that's before they reach the edge; when they're just about to pitch into the void, they say, "Yes, it's up to me, but I need support." When a student says, "I don't need any help," we should worry.

They really don't want to fail.

CONCLUSION

The word *assessment* is often used interchangeably with the words *examination* and *test*. Assessing generally refers to something larger than testing, with a test being just one means of assessing. As Grant Wiggins (1989) pointed out, *testum,* from which we derive *test,* means "any procedures for determining the worth of a person's effort" (p. 708). The root of the word *assessment* means *to sit with*. How nice it is to think of educators sitting with students for assessment. When you sit with someone, you focus, listen and observe, appreciate and wonder, question, and, yes, evaluate what you hear and see.

Examine has roots in Middle English, Old French, and Latin, eventually finding its original meaning in *ex-* which means *out* and *agere, to lead, act, or move*. One result of an examination, then, is taking action.

The two types of assessment discussed in this chapter are "sitting with" assessments and "taking action" assessments. Both students and educators learn through assessment and—as a result of their examination of learning—take action leading to success.

SO WHAT

Recall a work situation. How would you have liked to be evaluated in that work situation? What would have constituted an educative assessment for you?

NOW WHAT

Share this chapter with some colleagues. Have each mark a particularly effective sentence or idea and then get together to discuss what each has chosen, one at a time, first with reference to the chapter and then with reference to schools and students they know. (P.S. This is a version of a Socratic Seminar.)

Conclusion

The Importance of Looking at the Student as a Whole Person

This book started with the big picture, the importance of culture in a school and how culture influences everything else and is, in turn, influenced by everything else. It ends with a focus on educating the student as a whole person and how the goal of educating the whole person influences everything else (including culture) and is, in turn, influenced by everything else. On the one hand, decisions we make about structure, program, curriculum, instruction, and assessment both represent culture—and create it. On the other hand, the focus on the student as a whole person influences decisions about culture, structure, program, curriculum, instruction, and assessment—and these decisions also determine how well we can educate the student as a whole person. The Introduction and Conclusion in this book, then, are bookends for the strategies, techniques, and methods that come between them. Figure C.1 helps me understand the relationship of all of these elements of schooling.

It is sometimes overwhelming to be a teacher . . . or to be an administrator in a school, working with teachers and students. There are so many students. They have so many needs. Secondary school teachers, particularly, are crushed at the end of a day after they've seen as many as 150 students. Primary and elementary teachers don't see as many students in a day, but they see them for all subjects. Many principals are lucky to talk to ten students in a day, and mostly those are the ones who've drawn attention to themselves through some kind of mischief. District office people may go for weeks without really talking with students.

A visiting teacher cried, "Whole student?" when I mentioned that Eagle Rock's focus was on the whole student, not just the academic side. He added, "I can barely take care of the English side of them, and I see one hundred thirty-five students a day." I sympathized. I remember those days. I was lucky to know names by Thanksgiving.

Figure C.1   Culture and the Student as a Whole Person

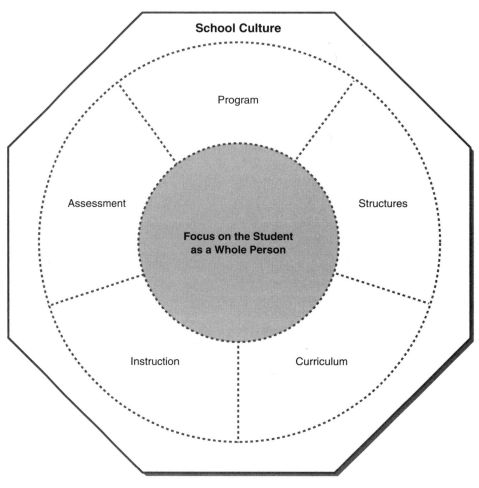

Whether or not we want to deal with young people as whole students, that's the way they come to us. They don't cast off their many selves when they cast off their coats each morning. They're still fretting about the insult they heard (or imagined they heard) on the bus. And Mom and Dad were fighting at breakfast. They hope they'll make the soccer team. They couldn't figure out the homework last night, even though they stayed up late to do it (well, they tried to do it after watching the horror movie on Channel 9). They are afraid they'll have to move. They imagine other students talking about them as they walk down the hall. They're wondering if they can make it until lunch. What about the party everyone's going to on Saturday night? Well, you get the idea. They're probably *not* thinking about commas when they walk into your room first period.

It's appropriate that we end this book with a close focus on students themselves. They've been part of every chapter leading up to this, but this one really counts, especially to them. This chapter focuses on why and how we need to educate the whole child.

A WHOLE STUDENT

Remember Sevi D. Foreman from Chapter 8? You read his POL packet from his first trimester at Eagle Rock. Here's part of his packet from the trimester before he graduated (which he did in April 2006).

Title Page

The Evolution of My Resolution
Presented in
Fulfillment of the
Requirements for
Presentations of Learning
Eagle Rock School
ER-36
Sevi D. Foreman
ER-28
November 6, 2005

Cover Letter

November 6, 2005

Dear Panel Members,

This trimester I found myself constantly re-evaluating myself and reviewing resolutions I had made for the trimester. Consistency with many of these goals was lacking, and the trimester seemed completely void of any real balance. There were those brief moments when I felt as though things were flowing smoothly. However, the feeling of ease in these moments may have simply been nothing more than me denying the reality of my situation.

Even through all of my struggles with motivation, stress and "presentness," this trimester has been very rewarding. I have had some amazing opportunities, had some great times, experienced some really interesting classes, as well as come to some very noteworthy conclusions and realizations about myself and other things.

Thank you for taking the time to read my packet.

Sincerely,
[signature]

Sevi D. Foreman

Autobiography

THE EVOLUTION OF MY RESOLUTION

Time flies; the last few trimesters at Eagle Rock have shown me that. It is hard to believe that it is already the end of the seventh week of the trimester. I have been a student here for about three years, and it seems that it blows by faster and faster the longer I am here. Though the trimester has sped by, the days have seemed slow. These last few months have been busy, fast, difficult, blurry, rewarding, awakening, full of self-observation, as well as a lack of complete consciousness. At times I was on top of things, while at other times I was lost in a sea of to-dos, and haven't-dones with tides of procrastination holding me back from getting to where I would have preferred to be. I came into this trimester with a refreshed mind and a rested spirit, though reluctance seemed still to fall like my shadow, dragging along behind me as if it were a sack of stones.

In spite of longing for a few more years of rest and relaxation, I decided that I was going to start off the trimester at a dash with hopes that I would not have to worry about catching up. Along with my goals for a fresh start lacking of procrastination, and the stress that comes with its consequences, I had also made up my mind over the break that I wanted to remedy my feelings of tediousness and sameness, and clammy eagerness to move on.

In writing this packet, I find myself hesitant to again speak on procrastination since it has been one of the major topics of my personal growth for the last few trimesters; yet I also know that it's still an issue that affects me and my freedom. My choice to allow procrastination to step in my way again and again only hinders my ability to do any of the things I want to do, including the things that need doing.

About the sixth week of the trimester many of the graduates were giving their personal growth presentations, and much of what was being said struck me. Martin's and Madison's presentations, in particular, got me to thinking. I was able to relate to the section in Madison's presentation in which she addressed her issues with procrastination. She said that she had realized procrastination had been nothing more than an excuse for her. I walked away with this thought and realized that I, too, had often used it as an excuse. I saw that I often allowed myself to, not justify, but excuse the fact that I often put things off until the last minute by basically saying, "That's how it is." It was not necessarily that I did not feel the need to change. In fact, since I began my career here, I have been trying to deal with this problem. Unfortunately, I would allow myself to fall back into this habit because I had grown accustomed to it being a habit. There is a line from a song that I wrote that says, "Sometimes it seems that we use the saying 'we are just human' as an excuse to make more mistakes." This is precisely what the root of this issue has been.

Martin's presentation also brought me to some conclusions, though this time about my motivation. I feel my work in the classroom is very good; it is rare that I don't participate or that I am not willing to accept the challenges that the class presents to me. I love to learn, I love to discuss, and I love to exchange, communicate, hear, and express ideas. Yet the instant I step away from the classroom and make my way to the LRC [Learning Resource Center or Library] to attempt to tackle whatever work was assigned, my motivation begins to deteriorate.

Martin addressed the issue of what he called "document production." As Martin expressed in his presentation, I too saw that one of the issues I had was not the learning but the process of reiterating what had been discussed in, say, a mathematics POW [Problem of the Week] or a science prompt, especially in situations where I felt the work did not truly build upon or relate to what was going on in the class. However, all this is an excuse as well. Instead of simply doing what I had to do, I chose to allow myself to become distracted, put it off, or complain about it in my head. I often found myself simply going over these things in my mind and would literally waste time thinking about all the things I would like to have been doing and the things I had to do instead of just doing what I needed to get them done so that I could move on.

The other side to this issue is that much of the time I would simply prefer to be doing what I am truly passionate about, playing music. This is another thing that has affected me over the last few trimesters. I am so eager to graduate and move on. I want to pursue my passions, I want to see the world, I want to learn, I want to play, I want to experience the world, and I want to do it through music. A constant thing I have to remind myself of is that, though it's OK to dream,

I must stay in touch with the reality that if I want to get to my dreams I need to build the foundations that will give me the tools and freedoms I will need to pursue them; that is exactly what Eagle Rock is. It is one of many stepping-stones I will have to use to get to where I want to be.

Overall I had really incredible classes this trimester. There was only one that I was not particularly fond of. In the mornings I had College Prep *for specials, a math class called* Do Bees Build It Best? *And then a science class called* Third Rock From the Sun. *For the first five weeks, my afternoon class was* Chicafrican Story, *and for the second five weeks I had a class called* Environmental Racism.

College Prep *was very eye-opening and a bit frightening, for I saw how much I am going to have to conquer if I want to go to college: Applying, financial aid, having only one college that I am interested in, SATs, ACTs, and the other various things I have to think about now that I am close to graduation. It's interesting because I am so eager to graduate, but I don't like dealing with all the paperwork. I just want to get into college so I can continue learning.*

Do Bees Build It Best? *was a math class in which we studied the principles of geometry in order to answer the question, "Are honeycombs the most efficient storage units?" This class was difficult to attend simply because each day seemed the same. We often spent what I thought was an unnecessary amount of time on very basic ideas. It was apparent that many of my classmates shared this point of view, for in week seven Andy and Jill, the instructors, stopped the class and allowed students to give them feedback on how they thought the class was going. It was at this point that many expressed their frustration with the structure. This is not to say I dislike the class. There were many things I found enjoyable and worthwhile, but I believe that I could have gained a lot more from it if it had progressed more steadily. Walking away from this class I realized that I really enjoy working with equations. I am not sure why, but the rare occasions that I allow myself to get into working with an equation my mind gets to play.*

Third Rock From the Sun *was an amazing class. The class was based around environmental science. Our focus was the effects of Hurricane Katrina, but we branched off in all sorts of directions, from global warming to the political, social, and economic repercussions of, not only Katrina, but nature in general. I have always been amazed at the power of nature. I am also very interested in politics, and learning about global warming and the different points of view around the issue, as well as the effects that are apparent in nature.*

In Chicafrican Story *we looked at the history of Chicano and African Americans in this country. Along with history, we dissected and discussed terms such as* identity, privilege, *and* race. *I would say the most rewarding thing about this class was learning about a side of history that is not usually taught or discussed. Also, the class was very personal for it touched each person in one way or another, which was great, for it created an environment in which people became comfortable with being uncomfortable. As a result, the discussions were very honest, and I personally walked away from this class having learned a great deal, and having a lot to think about.*

I am still only in the second week of Environmental Racism *so my opinion of the class is still being formed. So far I have really enjoyed it. The combination of this course and* Third Rock From the Sun *has been useful for it has tied the science, politics, and history around these topics together for me. During the last two weeks we have begun to define what environmental racism is. The most eye-opening experience thus far was our trip to part of Denver in which we got to see the many different hazards, such as oil refineries and hazardous waste dumps. I was both enlightened and appalled at the reality that many of these massive corporations place these very dangerous facilities so close to homes, schools, and parks. Many of these places were literally within a few blocks of a school or a home. The organization that gave us the tour of this part of the city has been successful at bettering a lot of the community by fighting the corporations, but the place is still quite unhealthy. Aside from the toxic mess that encircled this community, other things such as hospitals, supermarkets, and drug stores were nowhere to be found. I am looking forward to seeing how the class progresses, for I have already been exposed to many different ideas, and realities.*

Overall I have had a good trimester. It has been challenging in some ways, which is good, and relaxing in others. I am looking forward to seeing how my classes turn out in these last few weeks. In addition, I have renewed my resolution to not procrastinate and plan on following through for the rest of the trimester.

SOURCE: Used by permission from Sevi D. Foreman.

Résumé

Sevi's résumé has changed somewhat. He lists Berklee College of Music as his choice for higher education and is specific in terms of wanting to major in jazz composition and recording arts. He also mentions engineering, however. He lists several honors: Multiple 3P Awards (for being prepared, punctual, and participating) and two Eagle Rock Excellence Awards. He lists some activities related to music and some expanded technology skills, many related to creating and recording music.

At the time this book went to press, Sevi was completing his sophomore year at Berklee.

His list of service projects is now two pages long, as is his list of learning experiences. He has read up to six books each trimester. He has participated in a variety of Eagle Rock Ambassador Activities (mentoring, participating on a design committee, giving guitar lessons, being on a panel at an educators' conference in Florida, being on Peer Council, doing a benefit concert for Katrina victims).

Moral and Ethical Code

Life is the most precious gift one will ever receive, and not to embrace every moment is to fail one's self, and starve one's spirit. I have a passion for life, and I want to experience all its pains and joys so that I may become a wise being before death knocks at my door. Being in the present moment and embracing its struggles and pains is a constant struggle in itself, but the present moment is what is important to me for we are only guaranteed one life, so why not live it?

I believe that [it] is wise to keep an open mind in life for, otherwise, one will risk missing out on what could be a useful experience, rewarding relationship, or potential success.

I believe that pain can be a powerful teacher. Sometimes people must go through a painful experience in order to grow and learn, so that we do not make that same mistake again. I do believe it is possible for people to learn from observing or from watching someone else's mistakes, but there is more to gain from personal experience.

I believe that it is necessary for us to hold our selves to the same expectations that we hold others.

On a greater level, I believe in non-violence, though I also agree with an idea someone once expressed to me, "Peace without justice isn't truly peace at all."

I think that it is useful to take time to observe one's self so that one may evaluate whether one is where, who, and progressing towards what they want to be.

One line from a song I wrote states, "Sometimes it seems that we use the saying 'that we are just human' as an excuse to make more mistakes" also plays into what I believe. Although we are imperfect, it is not OK to let our imperfections stand in the way of our progress. This also ties in with much of the above. Just because we sometimes slip and lose sight of our personal morals does not mean we have the right to stop working to uphold those things, or grow in those areas.

I Used To Be . . . But Now I Am

I used to be a person who did not care about my education,
But now I am a person who has a passion for learning.

I used to be a person who did not feel the need to be aware of worldly issues,
But now I am a person who realizes the necessity of awareness.

I used to be someone who did not appreciate the relationships I had,
But now I am a person who embraces them.

I used to allow my low self-esteem to conflict with what I was striving for,
But now I am a person who allows my confidence to reign.

I used to be a person who limited myself with a closed mind,
But now I am a person who is willing and able to keep an open mind.

I used to be a person who was not willing to push myself outside of my bubble,
But now I am a person who is willing to try new things.

I used to be a person who attempted to mold myself to the expectations of others,
But now I am a person who seeks to find out who I am and does not allow others to dictate my reality.

I used to see the world through shattered glass and imprisoned myself in pain,
But now I am a person who realizes that I create how free my reality is.

I used to be a person who believed my dreams would not become realities,
But now I am a person who realizes that the sky is not the limit.

I used to be a person who felt "Why try? My opinion doesn't matter."
But now I am a person who realizes that I need to act in order to make the
changes I see fit.

THINKING ABOUT THE WHOLE PERSON

What do you most notice about Sevi, just one trimester away from graduation? Compare him to how he appeared to be (at least according to his packet) his first trimester. How is he different? How is he similar? Where is his focus? How does he think of himself as a person, as a learner? In what ways is he successful? In what ways does he still need to grow?

Hierarchy of Needs

It's useful to think about where school and learning might be in a hierarchy of needs. Here is the classic hierarchy from Maslow:

5. Actualization

4. Status (esteem)

3. Love/belonging

2. Safety

1. Physiological (biological needs) (see Simons, Irwin, & Drinnien, 1987)

Glasser (1990) hypothesized the rank order of basic needs slightly differently:

5. Fun

4. Freedom

3. Power

2. Belonging and love

1. Survival and reproduction

Going to school doesn't show up on either of these hierarchies, although we could argue that it is through learning that people achieve power, freedom, status, actualization, and more. But, the point of the hierarchies is that these higher-order needs are not important until the lower-level needs have been met. How can students care about academics—from naming the state capitals to logarithms—if they aren't sure where they'll sleep that night?

Eagle Rock staff have noticed that interest and success in academics do not occur until students have addressed some of their personal issues. Academic success that has eluded them for many years of school begins to seem possible once students address personal growth issues. This doesn't mean that a school holds off on academics until, suddenly, students have achieved personal growth. What it means is that work on personal growth is concurrent with work on academics. It also means that academic courses are infused with personal growth opportunities.

It's Not About Labeling

Many Eagle Rock students report that they were labeled in their former schools. Eagle Rock is small enough that labels don't matter much; all students learn in different ways. Blankstein (2004) presents in Table C.1 a chilling—but all-too-real picture—of what schools and others do when they use labels to define and respond to a "whole" child (p. 108).

Blankstein pointed out the number of words that label children that start with the letter "d" and called this chart the "Ten D's of Deviance."

So, no labels. Let's not seclude, punish, discharge, segregate, expel, or blame. There are other ways of working with the "whole" child.

Educating the Whole Person

What does it mean—to educate the whole person? The answer to this question may refer to physical or aesthetic education, as well as traditional academic education, but most often the words *whole child* conjure character development, morals, or values. For some, warning lights go off at those words. Some say schools have no business teaching character, morals, or values. Others point out that, even if they do not have an overt personal growth curriculum, schools teach character, morals, and values just by what they do: the culture they've established and the rules, programs, curriculum, instructional strategies, and even assessments that construct that culture. These all convey the beliefs that the school has about desirable human characteristics.

Educators and researchers such as Douglas Heath (1994) and Thomas Lickona (1991) point out that schools might as well specify and work toward what the school community believes, rather than let character, morals, or values develop willy-nilly. Heath describes apparent changes

Table C.1   Labeling Chart

Perspective	Problem Label	Typical Responses
Primitive	Deviant	Blame, attack, ostracize
Folk religion	Demonic	Chastise, exorcise, banish
Biophysical	Diseased	Diagnose, drug, hospitalize
Psychoanalytical	Disturbed	Analyze, treat, seclude
Behavioral	Disordered	Assess, condition, time out
Correctional	Delinquent	Adjudicate, punish, incarcerate
Sociological	Deprived	Study, resocialize, assimilate
Social Work	Dysfunctional	Intake, case manage, discharge
Educational	Disobedient	Reprimand, correct, expel
Special Education	Disabled	Label, remediate, segregate

SOURCE: From *Failure Is Not an Option* by A. Blankstein, 2004, p. 108. Reprinted with permission from Corwin Press.

in students that require schools to investigate the personal growth curriculum they unwittingly or consciously espouse. In interviews with California teachers, Heath discovered that students in the 1990s had the following strengths. They

- "Are more exposed to rich and varied experiences;
- "Hold adults in less awe, so are less inhibited and more honest in expressing feelings when around them;
- "Are less easily manipulated;
- "Have a stronger sense of fairness;
- "Are flexible, able to accept new ideas;
- "Are poised and self-confident; and
- "Are potentially as intellectually capable" [as students from decades preceding the 1990s]. (Heath, 1994, p. 4)

At the same time, they have new limitations. They

- "Need to be entertained; are more easily bored;
- "Operate more within a 'pragmatic moral parameter';
- "Are extremely competitive to get good grades;

- "Won't work on what they are not interested in;
- "Are more materialistic;
- "Lack a strong will;
- "Are covertly racist and sexist;
- "Have a 'false maturity'; and
- "Are less able to concentrate for long periods of time." (Heath, 1994, p. 4)

Thomas Lickona (1991) suggests two values few could oppose: respect and responsibility (p. 45). He maintains, "There are [others]—such as honesty, fairness, tolerance, prudence, self-discipline, helpfulness, compassion, cooperation, courage, and a host of democratic values. These specific values," however, "are forms of respect and/or responsibility or aids to acting respectfully and responsibly" (p. 45). See Chapter 4 for more about the values embedded in revered U.S. documents, such as the Declaration of Independence.

At Eagle Rock, the phrase *personal growth* represents the concept of educating the whole student. Personal growth encompasses a variety of behaviors that Eagle Rock graduates demonstrate, along with academic growth, in order to graduate. However, there's no magic list of the kind of growth Eagle Rock wants other than what's in 8 + 5 = 10. Personal growth is, by its very nature, *personal*. Just as students are not all required to know about the Franco-Prussian War (see Chapter 6), they might not all need to work on helpfulness or any other of a variety of behaviors that comprise personal growth.

If Eagle Rock *were* to have a list of personal growth goals, it would probably be based on the list Daniel Goleman (1995) presents as a result of research he did to write *Emotional Intelligence: Why It Can Matter More Than IQ*. According to Goleman, those who demonstrate emotional intelligence are able to do the following:

- Motivate themselves
- Persist in the face of frustrations
- Control impulses
- Delay gratification
- Regulate their moods
- Keep distress from swamping their ability to think
- Empathize
- Hope

As with academic requirements, personal growth is measured according to documentations. There are four documentations required for personal growth on the ILP (Individualized Learning Plan; see Chapter 6): Portfolio I, Portfolio II, Presentation, and Peer Mentoring. Portfolio I is required near the beginning of a student's career at Eagle Rock; it serves as a kind of pretest. Portfolio II is required just before graduation and is part of a Personal Growth Presentation of Learning, which the entire school community attends. Students mentor prospective students, continuing their mentorship for at least a trimester if the prospective student is admitted to Eagle Rock. They, their mentees, and staff evaluate students on their mentorship prowess.

The presentation of Portfolio II is the ultimate documentation of personal growth and—theoretically at least—students might find themselves in a place of not yet "mastering" personal growth according to their documentation. That never happens, but only because students have received quantities of formal and informal feedback before they even prepare their second portfolios and create a presentation to the school community. However, several times veteran students have wisely postponed graduation for a trimester or two, based on feedback prior to presenting Portfolio II.

Informally, students get feedback from their peers on a regular basis. Classes are small enough that individual harmful actions are not just managed (through discipline, for example) but discussed and resolved by the whole class. The community engages in so many interdependent activities—such as service, campus clean-up, hosting visitors, and kitchen patrol (fixing meals)—that no student's detrimental actions can go without notice, at least not for long. One advantage of being a residential school is that students get feedback from their housemates, too, and students use House Meetings to address individual behavior. Yet a school does not have to be residential to make personal growth consequential. Many schools help students understand personal growth through advisory systems, for example.

Formally, students present themselves as potential graduates a trimester or two before they graduate. They discuss their personal growth at community meetings and ask for feedback. (In fact, less-veteran students have taken up the practice, scheduling their own Gatherings to solicit commentary from the school community.) As they near graduation, veteran students also present their developing moral and ethical codes ... and receive feedback on these.

HOW SCHOOLS PROMOTE PERSONAL GROWTH

Many innovative schools craft Habits of Mind to promote personal and social as well as academic growth. You encountered some of these in Chapter 4 because they often serve as guiding principles for a school. The Habits of Mind from Francis W. Parker School in Massachusetts are expected to be demonstrated in both work and daily life: Inquiry, Expression, Critical Thinking, Collaboration, Organization, Attentiveness, Involvement, and Reflection (Parker School, n.d.).

Fenway High School in Boston has slightly different Habits of Mind, related to those developed by Central Park East Secondary School: Perspective, Evidence, Relevance, Connection, Supposition (Fenway High School, n.d.). Students at The School of the Future in New York City orient their school and personal lives around these: Point of View, Evidence, Connections, Alternatives, Significance, and Communication. At SOF the Habits of Mind are woven into rubrics that are used to evaluate portfolios and presentations (School of the Future, n.d.).

Wildwood School in California focuses on Life Skills and states that the development of these is "as important as his/her academic development" (Wildwood School, n.d.). Wildwood also expands Habits of Mind to include Habits of Heart.

Eagle Rock staff made a decision early in the development of the school *not* to have a personal growth class or trimester, not even a program on character development. No packaged materials, please. Their belief was that personal growth should infuse every aspect of Eagle Rock life. Everything about a school, they thought, should conspire to enhance personal growth. Beliefs (vision, mission, principles), culture, structures, program, curriculum, instruction, and assessment all work together in the environment to help students develop personally.

The danger in such an approach is, of course, that personal growth becomes so diffuse that it can get lost in everything else a school does. That danger is lessened, however, when a school is small or has found ways to be small. It's just harder to "get away with things" in a small school. A small incident during passing period in a large school can go unnoticed because the perpetrator and his or her victim are immediately swallowed up by the horde. Such an incident cannot be ignored as easily when the students are two of only a few and likely to see each other several times during a day. In one way or another, dealing with personal values and morals and resulting behaviors cannot be avoided in a small learning community.

Schools can promote the growth of the student as a whole person through beliefs and culture; structures; program; and curriculum, instruction, and assessment.

Beliefs and Culture

Beliefs and culture are expressed in 8 + 5 = 10, which you've already encountered in the Introduction and Chapter 4. The first four themes address individual integrity and citizenship. The expectations portray someone who is whole—who has an expanding knowledge base, communicates well, makes healthy life choices, participates as a global citizen, and takes on leadership roles in the interest of justice.

The commitments begin and end with requirements that are strikingly personal: Live in respectful harmony with others. Develop a moral and ethical code. Sandwiched between these are commitments that relate to the themes and expectations and are simultaneously academic and personal.

Vignette C.1   A School Vignette: The Student as a Whole Person

THE FUNDAMENTAL ATTRIBUTION ERROR

The Bronx Guild, NY

By Michael Soguero

The Bronx Guild, a charter high school in New York City, offers a program of learning that is based on internships. One of the most important strategies the Bronx Guild uses to work with struggling students is related to an assumption the school does *not* make. We don't assume we know what's "wrong" with students. We strive to avoid the "fundamental attribution error" that leads to blaming the student for lack of motivation or willpower.

The tool that has been very helpful to us in this effort is Kerry Patterson's *Crucial Confrontations.*[1] CC provides a six-cell model for human behavior. Even before we learned about CC, we found ourselves tapping into all six cells of his matrix; his work gave structure and vocabulary to our efforts.

Some examples: For the first cell (*Motivation—Self*), we have an extensive set of activities designed to get to the bottom of what interests a young person. When students are struggling, we ask what makes them tick? What do they really care about? Do we know? How can we find out?

	Motivation	*Ability*
Self	1. What motivates you in particular? NOTE: If this is the only place we go we are guilty of fundamental attribution error.	4. Do you have the skills necessary to accomplish what we are asking?
Others	2. How does the behavior of your peers and role models influence you?	5. Are you getting needed assistance to overcome obstacles?
Things	3. What does the incentive system look like and how does it play a role in your behavior?	6. What are the physical and/or programmatic structures that provide a bridge or barrier?

Justin (a student) was quite a challenge; he wouldn't even do the interest discovery activities. He seemed to be able to endure hours of doing nothing. He was

(Continued)

always smiling. No one could shame or anger him. He was implacable. Al, our apprenticeship coordinator, realized that we were not sure what Justin was interested in, visited the classroom, engaged Justin in conversations, and discovered his love of computer and video games. Coincidentally, Al was also our technology coordinator; he made Justin his apprentice and cocreated game design projects with him. Justin was interested—and also engaged in math, science and English performance expectations.

The second cell describes *motivation with others*. Are there activities the student sees others doing that are motivating or demotivating? Students who are consistently late to class may be demotivating, but peer pressure and models may be either. We teach students that they need to take charge of their lives and resist poor influences, and we also work to build a positive peer culture. For example, Stacey's crew had behavioral issues and showed little learning or engagement. A full-time Outward Bound educator—Juan—built a multi-month curriculum aimed at building positive social group identity. Activities included initiatives, challenges, field experiences, and contracting, etc. Within this positive social milieu, Stacy's crew became successful.

The third motivation cell involves *motivation through things*—extrinsic motivation. Here I must admit to a bias. Like Alfie Kohn, I do not believe that extrinsic incentives are useful in schools. However, external motivation is part of the system. By regulation, New York State has credits; at the Bronx Guild, we downplay credits. We were caught off-guard when we discovered that learning plans students and teachers were developing did not address the breadth of high school work and that students and their parents had no idea what credits were and, therefore, did not use them as a tool of any kind. Students were depending upon the adults to plan the sequences that would lead to graduation. At the Bronx Guild, we wanted the students to plan their sequences but did not educate them on the system.

We taught students and parents about how developing interest-based projects while consulting the state's list of required credits would put them in the driver's seat. They could take control of their progress towards graduation. Students moved from struggling to graduate to struggling with planners, learning plans and credit distribution sheets. At least they now had control and knowledge of their path towards graduation.

The fourth cell looks at *ability—self*. How much of a student's struggle is based on lack of skills or competence? Intervening in this area puts the focus on (1) instruction and (2) development of tasks and scaffolding. For example, the Bronx Guild did not have an English Language Learner (ELL) teacher. Another teacher attributed Govindra's struggles to a need for special language services. Born in Guayana, his English was halting. His crew leader, Priya learned that Govindra was actually a native English speaker, contrary to what they had believed. We had made false, assumptions about the source of his troubles. Priya decided he needed to be taught directly how to read and did so.

The fifth box looks at *ability and others*—how others can be a help or hindrance. IvyLee lost her mom to AIDS when IvyLee was in elementary school. With her father out of the picture, IvyLee's 20-year-old sister picked up the parenting duties, but soon married, had a baby and moved to Pennsylvania. By then, IvyLee was living with another sister who was a terrible influence. Parties all night. IvyLee had failed all 5 of her Regents exams—some of them more than once—and, in her senior year, confided to her crew leader, Dana, that she needed help. People in her life were hindering her. She committed to doing more work but needed someone to help her.

Dana, commuting an hour or more from and to Brooklyn each day, picked up IvyLee each morning, getting her to school a half hour early. IvyLee joined an afterschool program that provided work in an interest area (dance) as well as in test preparation. With Dana, IvyLee had a test prep plan for EVERY subject and graduated last week (as of this writing) having passed all five out of five Regents exams with a Regents diploma—meaning she did better than necessary to get an advanced distinction.

The sixth category looks at *ability as affected by things*—whether things are bridges or barriers to ability. This cell manifests itself in classroom routines, movement in and out of classrooms and hallways, and in transitions. A major problem for the Bronx Guild was entry into our large building. A cadre of school safety agents (SSA)—rule books in hand—confronted all students as they entered. Girls who had joined a knitting club were horrified when their knitting was dismantled by the SSA at entry because knitting needles were classified as weapons. Aware of how their first encounter at school soured these students, we argued successfully for a separate entrance for students, staffed by our own educators (in addition to SSA) who believed in treating students with dignity.

The Crucial Confrontations matrix helps us work with struggling students in ways that don't assume any cause-effect relationship.

NOTE

1. Patterson, K., Grenny, J., McMillan, R., & Switzler, A. (2004). *Crucial confrontations*. New York: McGraw-Hill.

SOURCE: Used by permission from Michael Soguero.

AUTHOR NOTE: Michael Soguero, founding principal of The Bronx Guild, is now Director of Professional Development at Eagle Rock School and Professional Development Center. You may reach him at msoguero@eaglerockschool.org or 970-586-0600. You may reach The Bronx Guild at 718-597-1587 or www.bronxguild.org.

Structures

Structures relate to use of time and space. Eagle Rock has times set aside to encourage personal growth, from morning Gatherings that are usually led by students to advisories held once a week. The agendas for these times focus on each student as a whole person. Even miniscule aspects of a school meeting, such as the Question of the Week, which might be "How are you contributing to community this week?" or "What does integrity have to do with when you're alone?" inspire students to center on their personal growth. Also, in terms of structure, there are places where the whole school community can meet.

What follows is an artifact of structure—one student's schedule for the day, a Tuesday, during her third trimester at Eagle Rock. Please read this with an eye to how Cybil's day promoted personal growth:

Cybil's Schedule

<u>6:25 am</u> *So I get up to go to morning exercise and work out for half an hour. I usually lift weights in the Human Performance Center [HPC]. I have a weight training circuit and I got up to 190 pounds on the leg press! From 7 to 8 is when I squeeze in getting dressed, taking a shower, and all that good stuff.*

<u>8:00 am</u> *Then I go to Gathering, which is the highlight of my day, it's probably my favorite thing. I really like starting off my morning with other members of the community, just enjoying the physical and spiritual closeness that I think we have. I especially like when we finish up with music and we're all singing together. It just starts the day on a positive note.*

<u>8:30 am</u> *After Gathering I go to Specials where I do various work in the greenhouse. I'm thankful for that time since I want to learn more about propagation and growing plants. Organic farming is something I definitely want to do with my life.*

<u>9:40 am</u> *I then go to first period, which is my science class, "Survival of the Fittest." I love learning science and how it's been used in society with theories of evolution and social Darwinism to warp the way people use science to put people down and further racism.*

<u>11:00 am</u> *Then I go to 2nd period, which is "Painting Words and Writing Pictures," a combination of visual arts and writing where we'll express impressions of written work using art and vice versa. It's a good integration because the two things go together well and it's a good class structure with a lot of spontaneity. We don't get in a rut of doing the same thing.*

<u>12:30 pm</u> *Before lunch I have Chores back in the greenhouse. I'm the only person in there and I get to take care of the plants and clean the greenhouse. I really enjoy that time because I chose to sign up for that chore and it's exactly what I want to do.*

<u>1:30 pm</u> *Normally I take a nap somewhere over the lunch break which is between 1.00 pm & 2.40 pm*

<u>2:40 pm</u> *I proceed to my third period class which is "To Devil With Opera." It's an incredible class where we're breaking down the opera* Faust *and having constant discussions about morals and ethics and what's right and wrong and what people should do. The class just opened my mind to ways people should do things and contradictions in my own beliefs.*

<u>4:15 pm</u> *Every other Tuesday I have a Service Learning Advisory Council to plan various projects in the community. Then I'll probably kick it in the lodge and drink tea or maybe go home and clean my area.*

<u>6:00 pm</u> *At dinner I usually sit with Bern, Sevi, Madden, and Heather where we like to have heated discussions about politics.*

> 7:30 pm *After dinner I will generally come home for a little bit and do some homework, then head to our Tuesday night Community, Gender, or House meeting.*
>
> 9:30 pm *At House Curfew I'll read and do some homework before I head to bed at 10.00 pm. I highly enjoy the fact that Wednesdays come after Tuesdays. I'll sometimes have so much homework that I'm tripping, but come ten o'clock I'll realize that I have intramurals the next day and I don't even have to trip.*

SOURCE: Used by permission from Cybil Martinez.

I know you are probably not associated with a residential school, but think about how some of the events that happen before and after classes at Eagle Rock could be incorporated into a school day, in different form, of course.

Program, Curriculum, Instruction, and Assessment

At an Eagle Rock staff workshop on data analysis, participants studied four aspects of data, as described by Vicky Bernhardt (2004a). These four aspects are demographics, perceptions, student learning data, and processes (by which she meant programs that affect student learning). Bernhardt maintains that investigating all four aspects, especially looking for trends or themes across the four, makes for the most effective data analysis. Readying itself for accreditation, Eagle Rock staff analyzed data, including processes, and found these processes operating at Eagle Rock. All of them have an effect on how Eagle Rock focuses on the student as a whole person (see Table C.2). You can generate a similar list for your own school or a school you know well.

THE BOTTOM LINE

Educating the student as a whole person means focusing on personal and social, as well as academic growth. Focusing on the whole person means focusing on how we treat young people and how we expect them to treat each other and us. Blankstein (2004, p. 111) charts the differences between effective and ineffective interactions (see Table C.3).

CONCLUSION

Remember the movie *The Wizard of Oz*? Dorothy meets a lion that needs courage, a scarecrow that needs a brain, and a tin man that wants a heart.

Table C.2   What Eagle Rock Does to Help Young People Learn

Active learning	Morning gatherings
Advisories	Outdoors education
Adult involvement in intramurals, band, orchestra, plays, musicals	Presentations of Learning (POLs) three times a year
Block schedule (3 classes/day)	Professional development center
Community meetings	Prospective students visit
Constructivist philosophy	Residential
Diverse student body, faculty—purposeful	Rubrics
Documentation of learning versus seat-time and grades	Scholarship (full)
Explore Week	Self-directed students
Graduation Presentations of Learning (Exhibitions)	Service learning
High school–age students	Standards, graduation expectations related to
Houses (dormitories)	Student roles in governance, meetings, hirings, etc.
Integrated/interdisciplinary classes	Struggling students
Interactive learning	Testing (TAP, Iowa Test of Basic Skills, on entering & graduating; SAT; ACT)
Intramurals rather than interscholastic sports	Trimesters
Internships	Twenty-four/seven
Mastery expectations (rubrics)	Wilderness expedition for all new students
Mentors	Year-round schedule

Together with Dorothy and her dog, Toto, this trio seeks the Wizard of Oz who will give them what they want. Of course, along the way, the lion demonstrates courage, the scarecrow smarts, and the tin man a heart of gold. Imagine the school as the Wizard, and the yellow brick road the way schools help students reach their potential, their whole potential.

Table C.3   Effective and Ineffective Practices

Connection	Disconnection
Welcoming students even when they are late.	Sending students to the principal's office, regardless of circumstances of late arrival.
Greeting students warmly at classroom door.	Working on paper at desk until all students are seated and the start bell rings.
Systematically assuring every student is positively connected to an adult.	Leaving personal connections to chance.
Using extracurricular engagement data of all students as a measure of student success.	Assuming most students are involved in extracurricular activities.
Developing Competence	Building Incompetence
Allowing makeup work.	Having "One chance" policies.
Demanding mastery of material.	Averaging zeros into semester grades.
Testing what is taught.	"Surprise" tests and pop quizzes.
Finding and emphasizing strengths.	Focusing on weaknesses.
Self-Control	Compliance and Obedience
Allowing students to help create class rules.	Telling students what the rules are.
Eliciting input on class projects and readings.	Recycling prior year's projects.
Teaching empathy, self-awareness, and other emotional intelligences.	Keeping emotional learning apart from academics.
Contribution	Self-Centeredness
Allowing older students to teach younger ones.	No student-led mentoring.
Creating community service and learning opportunities.	Holding learning within the school.
Encouraging cooperative learning.	Teacher directs all learning.

SOURCE: From *Failure Is Not an Option* by A. Blankstein, 2004, p. 111. Reprinted with permission from Corwin Press.

SO WHAT

Struggle is common in our lives. To a certain extent, we would be lost if we did not have struggles of some kind to give us an edge. We feel more alive when we struggle, all of our systems on "go." Too many struggles, of course, and we may collapse.

Think about your own struggles. What is it you're struggling against? To what extent is your struggle a personal one? A social one? An academic one? A political one? A philosophical/moral one? How do you struggle? What is it like for you to struggle?

How does understanding your own struggles help you understand young people who struggle?

NOW WHAT

One way to assess the focus of any organization is by walking into its public space—a reception area or front office or foyer. Walk into a school you have never visited before. What do you notice? What feeling does the place have? What sense do you have about the people inside? "Read the walls" to get a view of the culture. What's up there? Canned posters about courage and discipline? Real student work? Student awards? Pictures of students and staff? What are they doing?

Stop people you meet and ask them to tell you about the school. How do they describe it? Ask them to tell you about the students in the school. What are they like? Ask them to name a student they've been thinking about. What's that student like? To what extent do you think this school focuses on the whole student?

Now do the same in your own school or a school you think you know well, but try to visit as if you had never been there. Notice everything in the reception area. What does this area "say" about your school? Is this a good place for students—as whole persons? Do the same in the hallways. The next time you talk with staff members, perhaps in the staff lounge, ask them to name a student they've been thinking about. Listen for whether or not they are thinking of students as whole persons or as students with academic concerns only.

Resource A

About Eagle Rock School and Professional Development Center

PURPOSES OF EAGLE ROCK

Eagle Rock School and Professional Development Center was developed as a philanthropic project to serve two purposes:

1. To graduate young people who have the desire and are prepared to make a difference in the world.

2. To have a positive effect on education, primarily in the United States.

These seem like simple enough goals until you realize that Eagle Rock intentionally enrolls students whom many people think are the hardest to educate in American schools—those who have dropped out and, perhaps, made decisions that have put their lives (and others') in danger. The second purpose of Eagle Rock School (ERS) and Professional Development Center to some extent explains the first goal. Besides wanting to do something to help students who have been lost to the education system, the founders of Eagle Rock also wanted to have an effect on education, especially in the United States. By selecting hard-to-educate young people—rather than those who are successful in school, no matter what the conditions are—Eagle Rock gains credibility. The strategies that work at Eagle Rock have validity because they work for those for whom success in traditional schools has been elusive.

The school would probably not exist were it not for the second purpose, improving education, not just in the United States but worldwide. The Professional Development Center would probably not work were it not for the school, which is a living laboratory for educators.

Although Eagle Rock is an independent school because its founders wanted to free it from policies and regulations that might hamper its staff in finding the best ways to educate young people, Eagle Rock attends to most state policies, including the Colorado Model Content Standards

BARE FACTS

Eagle Rock

- Is an initiative of the American Honda Education Corporation, a 501(c)3, a nonprofit subsidiary of the American Honda Motor Company
- Is a full-scholarship high school for students and a low-cost professional development center for adults
- Is located in the mountain resort community of Estes Park, Colorado, gateway to Rocky Mountain National Park
- Opened in the fall of 1993
- Admits and graduates students three times a year
- Is year-round (three trimesters) and residential
- Is purposefully small, capacity of 96 students
- Is fully accredited by the North Central Association Commission on Accreditation and School Improvement and the Association of Colorado Independent Schools, as well as by the Association for Experiential Education; its alternative licensure program is accredited by the Colorado State Department of Education

HISTORY AND BACKGROUND[1]

In May 1989 the American Honda Motor Company began investigating nontraditional ways to expand on the philanthropic contributions made through the company's community relations department and the American Honda Foundation. Thomas A. Dean, who holds a doctorate in education and helped design Honda's innovative technical and corporate education programs, and Makoto Itabashi, an engineer, crisscrossed America searching for an appropriate education initiative.

On April 12, 1990, American Honda approved the concept of a professional development school, a school for young people who had not been successful in conventional school settings and needed a fresh start in a new environment. The school would help these students become successful, productive members of society and at the same time further educators' research and professional development. To fund this initiative, the company established a nonprofit corporation, the American Honda Education Corporation (AHEd). This support from within the corporate structure rather than through a foundation is unique in the world of philanthropy and clearly demonstrates a strong level of commitment to social investment. Dean and Itabashi crisscrossed the country again, talking with educators, parents, students, and others who had an interest in restructuring high schools so that they better served young people. They collected recommendations that led to the general framework of the Eagle Rock School and Professional Development Center.

During 1991–1992, AHEd hired its initial administrative staff. It also found 640 acres near Estes Park, Colorado (a small mountain resort town about two hours northwest of Denver and an hour northwest of Boulder, and the gateway to the Rocky Mountain National Park). The school is named after a prominent rock formation adjacent to the property, which resembles an eagle in profile. A governing board composed of Honda associates oversees the school much as a district board oversees a school district.

In the fall of 1993, the school opened unofficially with sixteen students, two and a half buildings, a set of thematic underpinnings, and a general curricular concept. As the school grew that year, so did its culture, programs, and curriculum—and the students participated in the development process. In the fall of 1994, when the school held its official grand opening, most of the buildings were finished, and the school culture and curriculum had been considerably refined. In the spring of 1995, the first two students graduated. As of August 2006, there have been 114 graduates; approximately half of them have enrolled in colleges or universities; the others have worked after graduation (sometimes to finance higher education), joined the armed forces, or participated in service organizations such as the California Conservation Corps or Public Allies. More than 15 Eagle Rock alums have college degrees, over 50 more are still working on them part- or full-time, and two have graduate degrees.

Demographics of ERS Graduates:

58% women, 42% men;

56% Caucasian, 44% students of color (47% African American, 37% Hispanic or Latino, 13% Asian, Native Hawaiian, or Other Pacific Islander, 3% American Indian or Alaska Native).

They have come from 26 states.

Although not all students who attend Eagle Rock graduate from ERS, they do graduate. Based on follow-up research done in 1999 and again in 2003, most (over 95%) of students who attend Eagle Rock graduate from a high school. Others earn their GEDs. Remember that none of the students who enrolled at Eagle Rock expected to graduate from high school.

The Professional Development Center hosts as many as two hundred events a year, welcoming as many as two thousand visitors to the facility. These visitors become immersed in the school, learning both cognitively and emotionally what it feels like to be a student at Eagle Rock. They take their learning with them, reforming specific elements of their own environments or restructuring their educational programs. Although not designed to be replicated, Eagle Rock has influenced the design of numerous alternative high schools, high school alternative programs, charter schools, independent schools, and public schools within a school.

As a Mentor School for the Small Schools Project of the Coalition of Essential Schools, Eagle Rock has worked closely to help develop schools reopening as small schools and other schools that are starting up as small schools. As a founding member of the League of Small Democratic Schools, Eagle Rock has worked similarly with other schools from around the country.

What is most remarkable about the Professional Development Center is how its activities serve Eagle Rock as a mirror, providing continuous feedback, leading to constant self-evaluation. Visitors, through their comments and questions, keep the school involved in the continual development found in thriving organizations of any kind.

THE STUDENTS

Eagle Rock's students are between the ages of fifteen and twenty-one and have one thing in common: They did not expect to graduate from high school. They have sat in the back of classroom after classroom, disengaged or belligerent. Many have dropped out or been expelled, sometimes from several schools, several times, before coming to Eagle Rock. Apart from that, Eagle Rock students share the diversity found in any American high school. The school strives to maintain an even balance of males and females, and of Colorado and out-of-state students. About half the population is white, the rest of color, mostly Hispanic and African American students.

Some students come from fully functional and caring families; others have been abused, neglected, or abandoned or are the products of messy divorces. Some have turned to drugs or alcohol; others have not. Some have run away or joined gangs; some have committed petty crimes. Students themselves must commit to Eagle Rock; no matter how committed their families are, students will not be admitted unless they choose to enroll.

Many Eagle Rock students have been labeled in their previous schools: ADD, ADHD, special education, LD, gifted and talented, dyslexic. Some have not. Some had low skills in reading and writing and mathematics before coming to Eagle Rock. Others were adept students, earning high grades but not sure they were learning anything. Nevertheless, Eagle Rock is a high school, not a therapy or rehabilitation center; students admitted to Eagle Rock must have dealt with their addictions and addressed emotional and psychological issues before enrolling. Once admitted, however, students receive support as they continue to stay sober or nonaddicted or as they continue to work through their issues.

Head of school Robert Burkhardt describes Eagle Rock students this way:

> Imagine a continuum. At one end are the students guaranteed from birth a spot at Harvard and probably editorship of the *Law Review,* too. At the other end are students guaranteed a bunk at Folsom Prison. If Harvard is 0 and Folsom 100, our students are between 60 and 80.

In part, this profile stems from the Professional Development Center—educators need to see whether strategies work with the most difficult-to-reach students.

ADMISSIONS PROCESS

Eagle Rock admits students between the ages of fifteen and seventeen. There is no cost to students and their families or to the schools or districts the students come from. Students are admitted three times a year. They complete applications, including letters in which they and an adult in their lives (students need either a parent or a sponsor to support them actively while they are at Eagle Rock) write about why they think Eagle Rock is the right school for them. There is no waiting list at Eagle Rock; each student's application is considered against all other applications for that admissions date, and students who do not get admitted for one admissions date may reapply for the next. Often, Eagle Rock admissions counselors give applicants work to do before they reapply: take a class at a community college, get a job, try to give up cigarettes, get counseling, go through a drug or alcohol rehabilitation program, get up before noon. Sometimes students are just not ready to make the commitment Eagle Rock requires.

Students who fit the profile and seem ready to make a commitment are interviewed in person; those who remain promising candidates for admission are then brought to the school for a prospective visit. As prospective students, they are mentored by and live the life of an Eagle Rock student. They do KP (kitchen work), go to classes, do service, sweat through 6:00 a.m. exercise, and take a hike that previews the wilderness trip. In addition, they meet in small groups and one-to-one with the admissions counselors. In these meetings, they are asked if they are prepared to give up their addictions, leave their cars at home, forgo "hanging out," be in residence 24 hours a day, seven days a week, go to school during the summer, get serious, and give up partying. They also need to realize they'll be living in a fishbowl because the school is also a Professional Development Center. Prospective students get a three-day chance to live the life of Eagle Rock and decide whether it's right for them—and Eagle Rock students and staff members get a chance to observe students in action and gauge their level of commitment.

Since grades and records are not the best indicators of whether or not a student should be admitted, admissions decisions ultimately come down to these considerations:

1. The student's commitment to making a change. Even if the student's parent or sponsor is convinced that Eagle Rock is the right place, only the student's conviction that change must be made and that Eagle Rock is the right place for that change to be made is a good indicator that the student will succeed at Eagle Rock. All students CHOOSE to come to Eagle Rock; however, they will continually reconsider that decision as they grow and learn. A traditional saying on the Eagle Rock campus is, "You choose each day to stay at Eagle Rock."

2. The student's understanding of Eagle Rock. Students need to realize that they give up much to come to Eagle Rock (no cars; no mall for hanging out; no alcohol, drugs, tobacco, violence, or sexual relationships) but they gain much, too, in terms of support and love. Expectations for personal and academic growth are high. Eagle Rock is not summer camp.

3. Diversity. With each group it admits, Eagle Rock seeks to balance gender, racial and ethnic characteristics, geographical origins, and economic backgrounds.

4. Options. Eagle Rock tends to admit students who have few or no other options available for completing their high school diploma.

Key questions for prospective students include these: "Are you satisfied with the direction your life is going?" and, "What are you willing to do about it?"
According to L'Tanya Perkins, Admissions Counselor,

A primary criterion is a willingness to actively pursue intellectual and personal growth. A young person must have an exceptional capacity to persevere when faced with difficult personal and emotional challenges. A secondary criterion is a willingness to attain personal achievement outside the classroom in a range of pursuits including academic activities. These include: community service, creative and performing arts, athletics, speaking at conferences and workshops and other extra-curricular areas.

The Director of Students declares,

We are a high school, not a therapy or treatment program. As a school we highly value academic rigor and personal growth and character. We do not have a preexisting mold into which all young people must fit.

We are not a college prep school. We are a prep-for-life school. We want our young people to value learning. We entreat them to do so in many ways. Ultimately, we want them to use their learning to better their immediate community and by extension society. Our desire is to graduate young people who have the will and are prepared to make a difference in the world.

We are a Professional Development school. Since we will never have a large student population, our greater purpose and good is to assist educators to better their craft. After they have worked with us here, we invite visiting educators to go out and influence change in their school and community.

We are not a dumping ground. A young person must want to be here. No one can make that choice for a young person (e.g., parent, judge, relative, or any well-intentioned adult). Eagle Rock cannot be a forced choice because there are no other options available. A young person cannot choose Eagle Rock in lieu of incarceration.

NOTE

1. Parts reprinted with permission from Easton, L. B. (2002). *The other side of curriculum: Lessons from learners.* Portsmouth, NH: Heinemann.

Resource B

Test Score Data From Eagle Rock School and Professional Development Center

Eagle Rock, with its population of students predicted to fail, serves as my chief example of how a school can teach for learning, not testing, and still do well on tests. Eagle Rock students took the Tests of Achievement and Proficiency (TAP) from 1993 to 2000; they currently take the Iowa Test of Educational Development when they first enroll at Eagle Rock. These are considered their *pretests* (Table R.1). They take the same test when they graduate; these are considered their *posttests* (Table R.2).

Table R.1   Pretest Distribution Scores by Percentage

	Percentage Below 50%	*Percentage Above 50%*
Vocabulary	47	53
Reading	46	54
Writing	52	48
Math Concepts	55	45
Social Studies	60	40
Science	48	52
Information Processing	56	44
Math Computation	76	24

Even more meaningful is to look at the percentage of students who scored in the range from the 76th percentile to the 100th percentile on pretests and posttests (Table R.3).

Table R.2 Posttest Distribution Scores by Percentage

	Percentage Below 50%	*Percentage Above 50%*
Vocabulary	27	73
Reading	28	72
Writing	37	63
Math Concepts	38	62
Social Studies	41	59
Science	31	69
Information Processing	34	66
Math Computation	63	37

Table R.3 Percentage of Students Scoring in the 76th–100th Percentiles

	Pretest	*Posttest*
Vocabulary	34	44
Reading	34	46
Writing	22	24
Math Concepts	10	20
Social Studies	20	36
Science	24	35
Information Processing	29	30
Math Computation	9	10

Another way to compare the pre- and posttest scores is to look at the difference in the percentage of students who scored in the cellar (0–25th percentile) (Table R.4). Significance test results are shown in Table R.5.

Table R.4 Number of Students Who Scored in the 0–25th Percentiles

	Pretest	*Posttest*
Vocabulary	20	11
Reading	22	11
Writing	25	14
Math Concepts	30	16
Social Studies	32	13
Science	31	13
Information Processing	34	17
Math Computation	52	42

Table R.5   Significance Test Results

Comparison	Category	Mean Change	Median Change	Significance	
Vocabulary	All	11.4	7	t: 0.0001 Sign: 0.0001 Signed rank: 0.0001	***
	Males	12.0	7	t: 0.0009 Sign: 0.0001 Signed rank: 0.0001	***
	Females	11.0	7	t: 0.0001 Sign: 0.0001 Signed rank: 0.0001	***
Reading	All	13.2	10.5	t: 0.0001 Sign: 0.0001 Signed rank: 0.0001	***
	Males	15.6	14	t: 0.0001 Sign: 0.0001 Signed rank: 0.0001	***
	Females	11.4	7	t: 0.0001 Sign: 0.0001 Signed rank: 0.0001	***
Writing	All	9.1	6.5	t: 0.0001 Sign: 0.0022 Signed rank: 0.0001	***
	Males	13.0	13	t: 0.0001 Sign: 0.0008 Signed rank: 0.0001	**
	Females	6.1	4	t: 0.0512 Sign: 0.3123 Signed rank: 0.0514	+
Math Concepts	All	12.2	12	t: 0.0001 Sign: 0.0001 Signed rank: 0.0001	***
	Males	15.3	15	t: 0.0001 Sign: 0.0008 Signed rank: 0.0001	**
	Females	9.9	11	t: 0.0003 Sign: 0.0001 Signed rank: 0.0001	***

Comparison	Category	Mean Change	Median Change	Significance	
Social Studies	All	16.7	14	t: 0.0001 Sign: 0.0001 Signed rank: 0.0001	***
	Males	21.2	28	t: 0.0009 Sign: 0.0039 Signed rank: 0.0004	**
	Females	13.3	11	t: 0.0002 Sign: 0.0021 Signed rank: 0.0001	***
Science	All	10.9	11	t: 0.0003 Sign: 0.0016 Signed rank: 0.0001	***
	Males	11.7	11	t: 0.0152 Sign: 0.0989 Signed rank: 0.0058	*
	Females	10.4	11	t: 0.0072 Sign: 0.0094 Signed rank: 0.0021	**
Information Processing	All	9.2	9	t: 0.0003 Sign: 0.0352 Signed rank: 0.0001	***
	Males	9.4	10	t: 0.0427 Sign: 0.1325 Signed rank: 0.0173	*
	Females	9.1	3	t: 0.0012 Sign: 0.1839 Signed rank: 0.0023	**
Math Computation	All	5.4	4	t: 0.0175 Sign: 0.1507 Signed rank: 0.0512	*
	Males	7.8	7	t: 0.0225 Sign: 0.1755 Signed rank: 0.0386	**
	Females	3.6	3	t: 0.2447 Sign: 0.5601 Signed rank: 0.4518	—

* Indicates mean/median changes are significantly different from 0
** Indicates mean/median changes are highly significantly different from 0
*** Indicates mean/median changes are *very* highly significantly different from 0

References

Abcarian, R., & Horn, J. (2006, August 7). Underwhelmed by it all. *Los Angeles Times*, p. A1.

Abdullah, M. H. (2001). Self-directed learning [ERIC Digest No. 169]. Bloomington, IN: ERIC Clearinghouse on Reading English, and Communication. (ERIC Document Reproduction Service No. ED459458)

About the project. (2007). Retrieved June 1, 2007, from http://www.firstamendment schools.org/about/aboutindex.aspx

Adler, M. J. (1982). *The Paideia proposal: An educational manifesto.* New York: Macmillan.

Alverno College. (n.d.). Retrieved January 24, 2007, from http://www.alverno.edu

Amy Biehl High School. (2007). Retrieved November 6, 2006, from http://www.abhs .k12.nm.us

ATLAS Communities. (n.d.). Retrieved January 28, 2007, from http://www.atlascommunities .org

Bailey, S. (2000). *Making progress visible: Implementing standards and other large scale change initiatives: Visual dialogue tools with a system view.* Vacaville, CA: Bailey Alliance.

Bailey, S. (2004). Visual dialogue. In L. B. Easton (Ed.), *Powerful designs for professional learning.* Oxford, OH: National Staff Development Council.

Bernhardt, V. (2004a). Data analysis. In L. B. Easton (Ed.), *Powerful designs for professional learning.* Oxford, OH: The National Staff Development Council.

Bernhardt, V. (2004b). *Data analysis for continuous school improvement* (2nd ed.). Larchmont, NY: Eye on Education.

Bjorklund, D. F. (1989). *Children's thinking: Developmental function and individual differences.* Pacific Grove, CA: Brooks/Cole.

Blankstein, A. (2004). *Failure is not an option: Six principles that guide student achievement in high-performing schools.* Thousand Oaks, CA: Corwin Press and The HOPE Foundation.

Boston Arts Academy. (n.d.). Retrieved January 28, 2007, from http://www.boston-arts-academy.org

Brooks, J. G., & Brooks, M. G. (1993*). In search of understanding: The case for constructivist classrooms.* Alexandria, VA: Association for Supervision and Curriculum Development.

Brown, A. L., & Campione, J. C. (1998). Designing a community of young learners: Theoretical and practical lessons. In N. M. Lambert & B. L. McCombs (Eds.), *How students learn: Reforming schools through learner-centered education.* Washington, DC: American Psychological Association.

Bruya, B., & Olwell, R. (2006, December 20). Schools that "flow." *Education Week, 26*(16), 31.

Caine, R. M., & Caine, G. (1991). *Making connections: Teaching and the human brain.* Alexandria, VA: Association for Supervision and Curriculum Development.

California Department of Education. (2006). Retrieved December 11, 2006, from http://www.cde.ca.gov/ci/gs/hs/hsgrmin.asp

Carbo, M. (1987, October). Matching reading styles: Correcting ineffective instruction, *Educational Leadership, 45*(2), 55–62.

Carnegie Foundation. (2006). Retrieved November 2, 2007, from http://www.carnegie foundation.org

Clark, R. (2003). *Goodlad's agenda for education in a democracy: A framework for school renewal.* Seattle, WA: Institute for Educational Inquiry.

Clinchy, E. (2000*). Creating new schools: How small schools are changing American education.* New York: Teachers College Press.

Close Up. (2005). Retrieved September 13, 2006, from http://www.closeup.org

Coalition of Essential Schools (CES) Habits of Mind. (2002a). Retrieved August 8, 2006, from http://www.essentialschools.org

Coalition of Essential Schools (CES) Small Schools Project. (2002b). Retrieved January 28, 2007, from http://www.essentialschools.org

Colorado model content standards. (2007). Retrieved May 20, 2007, from http://www.cde .state.co.us/cdeassess/documents/OLR/k12_standards.html

Cooper, C. R. (1977). Holistic evaluation of writing. In C. R. Cooper & L. Odell (Eds.), *Evaluating writing: Describing, measuring, judging,* Urbana, IL: National Council of Teachers of English.

Cotton, K. (1996a). *Affective and social benefits of small-scale schooling.* Charleston, WV: ERIC Clearinghouse on Rural Education and Small Schools. (ERIC Document Reproduction Service No. ED401088)

Cotton, K. (1996b). *School size, school climate, and student performance* [Close-up No. 20]. Portland, OR: Northwest Regional Educational Laboratory.

Covey, S. R. (1989). *The 7 habits of highly effective people: Powerful lessons in personal change.* New York: Free Press.

Covey, S. R. (2004). *The 7 habits of highly effective people: Powerful lessons in personal change* (Rev. ed.). New York: Free Press.

Csikszentmihalyi, M. (1990). *Flow: The psychology of optimal experience.* New York: Harper Perennial.

Cushman, K. (1989, June). Asking the essential questions: Curriculum development. *Horace, 5*(5). Retrieved May 22, 2007, from http://www.essentialschools.org/cs/ resources/view/ces_res/137

Cushman, K. (1993, November). Another way of measuring up: One school's graduation requirements. *Horace, 10*(2), 5.

Cushman, K. (1994, May). College admissions and the essential school. *Horace, 10*(5). Retrieved May 22, 2007, from http://www.essentialschools.org/cs/resources/view/ces_res/134

Cushman, K. (1998, January). Democracy and equity: CES's tenth common principle. *Horace, 14*(3). Retrieved May 22, 2007, from http://www.essentialschools.org/cs/ resources/view/ces_res/114

Cushman, K. (2001, June). Looking back on 15 years of essential school designs. *Horace, 17*(3).

Dale, E. (1996). The cone of learning. In D. P. Ely & T. Plomp (Eds.), *Classic writings on educational technology.* Englewood, CO: Libraries Unlimited. (Original work published 1946)

Daniels, H. (2002). *Literature circles: Voice and choice in book clubs & reading groups.* Portland, ME: Stenhouse.

Dator, J. (1992, August 5). Emerging trends in democratic participation: The many faces of democracy. Paper presented at the 13th Annual Citizenship Institute, Richardson School of Law, Hawaii. Available online at http://www.futures.hawaii.edu/dator/ governance/emerging.html

Deal, T. E., & Peterson, K. D. (1999). *Shaping school culture: The heart of leadership.* San Francisco: Jossey-Bass.

Dewey, J. (1938). *Experience and education.* New York: Macmillan.

Downey, C. J., Steffy, B. E., English, F. W., Frase, L. E., & Poston, W. K., Jr. (2004). *The three-minute classroom walk-through: Changing school supervisory practice one teacher at a time.* Thousand Oaks, CA: Corwin Press.

Duffrin, E. (2001, June). Grade-school dropouts with nowhere to go. *Catalyst Chicago*. Retrieved on July 20, 2006, from http://www.catalyst-chicago.org/arch/06-01/0601 main1.htm

DuFour, R. (2000). *Failure is not an option*. National Education Service/Solution Tree Video Series.

DuFour, R., DuFour, R., Eaker, R., & Karhanek, G. (2004). *Whatever it takes: How professional learning communities respond when kids don't learn*. Bloomington, IN: Solution Tree.

DuFour, R., & Eaker, R. (1998). *Professional learning communities at work: Best practices for enhancing student achievement*. Reston, VA: Association for Supervision and Curriculum Development & Solution Tree.

Dumke, M. (2001, June). Thousands of troubled students drop out before high school. *Chicago Reporter*. Retrieved November 3, 2006, from www.chicagoreporter.com/2001/ 6-2001/dropouts/dropouts1.htm

Dunn, R. (1990, October). Rita Dunn answers questions on learning styles. *Educational Leadership, 48*(2), 15–19.

Eagle Rock School and Professional Development Center (2006). *Eagle Rock accreditation report*. Estes Park, CO: Author.

Eagle Rock School and Professional Development Center. (n.d.). Retrieved January 3, 2007, from http://www.eaglerockschool.org

Easton, L. (1999, Summer). Tuning protocols. *Journal of Staff Development, 20*(3), 54–55.

Easton, L. (2000, April 12). If standards are absolute . . . How one school varies the old "absolutes" to make sure everyone can learn. *Education Week, 19*(31), pp. 50, 52–53.

Easton, L. (2002, March). How the tuning protocol works. *Educational Leadership, 59*(6), 28–30.

Easton, L. (2005, May). Democracy in schools: Truly a matter of voice. *English Journal, 94*(5), 52–56.

Easton, L. B. (1991). The Arizona State Assessment Program (ASAP) as educational policy. (Doctoral dissertation, University of Arizona, 1991). Ann Arbor, MI: University Microfilm International. (UMI 5032, Order number 9210317)

Easton, L. B. (2002). *The other side of curriculum: Lessons from learners*. Portsmouth, NH: Heinemann.

Easton, L. B. (2004a). Context: Establishing the environment for professional development. In L. B. Easton (Ed.), *Powerful designs for professional learning*. Oxford, OH: National Staff Development Council.

Easton, L. B. (Ed.). (2004b). *Powerful designs for professional learning*. Oxford, OH: National Staff Development Council.

Easton, L. B. (2004c). Shadowing students. In L. B. Easton (Ed.), *Powerful designs for professional learning*. Oxford, OH: National Staff Development Council.

Easton, L. B. (2004d). The tuning protocol. In L. B. Easton (Ed.), *Powerful designs for professional learning*. Oxford, OH: National Staff Development Council.

Easton, L. B. (2007, January). Walking our talk about standards. *Phi Delta Kappan, 88*(5), 310–314.

Education Trust. (2005, June 23). *Getting honest about grad rates: Too many states hide behind false data* [Press release]. Retrieved June 22, 2006, from http://www.edtrust.org

Etzioni, A. (1995). *The spirit of community. Rights responsibilities and the communitarian agenda*. London: Fontana Press.

Expeditionary Learning Schools Outward Bound. (n.d.). Retrieved January 27, 2007, from http://www.elob.org

FairTest (The National Center for Fair & Open Testing). (n.d.) Will more testing improve schools? Retrieved May 30, 2007, from http://www.fairtest.org/facts/main.htm

Federal Hocking High School. (n.d.). Retrieved January 12, 2007, from http://www.federal hocking.k12.oh.us

Fenway High School. (n.d.). Retrieved October 11, 2006, from http://www.fenwayhs.org/

Finn, J. D. (1998). *Class size and students at risk: What is known? What is next?* Retrieved January 17, 2007, from http://www.ed.gov/PDFDocs/class.pdf

First Amendment Schools. (2007). Retrieved April 4, 2006, from http://www.firstamendment schools.org

Foster, J. E. (1993). Reviews of research: Retaining children in grade. *Childhood Education, 70*(1), 38–43.

Foxfire. (2002). Retrieved February 7, 2006, from http://www.foxfire.org

Gagnon, G. W., Jr., & Collay, M. (2006). *Constructivist learning design: Key questions for teaching to standards.* Thousand Oaks, CA: Corwin Press.

Gardner, H. (1993). *Multiple intelligences: The theory in practice.* New York: Basic Books.

Garmston, R., & Wellman, B. (1999). *The adaptive school: A sourcebook for developing collaborative groups.* Norwood, MA: Christopher-Gordon.

Gendler, T. (1989, January). The testing paradox: Do we really test what we measure? *Basic Education, 33,* p. 9.

Gina, R. M. (2004, Winter). New Mission High School's response to the challenge of designing and supporting a meaningful mathematics curriculum. *Horace, 20*(2).

Ginsburg, M. (2004). Classroom walkthroughs. In L. B. Easton (Ed.), *Powerful designs for professional learning.* Oxford, OH: National Staff Development Council.

Glasser, W. (1990). *The quality school: Managing students without coercion.* New York: HarperPerennial.

Goleman, D. (1995). *Emotional intelligence: Why it can matter more than IQ.* New York: Bantam Books.

Goodlad, J. I., Mantle-Bromley, C., & Goodlad, S. J. (2004). *Education for everyone: Agenda for education in a democracy.* San Francisco: Jossey-Bass.

Greene, J. P. (2002). *High school graduation rates in the United States.* New York: Manhattan Institute. Retrieved January 12, 2007, from http://www.manhattan-institute.org/html/cr_baeo.htm

Hampel, B. (1986). *The last little citadel: American high schools since 1940 (Study of high schools).* New York: Houghton Mifflin.

Heath, D. H. (1994). *Schools of hope: Developing mind and character in today's youth.* San Francisco: Jossey-Bass.

High School for Recording Arts. (2007). Retrieved December 11, 2006, from http://www.hsra.org

High Tech High. (n.d.). Retrieved December 11, 2006, from http://www.hightechhigh.org

Hill, D. (2005, June). *Getting honest about grad rates: How states play the numbers and students lose.* Washington, DC: Education Trust.

Hobby, R. (2004, March). *A culture for learning: An investigation into the values and beliefs associated with effective schools.* London: Hay Group Management. Retrieved December 15, 2006, from http://www.haygroup.co.uk/downloads/Culture_for_Learning.pdf

Hord, S. M. (1997a). *Professional learning communities: Communities of continuous inquiry and improvement.* Austin, TX: Southwest Educational Development Laboratory.

Hord, S. M. (1997b). Professional learning communities: What are they and why are they important. *SEDL Issues . . . about change, 6*(1).

Hord, S. M. (Ed.). (2004). *Learning together, leading together: Changing schools through professional learning communities* (Critical Issues in Education Leadership, Vol. 11). New York: Teachers College Press.

Humanities Preparatory Academy. (n.d.). Retrieved October 23, 2006, from http://www.humanitiesprep.org

Isaacson, N., & Bamburg, J. (1992). Can schools become learning organizations? *Educational Leadership, 50*(3), 42–44.

Jerald, C. D. (2007, January). *School culture: The hidden curriculum* [Issue Brief]. Learning Point Associates in Partnership with the Southwest Educational Development Laboratory (SEDL) and WestEd. Retrieved January 13, 2007, from http://www.centerforcsri.org/files/Center_IB_Dec06_C.pdf

Kentucky Department of Education. (2003). KDE dropout prevention resource guide. Retrieved January 8, 2007, from http://www.ihdi.uky.edu/dropout-prevention

Killion, J. (2002). *Assessing impact: Evaluating staff development*. Oxford, OH: National Staff Development Council.

Killion, J. (2003, Fall). Solid footwork makes evaluation of staff development programs a song. *Journal of Staff Development, 24*(4).

Kise, J. A. G. (2006). *Differentiation through personality types: A framework for instruction, assessment, and classroom management*. Thousand Oaks, CA: Corwin Press.

Kraft, D., & Sakofs, M. (Eds.). (1988). *The theory of experiential education*. Boulder, CO: Association for Experiential Education.

Leadership High School. (2003). Retrieved December 16, 2006, from http://www.leader shiphigh.org

Lickona, T. (1991). *Educating for character: How our schools can teach respect and responsibility*. New York: Bantam Books.

Lionni, L. (1970). *Fish is fish*. New York: Knopf Books for Young Readers.

McCarthy, B. (1990, October). Using the 4MAT system to bring learning styles to schools. *Educational Leadership, 48*(2), 31–37.

Macrorie, K. (1988). *The I-search paper: Revised edition of Searching writing*. Portsmouth, NH: Boynton/Cook.

Martin, R. A. (2006, Winter). Wake-up call brings a jolt of alignment to the curriculum. *Journal of Staff Development, 27*(1), 53–55.

Martinez, M., & Klopott, S. (2005). *The link between high school reform and college access and success for low-income and minority youth*. Washington, DC: American Youth Policy Forum and Pathways to College Network.

Maslow's hierarchy. (2007). Retrieved January 28, 2007, from http://changingminds .org/explanations/needs/maslow.htm

Mayer, R. E. (1998). Cognitive theory for education: What teachers need to know. In N. M. Lambert & B. L. McCombs (Eds.), *How students learn: Reforming schools through learner-centered education*. Washington, DC: American Psychological Association.

McCourt, F. (2005). *Teacher man*. New York: Scribner.

Meier, D. (1995). *The power of their ideas: Lessons for America from a small school in Harlem*. Boston: Beacon.

Meier, D., Sizer, T. R., & Sizer, N. F. (2004). *Keeping school: Letters to families from the principals of two small schools*. Boston: Beacon.

The Met. (2006). Retrieved August 8, 2006, from http://www.metcenter.org

Murphy, D., & Rosenberg, B. (1998, June). Recent research shows major benefits of small class size [Electronic version]. *Educational Issues Policy Brief*, No. 3. Washington, DC: American Federation of Teachers. Retrieved January 17, 2007, from http://www.aft .org/pugs-reports/downloads/teachers/Policy3.pdf

National Association of School Psychologists (NASP). (2003). Position statement on student grade retention and social promotion. Retrieved December 8, 2006, from http://www .nasponline.org/about_nasp/pospaper_graderetent.aspx

National Association of Secondary School Principals (NASSP). (2004). *Breaking ranks II: Strategies for leading high school reform*. Reston, VA: Author.

National Center for Educational Statistics (NCES). (2000). *Dropout rates in the United States 2000*. Washington, DC: Author. Retrieved December 8, 2006, from http://nces.ed.gov/ pubs2006/dropout/

National Education Association. (2006). What the research says [About class size]. Retrieved October 14, 2006, from http://www.nea.org/classsize/research-classsize .html

National Research Council. (2000). *How people learn: Brain, mind, experience, and school*. Washington, DC: National Academy Press.

National Youth Leadership Council. (2007). Retrieved January 7, 2007, from www.nylc.org/ discover.cfm?oid=3152

Northwest Regional Educational Laboratory (NWREL). (2002). *Developing self-directed learners*. Portland, OR: Author. Retrieved November 6, 2006, from http://www.nwrel.org/ planning/rna2000.html

O'Connell, J., & Smith, S. C. (2000, April). *Capitalizing on small class size.* Eugene, OR: Clearinghouse on Educational Policy and Management. (ERIC Digest 136)

Olson, L. (2006, June 22). Opening doors: Keeping close track of students' progress would help more teenagers leave high school with diplomas. *Education Week, 25*(41s), 23–30.

Osofsky, D., Sinner, G., & Wolk, D. (2003). *Changing systems to personalize learning: The power of advisories.* Providence, RI: Brown University, Education Alliance.

Paideia active learning. (2006). Retrieved July 7, 2006, from http://www.paideia.org/content.php/system/index.htm

Palmer, P. (1991). The courage to teach. *The National Teaching & Learning Forum, 1*(2), 1–3.

Palmer, P. (1998). *The courage to teach: Exploring the landscape of a teacher's life.* San Francisco: Jossey-Bass.

Parker School. (n.d.). Retrieved April 7, 2006, from http://www.parker.org

Piercy, M. (1982). *Circles on the water: Selected poems of Marge Piercy.* New York: Knopf.

Pierson, L. H., & Connell, J. P. (1992, September). Effect of grade retention on self-system processes, school engagement, and academic performance. *Journal of Educational Psychology, 84*(3), 300–307.

Pilot network. (n.d.). Retrieved May 22, 2007, from http://www.boston-arts-academy.org/pages/baa_about/pilotnetwork

Poland Regional High School. (2007). Retrieved April 20, 2006, from http://www.polandhs.u29.k12.me.us

Powell, A. G., Farrar, E., & Cohen, D. K. (1985). *The shopping mall high school: Winners and losers in the educational marketplace.* Boston: Houghton Mifflin.

Testing our schools: A guide for parents. (2002). *Frontline.* Retrieved December 18, 2006, from http://www.pbs.org/wgbh/pages/frontline/shows/schools/etc/guide.html

Pritchard, I. (1999, March). *Reducing class size: What do we know?* Retrieved May 31, 2007, from http://www.ed.gov/pubs/ReducingClass/title.html

Professional development: Changing times. (1994). *North Central Regional Educational Laboratory Policy Brief* (Report No. 4). Retrieved June 1, 2007, from http://www.ncrel.org/sdrs/areas/issues/envrnmnt/go/94-4cent.htm

Pugh, K. J., & Bergin, D. A. (2005, December). The effect of schooling on students' out-of-school experience. *Educational Researcher, 34*(9), 15.

Quest High School. (n.d.). Retrieved September 4, 2006, from http://qhs.humble.k12.tx.us

Reeves, D. B. (2006). *The learning leader: How to focus school improvement for better results.* Alexandria, VA: Association for Supervision and Curriculum Development.

Resnick, D. P., & Resnick, L. B. (1985, April). Standards, curriculum, and performance: A historical and comparative perspective. *Educational Researcher 14*(10), 5–20.

Restitution program, Maine Township, Illinois. (n.d.). Retrieved May 30, 2007, from http://www.mainetownship.com/youth.html#mainetrac

Schlecty, P. (1997). *Inventing better schools: An action plan for educational reform.* San Francisco: Jossey-Bass.

Schlecty, P. C. (2002). *Working on the work: An action plan for teachers, principals, and superintendents.* San Francisco: Jossey-Bass.

Schmoker, M. (2006). *Results now: How we can achieve unprecedented improvements in teaching and learning.* Alexandria, VA: Association for Supervision and Curriculum Development.

School of the Future. (n.d.). Retrieved October 10, 2006, from http://www.sof.edu

Senge, P. M. (1990). *The fifth discipline: The art and practice of the learning organization.* New York: Doubleday Currency.

Shaughnessy, M. P. (1977). *Errors and expectations: A guide for the teacher of basic writing.* New York: Oxford University Press.

Shepard, L., & Smith, M. L. (1989). *Flunking grades: Research and policies on retention.* Bristol, PA: Falmer.

Simons, J. A., Irwin, D. B., & Drinnien, B. A. (1987). *Psychology: The search for understanding.* New York: West.

Singleton, G. E., & Linton, C. (2006). *Courageous conversations about race: A field guide for achieving equity in schools.* Thousand Oaks, CA: Corwin Press.

Sizer, T. R. (1984). *Horace's compromise: The dilemma of the American high school.* Boston: Houghton Mifflin.

Sizer, T. R. (1992). *Horace's school: Redesigning the American high school.* Boston: Houghton Mifflin.

Sizer, T. R., & Sizer, N. S. (1999). *The students are watching: Schools and the moral contract.* Boston: Beacon.

Skube, M. (2006, August 26). Commentary: Writing off reading. *Boulder Daily Camera,* p. 15A.

Skyview High School. Retrieved November 8, 2006, from http://www.acsd1.k12.co.us/schools/skyviewgeneral.html

Small Schools Project. (n.d.) Retrieved October 10, 2006, from http://www.smallschools project.org

Smith, M. K. (2001). Communitarianism and education. *The encyclopaedia of informal information.* Retrieved January 22, 2007, from http://www.infed.org/biblio/communitarianism .htm

Soguero, M. (2007). Community tackles non-negotiable process. *Eagle Eyes, 14,* 3, 6, 10. Retrieved January 28, 2007, from http://www.eaglerockschool.org

Sparks, D. (1999, Spring). Assessment without victims: An interview with Rick Stiggins. *Journal of Staff Development, 20*(2), 54–56.

Sparks, D. (2001, March). Advocating for powerful forms of professional development. *Results.* National Staff Development Council.

Spencer Foundation. (2001, May 18). Studying the Urban High School conference. Retrieved January 11, 2007, from http://www.spencer.org/publications/conferences/urban_high_schools/uhsfinalreport.htm

Sternberg, R. J. (1994, November). Allowing for thinking styles. *Educational Leadership, 52*(3), 36–40.

Stevens, P. W., & Richards, A. (1992). *Changing schools through experiential education.* Charleston, WV: ERIC Clearinghouse on Rural Education and Small Schools. (ERIC Digest No. ED345929)

Symonds, W. C. (2006, June 16). A school makeover in Mapleton. *Business Week.* Retrieved May 22, 2007, from http://www.businessweek.com/investor/content/jun2006/pi20060615_730385.htm?chan=search

Taylor, H. (2000, October 4). *Huge differences between values of young adults and older adults.* Harris Interactive. Retrieved May 20, 2007, from http://www.harrisinteractive.com/harris_poll/index.asp?PID=120

Urban Academy. (n.d.). Retrieved April 8, 2006, from http://www.urbanacademy.org

U.S. Census Bureau. (2007). *Current population survey* [November 1996, 2000, 2004]. Retrieved October 7, 2006, from http://www.census.gov/population/www/socdemo/voting.html

VARK: A guide to learning styles. (2006). (visual, auditory, kinesthetic or tactile, and reading). Retrieved October 1, 2006, from http://www.vark-learn.com

Viadero, D. (2006, June 22). Signs of early exit for dropouts abound. *Education Week, 25*(41s), 20.

Vygotsky, L. S. (1978). *Mind in society: The development of higher psychological processes* (M. Cole, V. John-Styeiner, S. Scribner, & E. Souberman, Eds. & Trans.). Cambridge, MA: Harvard University Press.

Wadley, J. (2004, August 16). Late night talk shows can turn young adults into cynics. *The University Record Online.* Retrieved October 1, 2006, from http://www.umich.edu/~urecord/0304/Aug16_04/13.shtml

Wasley, P. A., Fine, M., Gladden, M., Holland, N. E., King, S. P., Mosak, E., & Powell, L. C. (2000). *Small schools, great strides: A study of new small schools in Chicago.* New York: Bank Street College of Education Press.

Weiser, C. (2004, July 14). Young people answer call of political action, run for office. *USA Today*. Retrieved May 22, 2007, from http://www.usatoday.com/news/politicselections/nation/2004-07-14-young-pols_x.html

Westerberg, T., & Webb, L. D. (1997). Providing focus and direction through essential learnings. In National Association of Secondary School Principals, *Breaking ranks II: Strategies for leading high school reform*. Reston, VA: NASSP.

Wiggins, G. (1998). *Educative assessment: Designing assessments to inform and improve student performance*. San Francisco: Jossey-Bass.

Wiggins, G., & McTighe, J. (2005). *Understanding by design* (2nd ed.). New York: Prentice Hall.

Wildwood School. (n.d.). Retrieved July 8, 2006, from http://www.wildwood.org

Wisconsin Department of Education. (2006). Retrieved May 22, 2007, from http://dpi.state.wi.us/ec/ecboyrpg.html

Young Women's Leadership Charter School of Chicago. (n.d.). Retrieved June 1, 2007, from http://www.ywlfoundation.org/network_schl_chi.htm

ADDITIONAL READING

Arthur, J. (with Bailey, R.). (2000). *Schools and community: The communitarian agenda in education*. London: Falmer.

Center for Policy Research in Education. (1990). *Repeating grades in school: Current practice and research evidence* (CRPE Policy Brief). Retrieved October 8, 2006, from http://www.cpre.org/images/stories/cpre_pdfs/rb04.pdf

Cizek, G. J. (1991, May). Innovation or enervation? Performance assessment in perspective. *Phi Delta Kappan, 72*, 695.

Editorial Projects in Education. (2006, June 22). Diplomas count: An essential guide to graduation policy and rates. *Education Week, 25*(41s), 1–30.

Sizer, T. R. (1996). *Horace's hope: What works for the American high school*. Boston: Houghton Mifflin.

Smith, A. (2006, July 7). Political realist: An interview with Ben Barnes. *Austin Chronicle*. Retrieved May 22, 2007, from http://www.austinchronicle.com/gyrobase/Issue/story?oid=oid%3A384121

Sparks, D. (2005). *Leading for results: Transforming teaching, learning, and relationships in schools*. Thousand Oaks, CA: Corwin Press, NSDC and NASSP.

Index

CORWIN PRESS

The Corwin Press logo—a raven striding across an open book—represents the union of courage and learning. Corwin Press is committed to improving education for all learners by publishing books and other professional development resources for those serving the field of PreK–12 education. By providing practical, hands-on materials, Corwin Press continues to carry out the promise of its motto: **"Helping Educators Do Their Work Better."**